MW00442743

HOUSE COLORS

HOUSE COLORS

Exterior Color by Style of Architecture

text and photography by

Susan Hershman

Gibbs Smith, Publisher
TO ENRICH AND INSPIRE HUMANKIND
Salt Lake City | Charleston | Santa Fe | Santa Barbara

First Edition
11 10 09 08   5 4 3 2

Text © 2007 Susan Hershman
Photographs © 2007 Susan Hershman and as noted on page 336

All rights reserved. No part of this book may be reproduced by any means whatsoever without written permission from the publisher, except brief portions quoted for purpose of review.

The publisher or author cannot accept responsibility for any consequences arising from the use of this book. Every effort has been made to ensure accuracy of information. If inaccuracies in paint specifications are discovered, please contact the publisher.

Published by
Gibbs Smith
P.O. Box 667
Layton, Utah 84041

Orders: 1.800.835.4993
www.gibbs-smith.com

Susan Hershman
STUDIO+ONE:DESIGN
1395 Trestle Glen Rd.
Oakland, CA 94610
Phone: 877-832-9990
Phone/Fax: 510-986-0200
susan@studio-one-design.com, shershman@pacbell.net
www.studio-one-design.com

Designed by Kurt Wahlner
Printed and bound in China

Library of Congress Cataloging-in-Publication Data

Hershman, Susan.
  House colors : exterior color by style of architecture / text and photographs by Susan Hershman. —1st ed.
     p. cm.
  Includes bibliographical references.
  ISBN-13: 978-1-58685-690-8
  ISBN-10: 1-58685-690-1
  1. Color in architecture—United States. 2. Architecture, Domestic—United States—Themes, motives. 3. Decoration and ornament, Architectural—United States. I. Title.

NA2795.H47 2007
698'.12—dc22
                                    2007017052

I dedicate this book to my husband, tech guy and hero, Rock Snyder, and to the homeowners who participated in the project. I couldn't have made this book without you.

Contents

Preface

Many people consider their home as one of their most valuable assets. In order to maintain and increase the value of those investments, homeowners have been focusing on beautifying their houses—and it shows in neighborhoods everywhere. Those who are selling want to take advantage of the profit that can be gleaned by upgrading a property, which can be significant. Whether rates in the real estate market are rising or falling, people are using color, good landscaping, and other design details to make their homes stand out with personality while adding value to their investments.

Maintaining the integrity of the home's exterior paint, stucco, or other hard-surface materials like brick or stone not only gives you a sense of pride of ownership but it also protects your investment by improving your home's curb appeal.

What is curb appeal? It's everything about the design and maintenance of the home that contribute to how attractive the property looks from the street. It's also the degree to which your house reflects its original, unaltered architectural style. Curb appeal is about the finished package. All details have been considered and implemented.

There are many ways to enhance a home's curb appeal. It starts with good color, but it goes much further. Good landscaping is critical to the finished look, but all details count. The selection of the door, door hardware, mailbox, gate, house numbers, planter boxes, railings, roof tile, and pavers all contribute to the finished appearance. An ever-expanding variety of innovative styles, colors, and new finishes are available. Homeowners are investing in high-end products that speak volumes about their concern for quality and design and have become an avenue for expressing personal taste. Manufacturers of these products are responding to this trend by regularly introducing inventive designs. The choices are seemingly endless. It's an exciting time to upgrade your home.

But it's not always easy to realize this goal. It's difficult to know where to begin the process of planning the project. It requires extensive knowledge of how to integrate color, finishes, and materials together harmoniously. The process can be overwhelming to the layman. This book is designed to give you specific information so that you can achieve results as painlessly as possible, without all the guesswork.

Selecting Colors for Your Home

When homeowners make the decision to color their homes with paint or color-embedded stucco, they have four options:

Option One: Using Paint Manufacturer Samples

This option involves a trip to the paint store to obtain a selection of manufacturers' available colors. Sample colors are typically presented on a small stock card with a selection of up to seven shades. A few manufacturers provide three-by-five-inch samples, but this is a rarity and most color samples are much smaller. Color-embedded stucco samples are usually chosen from a foldout brochure and are even smaller. They are usually ordered directly through the manufacturer.

The process of selecting colors can be overwhelming and you may not know where to begin. The color chips are certainly a starting place, but small samples can't help you understand what it will look like scaled to the entire house. Color-embedded stucco is even more difficult to choose because you must also select a surface texture. I've seen it happen over and over again—homeowners select a color they like, and then often find themselves surprised, bewildered, and disappointed with the results. The color chips don't look anything like the color painted on the house, and

the color combinations aren't working together either. What happened? The answer is that when enlarged to the scale of a house, the color will almost always look different. Color on a paint chip will often appear to be two shades darker than when viewed on the exterior of a house. It can even be unrecognizable when compared with the tiny color chip.

You may have more success when choosing colors from a manufacturer's brochure containing exterior color combinations that have been preselected by industry professionals. These brochures can provide examples of tried-and-true results. Still, wouldn't you like to know what it will really look like before you go ahead and paint the entire house?

Manufacturers have begun to understand the difficulty of choosing colors from small paint or stucco samples. Some manufacturers are now selling small containers of paint that cover a two-by-two-foot wall area. Some will even send larger paint samples. This is a step in the right direction, but it's still hard to know how it will look on a large scale.

Trust me—it's very difficult to tell what house colors will look like from these small paint samples. If you can't find a field color that you like, how are you ever going to figure out how to pick a trim and accent color that work

Color and Light Conditions

Exterior color is tricky for many reasons. A house is a very large object to paint (even a relatively small house), and color just looks different blown up to a large scale. More importantly, color seems to change dramatically under different light conditions, a phenomenon called metamerism. This changes everything. To see it for yourself, paint a minimum of four square feet (two feet by two feet) on an exterior wall. Allow yourself to look at it throughout the day. Over time, the weather may change from sunny to overcast to rainy to combinations of all three. Perhaps the sample will have southern exposure, or it may have shaded northern exposure. Look at the color in morning light, afternoon light, and at dusk and you will see a significant difference. If you view the paint in eight different conditions, you'll think that you are looking at eight different colors. Seasonal light affects color as well. Ever notice that winter sun casts a cool blue light, while summer sun casts a warm golden light on objects?

So how can you pick a color when it never seems to stay the same? Since we know that color will change, the best you can hope for is to make your decision by giving yourself time to look at the colors under as many different light conditions as possible. Paint as large an area as you can on every wall of the house. If you still like the color in all the different conditions and locations, then proceed with it. You have done the best that you can to determine if the color will work for you.

well together? I've seen homeowners go back to the paint store a dozen times, selecting and reselecting colors with the hope that it will look better the next time around.

Choosing house colors can create a great deal of stress and anxiety. Not only is it expensive to paint your house, but you also have a responsibility to your neighborhood to make quality color selections that are appropriate for the area in which you live. For most people, selecting a color from a small sample is a setup for failure.

Option Two: Hiring a Color Consultant

A less stressful option is to hire a color consultant or designer to lighten the load and help guide you in selecting just the right colors. This can work very well, but it can also be expensive. The cost varies from area to area and from expert to expert, but you may spend up to $1,500 or even more, depending on how complicated the job gets. The designer will discuss the colors you're considering and will assemble two to three color combinations for you to choose from. Sometimes designers can point you to color combinations that have worked on other houses and can put these colors together for you by matching it, which will help you to know more closely what you're getting, but this can be costly too.

A designer and homeowner develop a certain amount of trust when working together, so this can be a very comfortable option. Still, the reality is that even when you hire an expert, you can't be absolutely certain what the color will look like until your house is actually painted. When I established my own business as an interior designer, I was asked to help with exterior color consultation. I thought to myself, "No problem—I've been working with color all of my professional life, and it should be easy to pick out a few colors for exterior use." The truth is that even though I know what I'm looking for, it can be very difficult to find just the right color and intensity without a number of attempts.

Option Three: Matching Existing House Colors

This option involves driving around different neighborhoods to find houses with color that you like and think will work for the architectural style of your home. You can try to match it to the manufacturer's colors yourself, but better yet, knock on the homeowner's door to ask if he or she will share the color information with you. The homeowner may be willing to give it to you, but maybe not. This is the only option so far that allows you to see the finished product before you make a decision about it. If you like it and the details (trim, roof tile, pavers, etc.) are similar enough to your house, there is a good chance that it will work for you too. Keep in mind that it's important that the proportion of color used on both houses is similar or it won't work well. That means that if there is a lot of trim on the house that you like, then you should have about the same amount of trim on your own house. Look for as many architectural similarities as possible. This will ensure its success. Finally, as a courtesy to the homeowners who give you information (including the homeowners who have provided the information in this book), do not use the same house colors if you live within a two-mile radius of their home.

But there is a down side to this option. Houses with great color combinations are few and far between. Homeowners may not have saved the paint color information or may not even be the ones who painted the house, thus lacking the information you need. They may not want to share the information for their hard-earned results. Obtaining the information that you seek may ultimately become a grueling process that may not produce results.

Option Four: Using This Book

Option Four is where this book comes in—basically, it is Option Three, but I've done all the work for you. The concept is simple: a picture is worth a thousand words. In this case, the words contain exact information, not just inspirational ideas. Some houses are grand and some are modest, but they all have one thing in common—the homeowners have made good color and design choices for their homes and have created great curb appeal.

Many people are interested in achieving these same great results for their homes but don't trust themselves to do it well. They don't know how to begin to choose good neutrals, let alone more saturated colors, because of the

fear of bad results. They end up painting their homes with colors that they consider to be safe and are ultimately unsatisfied with the results.

The purpose of this book is to show you dozens of color possibilities and to give you valuable design information. It will not merely guide you in selecting colors; it will take the guesswork out of color selection and will give you the specifications for the successful color combinations used on each house. These specifications give you the kind of information that you would receive if you hired a designer. The photographs are keyed to the specifications section of the book and will tell you what you need to know to achieve similar design results. You will also find a resource section that will guide you to finding many of the products and services.

The houses are loosely divided into nine architectural styles so that you can hone in on colors that will work for your own home's style. By looking closely and following the design direction on each house, you can begin to understand why proportional use of color is so important and how it contributes to a successful balance of color.

You may find inspiring color in any part of the book, but it is important to pay attention to how trim divides color on a house. Keep your proportions about the same. This holds true for landscaping, too—the size and scale of green plants, flowers, and trees that shade the house change the proportion of color and the color itself when seen from the street. Keep it simple and follow these rules when using any of these house colors in the book.

I've wanted to create a vehicle that would bring good color and design ideas to the public for years, and I'm happy to achieve my goal with this book. Often, good design is exclusive; design books often show lots of photographs with inspiring images and great ideas, but they don't give the information about how to achieve it. This book will tell you what you need to know to attain results similar to what you see in the photographs. I hope that it helps you to achieve great success with your house colors.

What You Need to Know about Using This Book

• This massive reference book provides specific information so that you can achieve the look of any home you see here. This includes not only color, but also, in as many cases as possible, information about other materials, products, and services for each and every home. Each house has a designated number; to find its specific product information, turn to the Color and Product Specifications by House Number section at the back of the book. Following the specification section is a resource section with manufacturer and retailer contact information, making a seamless connection between what you see and how to achieve the same results.

• Every effort has been made to ensure accuracy of information. Color and design information has been supplied by the homeowners. The manufacturer's standard fan deck colors have been checked, but custom formulas (recipes) were not able to be confirmed. I have relied on the homeowners for accurate information.

• Your freshly painted colors may look different than the house colors in this book for several reasons. First and foremost, paint colors will naturally fade over time with exposure to the elements. Newly painted houses will have more color saturation and may be brighter or darker at first. Your house colors will fade, too, and at some point will more closely resemble the colors that you see in the photographs.

• A shift in color from the printing process and a myriad of different lighting conditions will also make the colors appear different. This is to be expected. The use of this book is meant to be a general guideline for choosing color. Carefully check your selections by painting a four-square-foot patch of the color on your house before making your final decision.

• Color and resource information was not always available from the homeowners. In such cases, I've matched the colors myself. This is indicated as "my match" in the specifications section.

• Roof tile availability will vary from area to area, depending on the local climate. Check with a dealer to ensure that the product is available in your area. Dealers can usually be located through the manufacturer's Web site.

- If the homeowner had roof color information, I have included it in the specifications section. If it hasn't been included, it is because the information wasn't available, I couldn't match it because the homeowner didn't keep track of it or because the roofing material was installed prior to the current homeowner's purchasing the house.

- Contact information for items like house numbers, doorbells, mailboxes, lighting, slate and stone, tile, doors, windows, planter boxes, and hardware are supplied in the resource section. Check with the manufacturer to find a dealer in your area.

- Depending on the climate, some of the paving materials will not be available for use in your area. Check with the manufacturer or a local dealer for more information about substitution options.

- Unless otherwise noted, paint should be mixed in a flat latex paint for the field color and satin or semi-gloss finish latex for trim. A higher sheen may be desirable for wood trim, but it must be in pristine condition or every imperfection will show. Sheen selection will change the color slightly. The rule is, the flatter the finish, the lighter the color will be and conversely, the higher the sheen, the darker the color.

- If you like a certain color but the paint manufacturer is not represented in your area, contact the manufacturer (see the resource section) to order color samples and then purchase the paint by mail. The manufacturer's paint chip can also be computer matched at your local paint store. Over time, manufacturers' standard colors may change or become discontinued. If this happens, ask the paint store clerk if he or she can check with the corporate office to get the formula. You may have to be persistent! Paint colors are discontinued and reintroduced on a regular basis, so corporate headquarters tend to keep track of all formulas.

- The homes that have been used in this book are everyday houses and were not staged for photography.

- We have a responsibility to fit the places where we live because we are part of a larger community. The choices that we make reflect on that community and should work for all of its members. When selecting your house colors, consider that your choice affects those around you. The neighbors across the street probably look at your home's exterior more than you do.

- Original formulas with "recipes" were mixed in the finish (i.e. gloss, semi-gloss, oil, flat) that was used in the given area on the homeowner's house. The formula will often (but not always) change if you switch to a different finish. Since there are exceptions, ask your paint mixing specialist how to transfer a formula to a different finish for your house (i.e., if the formula was mixed up in semi-gloss, but you want it in a flat finish). A specialist at your local paint store may need to match to an actual sample of the color with the finish as it is in this book. If you want to change it, you may need to have the paint mixed up and matched to a brush out (sample of the paint on a board) to assure color accuracy.

- Tinting bases change regularly. There isn't anything that can be done about it. Usually the color will only be slightly affected, but again, ask your paint specialist for advice about how it may affect your selected color.

Tip

Look for competitive pricing for items on the Internet by using a search engine. If you buy a product from out of state, currently you can often avoid sales tax. Some manufacturers cover shipping costs to encourage Internet and out-of-state business. This varies from company to company and state to state.

The Basics

Color

"Only those who love color are admitted to its beauty and immanent presence. It affords utility to all, but unveils its deeper mysteries only to its devotees."
—Johannes Itten

Color is a visual language. It sends a message that can attract attention in quiet reflection or with a passionate outburst. It speaks of how we feel about ourselves through creative expression. When we use color on the outside of the home, we throw out a wider net that speaks to the neighborhood and the larger community. Color says what your home means to you and the life that you create for yourself. It fulfills an important aspect in our lives because it affects a mood within us and outside of ourselves and reflects on who we are. It manifests itself as an opportunity that can bring harmony to our lives. It creates a visual experience pleasing to the mind and to the eye.

Reds, oranges, and yellows are warm colors associated with feelings of energy and passion. Blues, greens, and violets are cool colors that relate to feelings of peace and tranquility. There is a massive amount of highly developed research on the psychology of color that could take years to fully understand. What is important when choosing your house colors is simply to have faith that your spontaneous preference will guide you to a selection that is comforting to you. This is an instinct worth trusting. The resulting selection, with guidance from this book, will satisfy your desire for house colors that will work for your home.

The lightness or darkness of the color is something to consider too for visual and practical reasons. For instance, light house colors will make the house appear larger, while dark colors will do the opposite and will make the house appear to be smaller. In the warm summer months when the sun is the strongest, light paint colors will deflect the warmth of the sun to help keep the house cool inside. A house painted a dark color will draw the sun to it and do the opposite to make the interiors warmer. Also, light colors tend to last longer than dark colors. Earth tones tend to fade less from sun exposure than primary colors.

The Color Wheel

To fully understand the science of color requires study of the color wheel. The amount of information on this subject is virtually endless. For the purposes of this book, we will explore its basic principles for a rudimentary understanding of how it works.

The color wheel is an organized circular arrangement of the visible spectrum's continuum of color. It's divided into twelve colors. The primary colors are pure red, blue, and yellow. Secondary colors are a combination of two primary colors. They are orange (red and yellow), green (yellow and blue), and violet (blue and red). Tertiary colors are the six colors that fall between the primary and secondary colors on the color wheel. They are blue-green, yellow-green, blue-violet, red-violet, red-orange, and yellow-orange.

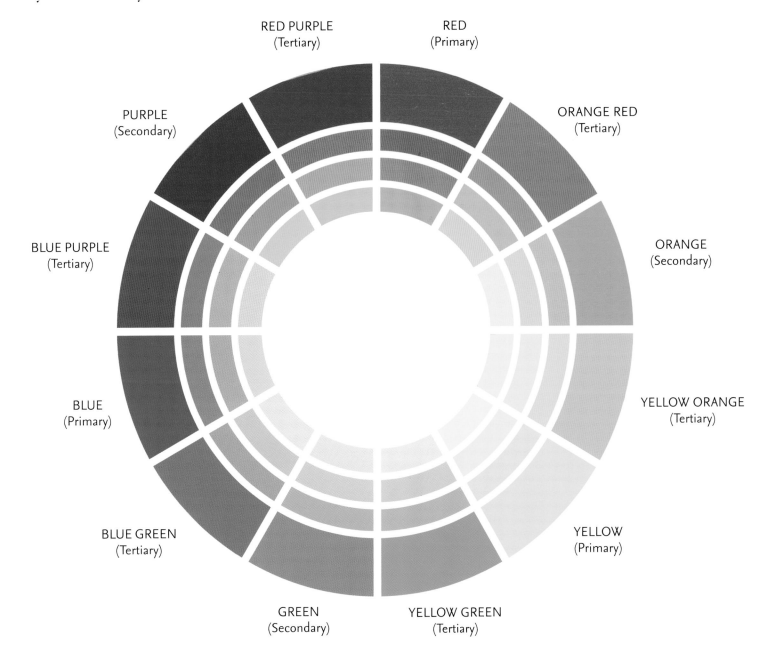

RED PURPLE
(Tertiary)

RED
(Primary)

PURPLE
(Secondary)

ORANGE RED
(Tertiary)

BLUE PURPLE
(Tertiary)

ORANGE
(Secondary)

BLUE
(Primary)

YELLOW ORANGE
(Tertiary)

BLUE GREEN
(Tertiary)

YELLOW
(Primary)

GREEN
(Secondary)

YELLOW GREEN
(Tertiary)

Within the color wheel are endless gradations of color created by the addition of white, gray, or black to the hue. **Shade** is the degree to which a pure color is mixed with black and is decreased into gradations of darkness. **Tint** is a gradation of color made lighter by adding white to a pure color, lessening its saturation. The general effect of shading or tinting a color with gray is known as **tone**.

Gradations of hue can be used to create harmonious color combinations. The theory of the color wheel is based on the location of the colors on the wheel and the relationship of one color to another. The resulting combinations are called color schemes and represent many of the well-balanced colors in this book.

We will discuss three of the simplest types of schemes—monochromatic, complementary, and analogous. The two remaining schemes are triadic—three equally spaced colors around the color wheel—and split complementary (or tetradic)—two complementary color pairs that produce four different colors. These schemes are more complex because they combine three to four color groups and use shades and tints from all of them. Let's start with easiest type to understand, the monochromatic scheme.

Monochromatic schemes use a variety of tints and shades from one single color, including neutrals like black and white. These are uncomplicated, soothing, sophisticated color schemes that lack contrasting color. For example, if we use a tertiary color like blue-green for the field color, a darker shaded tone for the windows, and a tinted lighter version for the trim, then we have created a scheme from one single color. Using any one of the twelve colors on the color wheel, in all of their gradations, will produce a monochromatic scheme.

Analogous schemes use colors that are right next to each other on the color wheel. These harmonious schemes use one dominant color and the two colors on either side. For example, if you use orange as the domi-

Monochromatic

nant house color and accent it with adjacent colors of yellow-orange and orange-red, the color scheme will be enriched. It's not unlike the monochromatic scheme, but offers more nuance and depth of color. Choosing colors that are all warm or all cool and colors that are next to each other on the wheel will provide the harmony that analogous colors generally create.

Complementary schemes use colors from opposite ends of the color wheel to create high contrast, dramatic color combinations that exude dynamic energy. Red and green, yellow and violet, and orange and blue are the colors that are across from each other on the color wheel. Select any one of the twelve colors on the wheel as the first color and the color directly across from it as the sec-

Analogous

Complementary

ond color. Use one as the dominant color and the other as an accent color. For a more dramatic appearance, use a primary or shaded hue, such as a robust, shaded red for the accent (like a door or shutters), and a tinted shade of its complement, green, for the house color. Three hues of the same green can be used too—the lightest tinted green for the trim, a darker tinted color for the field color, and perhaps a darker shade of the same green for the shutter color. Be careful when using two primary colors together on the same scheme, as it can be overwhelming if used in equal proportions. Equal amounts of primary red and green may look a little bit too much like Christmas colors.

Following these color scheme guidelines will provide

winning results, though you may need to study color wheel theory more to fully understand how to make it work with all of its nuances. Nonetheless, using this time-honored tool will create harmonious color combinations, resulting in the kind of visual interest and sense of order that give homes great curb appeal.

There are always exceptions to the rule, so interesting combinations that fall outside of the box can be applied with great results, too, if you know what you're doing. Fortunately, this book will take a lot of the pain out of understanding all of this by providing colors that work, making the process of selecting great house colors a whole lot easier.

Benjamin Moore Navajo White/OC-95

Classic creamy white. Works well with warm, saturated colors.

Sherwin Williams Inviting Ivory/SW6372

Has an orange cast. Works well with bright Mediterranean colors that have a bright yellow or orange cast.

Benjamin Moore Lancaster White/EXT.RM.

Classic white. Works well with field colors that have a gray tone.

Fuller O'Brien Siam Sand/3W16-1

Sand-colored white. Works well with warm earth tone colors.

Benjamin Moore Mountain Peak White/OC-121

Light white. Good with cool, light colors.

Benjamin Moore Canvas/267 (x1.5)

Creamy white. Works well with warm, saturated colors.

Benjamin Moore Elmira White/HC-84 (Historical Color)

Slightly grayed-down white. Works well with gray-toned, medium saturation colors.

Benjamin Moore Grand Teton White/OC-132

Grayed-down white with yellow cast. Works well with grayed-down, saturated colors.

Kelly-Moore Graystone/230

Darkest of the warm whites. Use this color when less contrast is desirable between the field color and the trim color.

Good Whites

Choosing a good white trim color can be challenging. The biggest mistake made by homeowners when picking house colors is selecting the wrong white. It's no wonder—the subtleties and nuances of the white color palette make it difficult to select from and can be an even more daunting task than choosing the field color.

Homeowners tend to settle and opt for a standard ready-mix white right off of the shelf in the paint store. Perhaps they think that "white is white," but that couldn't be further from the truth. Selecting the right white couldn't be more important. It has to have just the right shading, tint and tone to coordinate with the warmth or coolness of the field colors. Selecting the right white is an opportunity to unite the colors in harmony. Bright white works well with bright field colors, but not with many others. For example, a cool white and a warm earth-tone color would be at odds with each other.

The white you select can make or break the color scheme. As always, test all of your colors on an area of the house before you paint the entire house.

Roof Color Selection

Roof color selection is a significant part of the overall design of a house. It's important that the roof color work with the house color, though it doesn't have to "match" it. Since the roofing material will last a lot longer than the house color, keep in mind that the color you choose now will have to work with the house color through at least two changes in color, since most tiles last at least fifteen years and some a lot longer than that. Still, if you want to make sure that the color will work with future selections, pick a color that works with as many house color changes as possible. Stick with a good neutral, like black, gray, or even an earth tone color, and work future selections around whatever you pick. It's better to go darker than

the house color for the roof tile selection. Future selections can be made by starting with the roof color and working backwards. A general rule of thumb is: warm tile, warm house color. Cool tile, cool house color.

It's probably not a great idea to pick a tile that matches the house exactly. If you have a cool blue house, steer away from selecting a cool blue house tile, unless you're sure that the house will be blue for the life of the tile. Instead, select a darker neutral tone, like dark gray. This will open the possibility for a house color change that won't necessarily have to work with blue.

Sometimes you will see a roof color that is offbeat—like a cool roof with a warm house color. This can work, but it requires a special expertise to understand why. To be on the safe side, keep colors in the same warm or cool family and stick to a relatively safe selection for an overall scheme that is contiguous, purposeful, and appears to be made for each other.

Paint

A fresh coat of paint not only increases the curb appeal of your home, it also adds to the value of your house by protecting your investment from the elements.

Paint is made up of pigment, binders, additives, and a liquid material. Acrylic latex paint uses water for its liquid, and oil- or alkyd-based paints use mineral spirits. Product labels indicate the percentage of solids in a can of paint. The higher the percentage, the higher the quality of paint. The mixture becomes solid paint when the liquid evaporates.

Pigment provides the color. Eighty-five to ninety percent of the cost of manufacturing paint is spent on the pigment. The higher the percentage of pigment, the thicker the paint will be. Thicker paint means a better quality of paint because it allows for better coverage and uniform color. It wears better, lasts longer, and cleans more easily. Binders hold the pigment together. Additives supply traits like moisture resistance and extend the color so that it goes farther.

A good rule of thumb is that your house will need three coats of paint, including primer, but for areas that have southern exposure, you may consider adding one or two more coats. Window frames and trim exposed to direct sunlight may need an extra couple of coats as well. The first coat should be the primer (or conditioner, for stucco). It should always be used on new surfaces and re-painted surfaces whose previous color is darker than the new color. In general, it's recommended that a primer be used in all cases since it will give the color a more uniform appearance and will help the paint better adhere to the surface. Many factors will contribute to what works best for your home, so it's best to consult with a professional to determine the exact needs for your house.

Always clean surfaces with a power washer (they can be rented) before starting any paint job. Without this step, the paint won't stick properly and will ultimately peel and blister, shortening the life span of the paint and essentially making all of the effort a waste of time and money.

Painting Tips

1. Place the original batch of paint color in a five-gallon bucket. When it's about half gone, add a couple of gallons of the same color to the mix. Paint colors can vary from can to can, even with the same exact formula, so adding paint color this way will keep the color consistency the same.

2. Paint in a dry, moderate outside temperature with no wind. Don't paint in the rain or when the outside temperature is below fifty degrees. If you do, the paint will bubble and peel.

3. Paint from the top down and not the bottom up. This will avoid unnecessary dripping onto fresh paint.

4. Choose a low-sheen or flat finish for the field color

because it touches up better, doesn't show imperfections, and simply looks better. Shiny surfaces can look cold and industrial.

5. The sheen of the paint affects the color's appearance. A flat-finish color will look lighter than one with a higher-gloss finish.

6. Exterior paint can be mixed in an oil base, but is limited to quart-size containers in some states because of environmental safety concerns, thus inhibiting its use for the field color. Oil-based paint lasts longer and

> **Tip**
>
> For more great painting tips and guidance on estimating paint amounts, check out a paint manufacturer's Web site, such as www.dunnedwards.com or www.kellymoore.com.

looks better on wood trim because of its hard, glassy, smooth surface. Because of the harmful impact on the environment, it should be used sparingly on a small area, such as the front door or shutters.

7. Any manufacturer can match another manufacturer's paint colors. If you want to custom-color another manufacturer's paint, take the paint chip to the store and have it computer matched. If you want to paint your concrete pavers the same color as the house, match the color to a specialty floor paint product that's made for this purpose.

8. If you are using a semitransparent, semisolid stain for a front door, it should then be protected with an oil or polyurethane finish to protect both the stain and the wood.

9. As a good rule of thumb, highlight trim, windows, and doors, not minor architectural details like pipes,

vents, or small utility doors. These items should blend into the house colors rather than stick out by being highlighted with a different color.

10. Don't wait until the paint is peeling off of the windows and siding of the house before you paint. Paint while the house is still in good condition, if you can. It's very costly to patch and prep peeling paint and can raise the cost of your new paint job.

11. Prepping properly is the key to the longevity of a new paint job. The amount of preparation needed will depend on the condition of the existing surface. If the paint is old and peeling in patches, heavy sanding will be required to remove the failed material, and "feathering" with your old paint color will be needed to soften the remaining hard edges of the existing paint finish. Ideally, exposed, weathered wood should be sanded to reveal the original hard material. Then the house should be primed with paint, followed by caulking of any cracks and gaps. Every house is different. Seek the advice of an experienced painter to find a solution that will work if the house is in need of serious repair.

Estimating the Amount of Paint Needed

To determine the total amount of paint you will need, first calculate the surface to be painted: Multiply the length of the walls with the height, from foundation to roofline, for each side of the house. For example, 15 feet high by 25 feet long equals 375 square feet. Measure the square footage of all window openings and doors and deduct this number from the total square footage. Multiply this number by the number of coats you have determined you need. Next, divide this number by the estimated coverage rate of the paint that you're using. Manufacturers typically indicate the coverage rate on the back of the paint can.

If your house has trim, the general formula is 1 gallon of trim paint for every 8 gallons of field color paint. After estimating the amount of paint needed for each side of the house, add the numbers together. This is a simple formula, and your house may have complicated angles, nooks, crannies, and lots of window openings, but it's a good place to start. A painting contractor can help you to figure this out too. It can be tricky to determine because many factors affect how much paint needs to be purchased. Here are some reasons why it can be tricky:

1. A textured or porous surface will absorb more paint.
2. High-quality paint covers better than lower-quality paint, so you'll need to buy less of it.
3. Brushes and rollers will have a slightly higher coverage rate than paint sprayers.
4. An experienced painter will be able to get more coverage than an inexperienced painter.
5. Dark colors generally cover better than lighter colors.
6. Ready-mixed colors usually cover better than custom-mixed colors.

Testing Color

A good way to test colors on a house is to construct a 2-foot by 2-foot "brush out" from a material that closely matches the texture and finish of your home's exterior. Move the sample to different areas of the house exterior to see it in different light conditions. This will save you the trouble of painting samples on all four sides of your house. Still, the best way to test color is to take the time to paint the color on every wall of the house.

Paint Finishes

The paint's finish is essentially the degree of light reflectance in the paint. Manufacturers have different names for paint finishes, but exterior paints usually fall into one of the following categories:

Flat—Hides imperfections and spatters best. It's easy to touch up. There is little to no sheen (except for high-pigment colors, which tend to show some sheen).

Eggshell (sometimes called satin or low-luster)—The slight sheen of an eggshell finish shows more imperfections than a flat finish. On a home in good condition, however, eggshell is a good choice because moderate sheen allows the surface to be cleaned more easily. It will also flatten some over time.

Semigloss—Durable and easy to clean, semigloss has higher sheen than eggshell but less than gloss. It is often used for windows, window frames, and trim when a contrast in sheen is desirable.

Gloss—Used mostly on high-traffic areas, gloss is the easiest finish to clean. Imperfections show more with gloss than with any other finish, so it should be used on only well-prepped, clean surfaces. It can look harsh, so it should be limited to select areas where a shiny glass-like appearance is desirable. Gloss is a good choice for the front door. The mirror finish can add sophistication, and the cleanability is a plus since doors typically take a lot of wear and tear.

Finding a Painter

You may feel confident about painting your own house, but it requires quite a bit of skill to do it well, besides being a time-consuming project. Consider using an experienced painting contractor to do the job instead.

Many homeowners are stumped when it comes to finding a good contractor to paint their house. One of the

Elastomeric Terpolymer Paint

Developed by VIP Paints over 35 years ago, elastomeric paint is heavier bodied than acrylic latex and comes in a flat or low-sheen finish. This commercial-strength product has become popular for painting masonry and stucco homes because of its inherent elasticity, excellent adhesion, and durability. It can bridge small gaps and cracks on a properly primed surface without showing the usual caulking lines that are often visible with a latex product. Though the cost per gallon is about the same as acrylic latex, the painting costs are about twice as high—the thickness of the paint means application takes more time, which means more expense for labor. The plus side is that it lasts longer than latex, and with its ability to patch hairline cracks seamlessly, it is a very good product to consider for stucco homes.

best ways is to look for quality paint jobs on other houses in and around your neighborhood. Look for a house with no uncovered cracks, seams, or joints and with a smooth, seamless paint finish. With permission from the homeowner, examine the window sills to see if they've been painted smoothly. Check to see if the window frame has been completely painted or if the paint comes up onto the frame. Finally, inspect the overall finish to see that there is no cracking, blistering, or peeling anywhere on the house. Don't be afraid to knock on the door to ask who did the job and get the painting contractor's contact information. It's a nice way to meet your neighbors too!

Another source for contractors is your local homeowners association or a real estate agent who works in your neighborhood. They often have lists of tried-and-true professionals in the area.

Check to see if the painter offers a warranty. Ask how long the warranty is good for and get a written agreement to back it up, if you can. I've seen paint jobs that have blistered after a year or two, so you want to make sure that you have some recourse if you find yourself in this unfortunate circumstance. Know your rights.

A good paint job should last ten years, more or less. This number will vary depending on the weather conditions of your area, the amount of exposure to the sun and the elements, how well the house was prepped for painting, and the quality of the paint that was used for the job.

Warning

The paint on structures built before 1978 may contain lead or asbestos. If you think that this may apply to you, do not disturb the paint without contacting your local health officials for information on testing and safety precautions. Exposure to these elements is toxic and can be dangerous to your health, causing serious injury or even death. For more information about asbestos or lead, contact the U.S. Environmental Protection Agency or, if outside the U.S., your government's environmental department. You can also call the EPA's lead information hotline at 800-424-LEAD.

Roof Shingles

Roof shingles are important to your home's overall design. They're not just a functional cover, but also a design detail whose color needs to coordinate with the colors of the rest of the house. Besides adding color, roof shingles offer texture and pattern that add visual interest to the house. There are many different types at varying costs that are available in today's market:

Asphalt shingles—This is the least expensive option and the most commonly used of all shingle types. Asphalt shingles are made from fiberglass and asphalt, and though the selection used to be run-of-the-mill, these days you can choose from many different textures and patterns. Asphalt shingles last about fifteen to twenty years.

Laminated fiberglass shingles—A more expensive variety of asphalt shingles, laminated fiberglass shingles contain the same materials but have a pricey appearance because of their added thickness, pattern, and texture. They last about thirty years.

Wood shake shingles—These shingles are made of treated wood and give the house a more rustic appearance. They're commonly used on Cottage- and Tudor-style homes. They are less fire-resistant than asphalt shingles and are typically five times costlier. Consider using another type of shingle in areas where there is danger of fire. Check with professionals in your area. Wood shake shingles last about fifteen to twenty years.

Synthetic shake shingles—Made of man-made materials, high-quality synthetic shingles are hard to tell apart from the natural shake product. They have a better fire rating than natural shingles and have low-maintenance characteristics. The cost is about the same as for real wood shakes, meaning they are about five times costlier than asphalt shingles, but they last fifty years. These are new products for the marketplace and don't have the track record of natural shake shingles, so some research would be required before purchasing these products.

Metal panel roofing—Good for harsh weather conditions, this roofing is lightweight, easy to install, and comes in several different colors. Metal roofs last about twenty to fifty years, depending on their weight. They typically cost ten times the price of asphalt shingles, though more basic, lower-cost versions are available. Metal roofs are most often seen in areas that experience heavy snow because they can support the weight better than most other materials.

Clay tile—Often used on Mediterranean-style homes, clay shingles are often tube shaped, unglazed, and heavy. Clay tiles are pricey and can cost thirty times more than asphalt shingles. If you can get past the cost, they're a good investment because they last fifty years or more.

Slate roofing—Seen on many styles of homes, slate roofing is elegant and timeless. It's very heavy, so it must have proper reinforcement from rafters. Slate tiles come in single- and multicolor varieties. Since they're a natural product, the color can vary from quarry to quarry. About as expensive as clay tile, slate tiles will last one hundred years or more.

Synthetic slate roofing—High-quality synthetic slate looks like the real product but is about one-third the weight of real slate, which reduces the need to reinforce the structures that receive it. It's easier to install and has no maintenance requirements. Though it costs about six times more than asphalt shingles, the cost is considerably less than that of real slate. Synthetic slate doesn't last as long as real slate, but it will still hold up for fifty years. A new product on the market, synthetic slate doesn't have the same track record as its natural counterpart, so research the product carefully before purchasing.

1 | Colonial Color

House Number 22

1 This home's historical colors come from an old local paint company that draws on actual colors used in the colonial period in Philadelphia. The warm golden field color contrasts against the gray-blue shutters and garage door. The garage door color works especially well when viewed next to the cool gray stone wall that runs the length of the driveway. A punch of red on the front door is an exciting, unexpected selection.

2 Impeccable architectural detailing and landscaping with beautifully balanced colors are the reigning features of this Colonial house. Warm white details lighten the scheme, from the portico and window frames to smaller details like the flowers on the door, chair cushions, patio umbrellas, and garden flowers. The black door and shutters add a dramatic impact, and the house numbers and doorbell add further personality to the entry. All details have been considered on this lovely home, and it shows.

3 If color can make you feel better, this house will do the trick. The home's peaceful Zen-like garden is protected from the street by a gate that shields the house from the neighborhood and makes these colors personal and private for the taste and enjoyment of the homeowner. Bright blue meets navy blue in the inside corner of the courtyard, and the two colors play on each other in light and shadow. The backyard deck picks up the bright yellow accents in its striped yellow awning. A bowl of lemons on the table is a simple touch that emphasizes the playfulness and appreciation for color that this home embodies. What a delight!

4 The colors of this Colonial house present a bright, lighthearted, even somewhat eccentric view to the world. Light green paint color in the shutters' reveal lines adds a welcome detail and brightens the scheme. Red, the perfect complement to green, makes the screen door pop out. The window color is an unexpected pink that connects to the flowers in the window boxes. Sitting behind the red screen door is an unusual color that takes a leap away from the other colors of the house, allowing it to be interesting without offsetting the field color combinations. It's a very unexpected color addition. A final touch for this interesting and friendly old home is a ceramic goose at the entry, poised to greet visitors as they enter the house.

5 The saturated color of this Georgian-style home is sophisticated and, depending on the light, turns from brown to green taupe. The very dark green—almost black—portico and doorway create a dramatic focus that draws you down the steps to the entry. Once down to the house level, a second focal point of an Italian-inspired fountain and sitting area is revealed. Square black slate tiles are evenly scattered in the medium rock aggregate paving all around and connect in color to the entry and shutters. The house is set in a heavily wooded area and sits beautifully in its natural surroundings.

6 The earth tone colors of this Colonial Revival home blend brilliantly with each other and with the home's stone veneer facade. The asphalt roof shingles pick up all of the colors. Clapboard siding bookends either end of the house in a mossy green color. The yellow entry door and chocolate brown shutters are a refreshingly different color combination. A lushly landscaped mound with boulders creates a rugged, woodsy appearance and shields the entry of the house from the street, providing privacy for this sophisticated home.

7 The historical, rich saturated blue of this New England saltbox (named for its resemblance to a colonial-era box that was used to contain salt) is a strong and inviting color. The red door pops out and acts as a focal point for the perfectly balanced architecture. A replica plaque above the door is a reminder of times gone by—private insurance companies in colonial times would come by to put out a fire if a plaque was placed above the door. The setting of the house, placed deep into the property and surrounded by lush landscaping, helps to balance and soften the home's bright colors.

8 The rich green and warm white colors of this Colonial Revival home blend together beautifully. Painted a deep red, the door stands out as a complement to the field color. The plants in the garden are cued into the color combination, allowing the landscape to further enhance the home's curb appeal.

9 This old saltbox house was built in 1877. The fact that it has never been painted is not unusual for its time, but it's rare to see them unpainted today. The house has been stained and protected to keep it in its current pristine condition. The dark gray windows work well with the gray slate roof, while the historic green of the door and shutters blend well with the green slate pavers. A newer cottage in the backyard is picturesque and blends in seamlessly with the architectural style of the original house. This house has the charm of another time and, thankfully, has stayed this way for more than 125 years.

10 Here, classic colors are tweaked into an up-to-date combination. The front door is an especially refreshing offbeat color that singlehandedly spices up the home's neutral palette. The field, shutter, and trim colors are blended and balanced well to create a fresh color combination and eye-catching appeal.

11 A sophisticated combination of colors, texture, and landscaping come together effortlessly on this Colonial Revival house. The rough-cut cobbled limestone facade and warm gray asphalt tile roof lend contrast to the soft yellow house color and add texture to the facade. The blue shutters and door give a refreshing crispness to the scheme. The clear glass storm door functions well to protect the house from inclement weather, but it's also clean and attractive. It allows the front door color to be seen from the street without distraction. Every detail has been attended to on this pristine property, and it shows with its winning presence in its neighborhood.

12 The stone exterior of this early classical revival house has been brightened with the addition of a crayon-colored red door and shutters. This is a great example of how using a bright color in small doses can add pizzazz to the house colors without overwhelming it. The bed of flowers around the large tree in the garden picks up the red again, making an understated but important connection between the house color and landscaping.

13 This Colonial-style house has Craftsman detailing, resulting in an unusual, eclectic combination of the two architectural styles. The color selection is an outstanding, sophisticated combination of grayed-down greens and whites. Lush landscaping varies from small shrubs to overscaled plants to flowers with bursts of color, making the winding black slate path to the front door a study in scale and an interesting journey to the entrance of this delightful property.

14 Colonial homes often use different paint colors for upper and lower shutters, so that's not what makes this house unusual. What does make it unusual are the colors used for the shutters and front door—a fresh, decidedly contemporary palette of colors that are a welcome change from the stone houses of this era. The pastel colors work well with the warm tones of the stone facade. The front door wreath incorporates all the colors, bringing them together in a pretty focal point. It adds a nice touch to this lovely home.

15 The monochromatic scheme of fresh, watery blue-green colors of this Colonial Revival–style house creates a feeling of harmony that is restful to the eye. The darker front door and shutter colors punctuate the house with a welcome contrast and are balanced symmetrically on the facade of this pristine, classically handsome house.

16 This new Colonial Revival house looks like a stately older home because of the high quality of building materials used in its construction. The stone veneer facade is graphically strong in color and pattern, and the carefully chosen house colors blend in artfully with it. Shrubs marching along the entry path create a strong pattern and focal point that reinforces the home's symmetry while drawing you to the front door. There, flower-filled urns flanking the entry and a color-coordinated door wreath welcome you to this handsome home.

17 The nicely articulated detailing on the strong portal entrance, multipaned windows and sidelights, cut-out patterned shutters, and the fanlight over the front door make this sweet little Colonial Revival house a standout. The unusual color combination first calls attention to the front door because of its rich dark blue color, and then to the green cut-out shutters. There are many details for such a small house, but they are well done, bringing the home much-deserved attention.

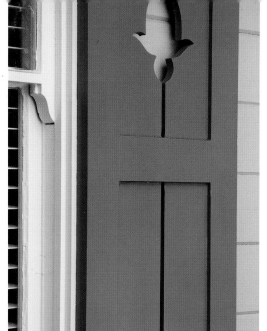

18 Color combinations like these are found far and wide on this style of house. They are chosen for good reason—the warm rust color and creamy white work well against the texture and color of the natural stone but have enough color contrast to highlight the door and shutters. It's a classic color combination that is warm and welcoming and also retains a striking appearance.

19 Stonework dominates the facade of this lovely Cape Cod-style home, adding texture and color variation. The two-toned soft putty trim, verdigris patina lantern, and teal door and shutters work together to successfully pull out these colors from the natural stone in an unusual and unexpected way. Fresh annual flowers are always a welcome touch of color for the entry.

20 A range of mauve tones works in symphony with the neutral trim color of this neo-eclectic style house. Though they are difficult colors to get right, this home succeeds in every way. Even the stone pavers leading up the entry connect well because they use the same colors. Colorful flowers and landscaping, including a Japanese maple with delicate leaves, brighten the scheme and add scale and softness to the property. The dark aubergine door, with its strong surrounding portal, adds depth of color to the palette and creates a strong focal point. The final touch is a door wreath that pulls in all of the house colors, reinforcing the sense of entry and making the focal point even stronger.

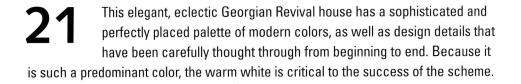

21 This elegant, eclectic Georgian Revival house has a sophisticated and perfectly placed palette of modern colors, as well as design details that have been carefully thought through from beginning to end. Because it is such a predominant color, the warm white is critical to the success of the scheme.

The strong architectural portal entry is reinforced with a dark green contrasting door color and complementary-colored red wreath, spiral topiaries, hanging light fixture, and red brick bordered black pavers that lead to it. Landscaping is an important consideration in the overall design of the property. It softens the hard lines of the architecture and makes the house softer and more welcoming. The final touch—round metallic medallions placed between the first- and second-story windows—adds a sophisticated and understated sparkle to a house that is already a gem.

22 Though the right side of this distinguished old Colonial was built in 1690 and the left side was added in 1830, the colors suit the twenty-first century. The palette definitely befits this wonderful old house, yet it also speaks of the present, with its contemporary muted color combinations. The roof tile demonstrates how the proper color selection can successfully tie into the house colors. You can't get much more charming than the ivy growing up the side of the house—except perhaps for the mailbox that mimics the property's freestanding garage. A little bit of levity is always welcome. This home has clearly been well maintained by its many owners over the last three hundred years. Quality construction and tender loving care have kept it in its present condition so it could survive and be here today for all of us to appreciate and enjoy.

2 | Cottage Color

House Number 38

23 Set below street grade, this charming bungalow is partially shielded from the street by its landscaping. Color-embedded stucco offers a dusty brown backdrop for the lush array of wild, colorful flowers in the garden. The large, rough cobblestone pavers come from the streets of San Francisco after the 1906 earthquake and offer a rich texture that contribute to the quaintness of this cottage.

24 Stylized accents such as lighting and porch furniture have transformed this pristine Victorian gem. The house colors are subtle and unusual: beige with a hint of cacke green with a dark cacke green for the porch floor paint. The white trim colors blend to perfection with the house color. Black adds a punch of dramatic contrast to the door, windows, and railing. Symmetry has not been overlooked; palm trees on either side of the steps and climbing vines covering the columns reinforce the "sense of entry" and act as a strong focal point while providing a softening device for the property.

25 & 26

These absolutely charming cottages, reminiscent of the French Normandy countryside, were built with irregular coursed rough rubble from the local quarry many years ago. Short walls run the length of the private road and connect one house to the other. Painted windows, shutters, and garage doors add unique color to each property. The dark-green-shuttered house is especially lovely with its view through french doors that reveals a lush garden and lily pond complete with goldfish and a visiting frog.

27 This once-plain 1950s cottage has been renovated with eclectic details that have taken it from ordinary to extraordinary. The 5-lite etched glass door, door hardware, and copper and redwood railing add a modern twist, while the trellis, light fixture, and beefed-up window frames lend themselves to more of a Craftsman feeling. Landscaping lends an Asian flair with bamboo, grasses, and a Japanese maple. Boulders and river rocks set organically into the steps add a sculptural element, while vines climbing and covering the entry act as a softening device and create a strong focal point. The green house color fits well with the natural redwood porch, steps, trellis, boulders, and river rocks and reinforces the colors of nature that have been incorporated on the property.

28 This pretty cottage takes a leap of faith with its bold, lively blue color. It is worth the jump. Because of the small scale of the house, it can take this intense bold color. White shutters and trim, along with trees and foliage in the front yard, help to break up the amount of blue color seen from the street. Heavy shade protects the house from the sun, which will minimize fading. Ultimately, colors used on the right scale and in correct proportions is the key to this home's success.

29 This French provincial cottage exudes charisma and curb appeal. Amazingly, it has never been painted—the homeowner has purposefully and carefully preserved the original 1928 exterior stucco finish by applying a waterproof, breathable silicone coating as needed. This has allowed the house to "breathe" and has created a natural patina with a complex depth of color that would be difficult to achieve otherwise. A soft shutter color adds a welcome fresh color to the neutral palette. A seasonal display of white roses add brightness, color, contrast, and texture to this exceptional property.

30 The light brown and gray colors of this small bungalow are an unusual combination and work well together because of important color connectors used on and around the property. Wood blinds in the front window pick up on the mustard front door color and the tree beside it, while the gray trim around the door and window frames make a connection to the metal in the contemporary glass awning. The garden landscaping picks up the colors of the clay roof tile, adding warmth to the scheme. Loosely planted landscaping fills the garden with colorful flowers and softens the hard lines of the house. Together, the colors create an interesting, offbeat collection that makes this simple house special.

31 This specialty "Devita Style" cottage was developed by a builder in the wine country of Northern California. The appeal is in its architectural simplicity, scale, and detailing. The soft pink-peach and warm grays work in harmony with each other and the surrounding picket fence, giving the property a feeling of "home sweet home."

32

The combination of color, architecture, and landscaping can set a mood and take us to another place, and this home proves it. The scale of the house, with its sloping cedar tile roof, gives the feeling of a small one-story cottage in the woods when the home is actually much larger. The field color is a creamy white-painted brick that brightens this house in the woods. Dark green trim fits the wooded environment and calls attention to the architectural details on the home. Attention to fine details are everywhere, including the paneled garage door, concrete pavers, short stone walls, antique bench, well-placed concrete planters at the entry, round boulders scattered around the tree, and beautifully layered landscaping. Color and architecture are in balance and work together like a charm.

33 This is an extremely unusual but very attractive color combination for a stone house. The turquoise adds a brightness that is at once bold yet also fitting, especially when seen alongside the pool color through the turquoise gated entrance. The color has a sense of elegance against the stone walls of the old house; it almost seems to pick up the color out of the stone. The color is repeated in the striped awning and lounge chair cushions. It's an exciting color choice because it's used in fairly small doses, takes a chance, and wins big on this delightful Cotswold cottage. The overscaled ferns planted on the streetscape, pink flowers in window boxes, and outlined red paint in the door panels add even more charm, if that's possible.

34 Rich camel and deep red create a striking combination that works beautifully on this sweet little cottage. The multipaned, plentiful windows open up the house to light. The repeated pattern on the paneled front door adds even more congruity and dimension to the facade. A winding stone path, with loosely landscaped arid plants and flowers on either side, relaxes and softens the symmetry of the house while adding curb appeal.

35 If you were traveling through the English countryside, you might see picturesque Tudor-style cottages just like this. The colors are neutral but sophisticated. The landscaping responds to the size of the small garden, with loosely structured, arid plants rather than a formal garden. This adds welcome dimension to the small plot and works to soften the house from the street. A small metal clover leaf added to the house number plaque brings a little extra personality to the entry of this charming house.

36 The rich gold and orange colors on this little Victorian cottage are fun and adventurous. The chestnut stained hardwood plank porch floor works great with the wicker chairs and warm colors of the house, adding a depth of color to the overall scheme. The dormer windows on the second floor and shutters on the first floor are inspired and serve to balance the colors on the house. Peach roses are a great color-connecting device that take the colors beyond the walls of the house onto the property. Attention to detail is apparent everywhere you look, giving this little gem of a house its eye-catching appeal.

37 Terra-cotta and sage dominate the colors of this adorable cottage that looks like a little dollhouse. Two tones on a door can sometimes be distracting, but in this case they are an interesting feature of the entry and give the door the appearance of being smaller, thus visually enhancing the small scale of the house by bringing added attention to the entry. Mimicking an old slate-tile roof, the asphalt shingle roof color cools off the warm colors and contributes to the home's allure.

38 This house is a showstopper. Designed with thoughtful detailing throughout the property, it features subtle, sophisticated colors. The field color is a warm, soft neutral with an occasional white-washed effect on the garage door and bay windows. The

light teal window and roof tile colors are a refreshing addition that suits the architecture and provides a bit of a punch. Rather than being a standard "gray" concrete, the stone aggregate paving is an integral buff color that blends with the house color. It's a subtle but extremely effective detail that elevates the concrete product to another level. The color and landscaping are combined differently on each part of the house, yet tie in beautifully with each other. A lush backyard invites relaxation, while old-growth trees soften the architecture, adding a casual elegance to the ambiance of the property.

39 The traditional Christmas colors of red and green have never looked so good! This artistic and enchanted cottage in the woods has a view to the world that's both rustic and sophisticated at the same time—a difficult characteristic to pull off, since the two qualities are generally at odds with each other. But not here. Charm abounds in the house colors as well as the abundant multicolored flowers used in every corner of the property, from the front of the house to the lush, sloped backyard complete with an attached greenhouse and two tiny shingled structures. One structure, with Christmas tree cut-out shutters, is a small, delightful storage unit. The other, lit from inside, is an artist's studio. Both can be reached by traversing the stairs that are shrouded in shade by trees and are surrounded by a lush array of blooming flowers. The charming ambiance and character of the property has been gained over the years with patience and tender loving care.

40 Great details abound on this soft ivory clapboard, stucco, and stone cottage, including three high-pitched rooftops, multiple leaded-glass windows, and stone veneer running up the outside corners of the house and surrounding the entry door. The windows are painted a softer shade of green than the frames and shutters. The worn color of the natural shake roof shingles blend with the stonework and add a soft earth tone to the scheme. All of these elements work together harmoniously to create a look of timeless appeal.

41 The addition of a winding garden path flanked by wildflowers and surrounded with a picket fence has enhanced this delightful cottage. Slate on the steps subtly pulls out the house colors. Equally subtle, the colors of the house and landscaped garden blend together harmoniously, creating an enchanting, idyllic property.

42 A tree-lined driveway and the strong horizontal lines of a louver-paneled garage door give this French-inspired cottage graphic interest and a unique allure. As you look past the house to the left and walk around the corner, you can see a French blue entry door, two French-inspired lanterns, and a figurative sculpture that is set in a lush green garden—all of which add more interest to the hidden courtyard. These added design elements make a fairly plain house quite extraordinary.

43 Newly constructed, this French country-style cottage features great detailing from the front to the back of the property. Color-embedded stucco on the ground floor adds a depth to the finish and serves as a golden, warm neutral that works well with the stonework that's used generously around the property. The stucco was given two coats of color, the lighter-colored second coat being applied over a wet first coat so that the colors would blend together and produce a mottled antique finish. A whitewashed redwood ceiling on the entry porch has a bright, rustic antique finish that keeps it light and airy. Cool sage green paint on the second-story clapboard adds a refreshing counterpoint to the stonework and neutral colors, while the unexpected pink door proves delightful among this collection of arid house colors and landscaping. Perennial 'Blue Star Creeper' permeates the Arizona flagstone for a rustic effect in the pool area behind the house, and the acid rusted steel gate to the area adds deep color and texture to the property. This new construction project with newly planted gardens will only get better with time.

44 Tall old-growth trees have helped to create a dramatic setting for this cottage in the woods. Bleaching oil has been used to protect the naturally brown cedar shingle siding and accelerate its natural weathering process, turning the surface of the house into a silvery gray color with a hint of green. The trellis in the front of the house softens the entry and creates privacy from the street. In the backyard, a raised circular ledge stone wall softens the hard lines of the architecture and creates an outdoor living space that overlooks the flower and vegetable gardens. Wood chips cover much of the grounds as pine needles would on a forest floor. Blending well into its natural environment, this property embodies the peaceful, relaxed feeling that has been created here as a joint effort by man and nature.

45 A cozy style emanates from this attractive ranch house, whose soft coordinated colors and brick porch setting provide a view of a quiet, simple setting. The front door color matches the flagstone path, red leaf maple tree, and red brick steps and porch. Monochromatic green window colors complement the soft red, so the two colors naturally work well together. The addition of a weather-worn redwood fence and a rickety old chair, stacked tree branches, and watering can that sit on the porch complete the picture of a down-home country farmhouse.

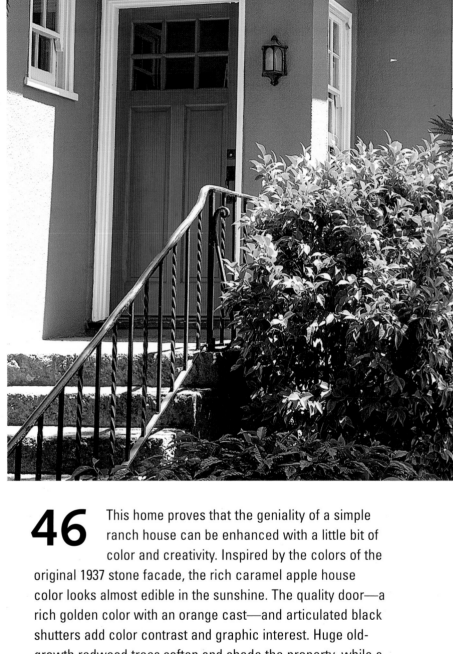

46 This home proves that the geniality of a simple ranch house can be enhanced with a little bit of color and creativity. Inspired by the colors of the original 1937 stone facade, the rich caramel apple house color looks almost edible in the sunshine. The quality door—a rich golden color with an orange cast—and articulated black shutters add color contrast and graphic interest. Huge old-growth redwood trees soften and shade the property, while a newly added redwood trellis and fence revitalize the view of the property and create a barrier between the house and street traffic, generating a great deal of curb appeal for this updated cottage.

3 | Craftsman/Bungalow Color

House Number 51

47 The fresh, saturated green and white colors on this charming Craftsman are seen through trees that separate the house from the city street. It's a refreshing change from colors that are typically seen on this style of shingle house. There is plenty of curb appeal, but what makes the house stand out most is the attention to detail paid to the home's entry. The steps lead to a periwinkle blue door that works beautifully with the row of potted hydrangeas lined up on the ledge. Multicolored flowers in planter boxes under the third-story double-hung windows add more color and a secondary focal point to this charming house.

48 This handsome Craftsman house has a sophisticated and complex paint formula color that reads both "warm" and "cool," depending on the light. Warm white trim complements the field color with just the right amount of contrast. The dark earth color sets a dramatic backdrop for brightly colored landscaping and draws positive attention to itself. The house is a great example of using color in the right proportions successfully—lots of windows and white trim break up this home's dark field color. Interesting, colorful landscaping and shade from trees soften the intensity of these dramatic colors. The house number, located over the front door, is also a light fixture and has been creatively adapted from an antique ship's spotlight, adding a personal touch to the entrance of this captivating, appealing house.

49 The out-of-the-ordinary combination of colors—an unusual pea green field color, dark brown trim, concrete roof tile, and multicolored slate paver tile—is the most unique characteristic of this house on the hill. The front door and patio area sit below street level, providing an alluring private space reached by descending steps. There, the nicely articulated Craftsman-style entry with its warm-colored cherry door, glass french doors, and a nicely landscaped seating area with extraordinary panoramic views are revealed.

50 This shingle Craftsman uses traditional complementary colors that are a classic combination on this style of house. They work so well that it's worth a second look. The cedar shingle color glows against the dark forest green window frames. Warm white interior shutters add a tailored appearance on the inside as well as the outside of the house. This illustrates why selecting the right colors for window treatments and having consistency from window to window are so important. The cottage red front door picks up on the colors of the brick path and budding red-leafed cherry tree. The herringbone brick pattern on the entry pavers meets a plain pattern on the steps, providing subtle sophistication and an extra level of interest. There is a good reason why the classics always seem to work successfully, and this house is no exception.

51 This grand Craftsman has a cozy quality by giving the illusion of being smaller than it actually is, a result of the dark charcoal gray used for its field color and large shade trees that break up its appearance visually. The lush landscaping softens the hard lines of the architecture. A white picket fence gives way to the garden path that leads to classic battered Craftsman columns on the porch, which is complete with wicker furniture. Here, the homeowners can sit and relax in an intimate living room-like setting. This peaceful setting gives the feeling that time stands still here.

52 Plant massing is a dramatic way to add modern style to your property that's also simple to create and maintain. A sweep of one single botanical variety—in this case, lavender—creates a field of sensational seasonal color. The flower color pops against the gray-toned house. Terra-cotta pavers, a stained cherry-wood door, a bronze doorbell, and a rusted lounge chair add warm earth tones to the scheme. Modern touches, including the doorbell, the perforated lounge chair, and a planter turned into a miniature koi pond, add eclectic interest. Marching ants over the curved bay window add a bit of unexpected whimsy. The green-painted embossed wreath relief above the entry is a nice touch too. It all adds up to a sophisticated combination of color, texture, and style.

53 "Brick red" paint on this bungalow house provides an exciting and dramatic backdrop for the landscaping that matches the home's harmonious red and green colors. Cleverly, the side walls of the neighboring home's two garages, visible from the homeowners' backyard, have been painted an upbeat green, affording the homeowners a backdrop that works with their own color palette. The scale of the landscaping helps to create small, private outdoor living spaces for the sitting areas in the backyard. This is an outstanding example of how landscaping can positively impact the curb appeal of a house.

54 This is an example of how a little creativity can go a long way to create great curb appeal on a plain little house. Bungalow and modern styles are mixed together, creating an interesting, eclectic result. Attention to detail at the front door, including the door style and color, doorbell, door hardware, and house numbers, makes a strong focal point that demands attention. Semitropical plants add a nice scale, soften the entry, and add welcome texture. Terra-cotta planter colors connect to the painted concrete path and add warmth to the cool house color. It's an offbeat collection of color and design—but it works very well and has fashioned the home into a chic urban property.

55 This sweet bungalow cottage uses an interesting mix of tropical, sun-drenched peach and a gray-sage color. Orange flowers pick up the field color and brighten the scheme further. The soft red door is an unusual and unexpected punch of color, but happily works quite well for this scheme. This is a good example of the importance of well-placed color. The idea of connecting roof color to house color is obviously not lost on the homeowner; the peach-colored stucco is sandwiched by neutral colors on the roof and the clapboard siding on the base of the house, providing balanced color. Landscaping helps to frame the house handsomely too. The well-placed details all come together to produce a home with attractive, pleasant appeal.

56 This delightful bungalow-style cottage features a redwood stain on its cedar shingle siding, railing, window frames, and steps, blending them together seamlessly into one color while letting the texture of the shingles become the main focus. This glowing stain color is nicely coordinated to complement the green paint used on the door and windows. The house numbers, doorbell, and lighting, all in bronze, blend with each other as well as with the entire color scheme to create a picture-perfect appearance.

57 The saturated bronze-green color of this Craftsman shingle house combines splendidly with the dark red on the door and windows. White on the beams and trim highlight the best details offered by a house of this style. It's a lovely home and is nicely balanced with its sophisticated color palette.

58 This stucco Briarwood bungalow home that's set below street level has a soft, warm gray field color. Since the facade of the house is so flat, most of the interest comes from the persimmon front door and planters that match each other flawlessly. These two items single-handedly give the home its strong color focus. The slate steps and colorful plants pull from this persimmon color, making an important connection that enhances the balance of color on the property. The large hand-poured cement steps add substantial scale to the garden. They make a dramatic statement as they lead visitors down the hill from the street to the strong, colorful entry.

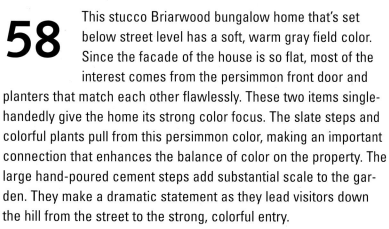

59 Three house colors—copper, green, and gray—dominate this eclectic modern/Santa Fe-style bungalow. A field of wildflowers fills the garden, picking up the house colors and adding loads of bright color to the property. Three-foot-long eaves protect the walls from rainwater and the wood-framed windows from sun and rain. Vertical rain chains lead water from the roof gutter to a basin filled with granite river rock and then out to the street, a feature that is simple to make, visually interesting, and very effective. The attention to detail on this home is abundant and gives this house a terrific presence on its street.

60 This distinguished farmhouse with Craftsman detailing looks impressive dressed in its dark blue field color. The sophisticated color works particularly well because it balances proportionally with the white window frames, porch railing, rose trellis, and picket fence. This helps to keep the house from becoming too oppressively dark. The property's stonework, flagstone pavers, and plaza fountain add welcome warm colors and texture, while the landscaping, including the rose-covered trellis, softens the architecture. With their matching blue-and-white-striped cushions, the white wicker chairs on the porch complement the whole scheme and add a relaxed, down-home atmosphere to this country house.

61 This modernized Arts and Crafts house that sits high in the hills has overscaled picture windows, deep eaves, and architectural detailing that give it dramatic flair. The eaves offer an opportunity for a darker contrasting color against the home's lighter field color. Although the home is actually quite large, the entry is intimate and gives it a smaller intimate feeling, contributing to its charm. The vines that shroud the front facade and climb up the rear foundation add lots of character while softening the hard lines of the architecture. The field color is a complex sun-kissed gold that lights up the house when the sun hits it, enhancing its Mediterranean flavor.

62 This enchanting Craftsman features a vine-covered wall surrounding the property, complete with unique antique gates recovered from a Korean temple. It creates a delightful private courtyard space with soft-colored Mexican saltillo pavers and a seating area. The dark house color acts as a dramatic backdrop for the pink and white flowers, which add vibrant color and contrast to this striking property.

63 This sophisticated Craftsman-style house was built in 1908, but the beefed-up arch and trellis were added on more recently and fit in as if they've always been there—the sign of a quality restoration project. The warm white trim colors provide strong visual interest that initially keeps the eye focused at the street level. Then, through the arched trellis and up terra-cotta steps flanked by plants, a secondary focal point is revealed of a Moravian star light fixture above a beautifully detailed red front door. It's a warm, welcoming entry to this lovely city home.

64 From the colors of the house, trim, and stucco garden wall to the door, gate, and wood caps, neutral colors with warm wood accents rule the clean lines of this striking Craftsman home. The garden wall with a redwood cap adds a horizontal line that relates to similar horizontal lines on the house. Once inside the garden walls, the color and texture of the flagstone paving, Japanese maple trees, flowers, and plants become apparent. The statuary figure at the back of the garden is a focal point that provides a place to rest the eye. A newly added wall was designed to work in unison with the architecture of the house and also serves to separate this peaceful Zen garden from street traffic. A pine gate, located in the garden wall, points visitors to the entry path of this attractive property.

65 This stunning shingled Craftsman home has skillfully blended detailing from one end of the property to the other. The light-colored stucco walls lift the house up and help to separate the heavily articulated upper portion of the house from the richly textured garden below. The shades of green—pea green and forest green—work very well together and complement the naturally aging redwood shingles, red brick steps, and stone walls. Through the breezeway, a patio area at the back of the property is revealed, while the opposite direction frames a breathtaking panoramic view through the archway.

66 This is a good example of how new construction materials can retain the integrity of the original style of architecture, right down to the battered piers. But there's no doubt that the colors are fresh and modern. The Mackintosh-inspired etched squares in the transom window above the door echo the four square windows in the door—an Arts and Crafts detail worth repeating. The door handle and knocker are authentic reproductions of the same style and add a distinguished finishing touch.

67 This bungalow-style house has four saturated colors used in assorted locations—gold, taupe, rust, and army green. The colors are applied in a fun way, almost as if they've been "colored in." What a delightful and inventive collection of colors. It's an unusual application, but it has great personality and the colors balance out beautifully on this charmer.

68

This handsome Victorian-turned-Craftsman/modern house fits easily into its eclectic urban neighborhood. The back of the house is an inspired modern renovation with large, open windows that make good use of city views. Richly colored cedar shingles and a cherry-stained mahogany front door add warmth and connect to the shingle color. A generous use of black accent paint makes a dramatic statement and articulates the details of the home. Concrete planter boxes at the entry add a

unique modern element to the architecture and help to connect it to the modern portions of the house. A dark charcoal color on the inset panels makes a visual connection to the modern slate steps and planter boxes. A tile replica of "She Who Watches," a reproduction of a petroglyph from the Chinook Indians of the Columbia River Gorge area, is embedded in the planter box and stands in waiting at the entry to the house. This detail adds a personal touch for the homeowners and neighbors to enjoy.

69 This little bungalow uses an attractive combination of cocoa brown for its field color and a deeper brown for the articulated Arts and Crafts windows, but what livens up the scheme most are the warm red door and flowers of the same color in the recessed entry. Carefully tended shrubs add color and texture to the property and help to soften the entryway, which is paved with oversized red bricks.

70 This charming brick and wood-framed bungalow is complete with rocking chairs on the porch, a throwback to simpler times. Other appealing features include a secondary seating niche, an old wood door, leaded-glass windows, flower pots, and oversized garden flowers in seasonal bloom. The house colors have well-coordinated earth tones that add to the timeless curb appeal of this Craftsman home.

71 The redwood entry gate and river rock stone pillars add rustic Craftsman detailing to this Prairie-style house and give the property an eclectic style that's quite unique. When the gate swings open, a delightful view to the entry of the house is revealed. Down a charming stone path past rubble walls, trees, and plants is a salmon-colored recessed wall at the entry to the house—an unexpected shot of color that's a pleasure to behold. Not only does it add a creative and unexpected splash of color to the neutral beige and white scheme, but it also draws attention to the entry by making it a strong focal point. The Japanese maple trees and pink tones in the stone seem to reflect this color, making a subtle connection and adding balance to the property. This is an exceptionally good example of how, when using the right color, a little bit can go a long way.

4 | Mediterranean Color

House Number **88**

72 This Monterey-style Colonial has been renovated into a Spanish Revival home, adding great personality and style to the original house. The fanciful and delicately sculpted entry gate gives way to an enchanting courtyard within the garden walls. Here, an elaborate lily pond, flagstone pavers, a diverse selection of potted plants, and a semitropical landscape offer an inviting outdoor space while also providing privacy. A winding path outside of the garden wall adds another layer between the courtyard and the street. Dusty blue planters on either side of the front door pick up the patterned multicolor ceramic tile and window color. The warm white house color provides a quiet backdrop for this beautifully landscaped property. There is no doubt that in every way, this home has successfully been transformed from ordinary to extraordinary.

73 Design has been thoughtfully considered from top to bottom on this charming Mediterranean home. The house color is a modern interpretation of what is generally seen on this style of house, though this version is brighter and considerably more luminous. The foggy weather of the area where this house is located was taken into consideration when the field color was chosen, and the vibrant hue will brighten up even the darkest of days. If selecting this color for a sunny area, consider that the color will be much brighter and livelier than in the photograph.

There is so much to look at on this property. The eye is first drawn to the trellised gate and then to the arched garage doors flanked with overscaled potted plants. A row of glass block windows adds a decidedly modern twist and eclectic interest to the architecture. The gated entry, covered with yellow-flowering vines, takes you through to a rustic courtyard that's tucked away from the street; with its lush foliage, rustic brick pavers, and colorful assorted flowers, it brings even more charm to this enchanting property. A well-placed plum tree helps to visually break up and divide color, and it also serves to connect to the trim color. The proportional use of house color to landscape color is well done and plays an important role in the success of this home's delightful appearance.

74 This enchanting Mediterranean home looks like it was plucked out of the hills of Tuscany. The faux finish used for the field color and verdigris front door adds depth and gives the look of a much older home. To achieve the same sophisticated subtleties, it's best to hire a professional specialty painter to do the job. Flagstone pavers lead up to painted steps that pull out a slightly purple hue from the stone pavers. It's an interesting shift of color that's inspired. Spiral topiaries on either side of the elaborate, broken-pediment portal entry and colorful flowers and landscaping lighting that line the path reinforce the home's strong central focal point. Wildflowers, a climbing vine, boulders that line the flower bed, and a graceful wooden bench contribute to the pastoral ambiance that's been created here.

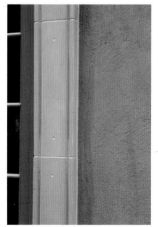

75 The patina of this French eclectic house appears to be old, but has been created using an old-world lime wash process. The decorative painting specialist for this project used brooms and huge brushes to apply the lime wash to the stucco, which was mixed with dried powder pigments from Tuscany and Provence. The wash soaked in and gave an immediate aged look that purposely features drips and uneven color. It was mixed at the job site without a formula to attain just the right color. This is a special method that should be applied by a skilled painting specialist to achieve top-notch results. The front door elevation of the house has experienced extreme sun exposure, and the window color has faded into a soft blue because of it, but it still works well with the overall color scheme.

The grille work in the small openings of the stucco walls was purchased from an antiques dealer, and the walls were built to accommodate its size. An extraordinary find—an antique French gate—was found at a salvage yard and the wall was also built to house it. The paint on both the grille work and gate has achieved a natural patina that complements the lime wash and the cast stone window surrounds harmoniously. The creative use of unique found items, color and patina, style, and landscaping have come together to create a picturesque appearance that evokes a southern French country ambiance.

76 The bold earth tone colors of gold, green, red, and terra-cotta on this exquisitely detailed urban Mediterranean-style house were inspired by the homeowner's visit in and around Bologna, Italy. Bronze door knockers like this are found all over the older neighborhoods of Florence. The homeowner discovered a reproduction at a local metalwork shop there and purchased it as a souvenir from the trip. It stands as a constant reminder of a memorable vacation while adding style to the house. Elaborately detailed grille work on the windows not only protects the house from burglars, but also enhances it with ornate and decorative architectural detailing. The addition of heavy-link swagged chains and large-leafed plants in oversized cast-stone planters complete the Italian villa motif. Bellisimo!

The ceramic tile above the garage door acts as the inspiration piece for the dusty, muted colors of this fetching Mediterranean-style home. French doors open onto a landscaped flagstone patio that's surrounded by a low stucco garden wall, creating a relaxing private space for the homeowners to dine al fresco. Articulated shutters and fanciful custom light fixtures and wrought-iron gates work together to create a charming ambiance with Tuscan style.

78 This house seems small until you open the arched plantation shutter doors and are transported to a lushly designed, Mediterranean-style courtyard that opens up to panoramic views. Seating areas to the left and right are complete with a unique wall-mounted water fountain, white Italian marble pavers, vine-covered walls, lush potted flowering plants, airy ferns, and a swagged drapery panel that softens the french door of the garage entry. The magnificent overscaled, elaborate curved-glass-paneled entry doors to the house were salvaged from an old department store and have found a new home here. A grand white marble staircase at the back of the house is brimming with bougainvillaea vines that top intricate iron railings and decorative fruit basket final posts. The bougainvillaea adds a substantial addition of color to the property, standing out against a backdrop of soft brown and white house colors. The Italian villa motif is complete, and it's a beauty.

79 Constructed on top of a rock formation, this home was designed to accommodate the property's unusual site. The portico, set deep into the property, helps guide visitors to the entry, which draws attention to itself with its richly saturated terra-cotta color. Other colors—gold, sage, forest green, and redwood—punctuate the house with bold colors that are typically found on homes in the Mediterranean. Colorful succulents, climbing vines, and wildflowers add a vibrant, complex landscape that ties into this out-of-the-ordinary, multi-hued home.

80 This casually elegant brick and stucco Mediterranean-style house is a terrific example of how color can be used to visually connect two different surface materials together seamlessly. Exposed brick provides an interesting texture and connects with the same color of the oyster-colored stucco walls. A refined green paint color is used on the portico entry walls, windows and window frames, and french doors off the patio. It ties in beautifully to the lush landscape while contributing a rich color to the scheme. Dark brown exposed rafters on the house and trellis add verticality and make a dramatic contrast against the light-colored wall behind them. Balanced and harmonious color rule in this textured, stylishly sophisticated setting.

81 The use of happy, sun-kissed colors on the irregular stucco walls enhance this Mediterranean-style house. It would have been safe to paint it neutral colors, but the vivid field color and green accent for the door and shutters are refreshingly bright and make the home friendly and welcoming. The red horse chestnut tree adds seasonal color, bringing a complementary hue to the scheme. These combinations, along with details like the flower-filled urns, topiaries on each side of the front door, and a bright yellow lemon tree transform the house into a cheery, tropical delight.

82 With eclectic style and discerning design, this Mediterranean home has elaborate architectural details everywhere you look. The color-embedded stucco walls have dimensional color that gives life to the flat surfaces of the house and provides it with eye-catching appeal. Black trim and accents add dramatic contrast. High-end products like cast-stone pavers, stair treads and molding, lavishly designed custom railings, french doors and windows, and a heavy mahogany door attest to the homeowners' commitment to quality of materials and design. Two dried squash sitting on the entry's cast-stone bench complement the front door color and give a lighthearted message to visitors. All details work together to create refined elegance for this ultra-chic city home.

83 An old patina on a stucco house can be simulated with faux finishes, but this one is the real deal. The house was built in 1993 and has developed a natural patina over time, one of the advantages of using a color-embedded stucco. The house looks much older, as if it has been there for ages. The glazed ceramic address tile is the inspiration for the house color. This terra-cotta and green combination always works well on a Mediterranean-style house, as the rich, full-bodied colors are perfect complements to each other. A trellised entry gate swings open to reveal steps leading through lush, large-leafed semitropical plants to a courtyard complete with Mexican saltillo pavers and hand-painted inset tiles. The columned entry, iron grille work on the windows, and quaint table and chairs complete the picture-perfect, rustic Mediterranean setting.

84 A great deal of attention has been paid to the design of this exquisite property. Nothing has been overlooked. As you move toward the wrought-iron gated entry, the finer details come into view. They provide a treasure trove of superior design elements, including a decorative entry with a graceful arched door, intricate balconies, arched windows, colorful flowers spilling from planter boxes, patterned brick and exposed aggregate paving, exquisite custom lights, and an elaborate ceramic tile mural at the entry. These tiles connect all of the house colors together and may have been their inspiration. The saturated colors of this picturesque home have been blended and balanced to perfection, creating the look and feel of a refined Mediterranean villa.

85 The subtle use of color and texture speak volumes about this house. The ambiance created is of an old Tuscan farmhouse with a granite cobblestone entry path, ceramic tile on the step risers, a deep walled entry with an old paneled wood door, and a few small windows with grilles that penetrate the thick walls of the house. Olive trees that line the front of the house and the general ease of the property's landscaping feel natural and unplanned. The paint on the front elevation of the house has aged and gained a subtle patina that works well for the home's rustic atmosphere. The back of the house is newly painted and has a modern redwood deck addition, a high tensile strength cable and redwood railing, and french doors that bring contemporary interest and sophistication to the mix.

86 This Spanish eclectic home has modified details of the classic style—a hipped terra-cotta roof, parapet, molded cornice, wrought-iron window railings, and enriched entry and window surrounds. The refined color selections blend with the roof tile effortlessly, while multicolored flowers and succulents keep the same muted tones as the house colors to create an overall consistency that is pleasing and restful to the eye. The front door continues with this theme; it is an old finish on the door, so the process of how it was achieved is an educated guess, but we do know that it was originally finished with a dark walnut stain and then was most likely water-blasted to create the grooves and irregularities in the grain. Finally, it was lightly sanded. The streaking is probably a result of the natural bleaching that occurs as sun exposure wears down the wood protectant over the years. To keep this desirable finish, the door is protected regularly with an exterior varnish. The rustic appearance and the muted quality fit right into the plan for this graceful Mediterranean home.

87 The high-end, durable materials used to build this picturesque Tuscan-style home in the hills will sustain its pristine condition for years to come. A dramatic stage is set from the start, with a passage to the steps reached by passing through pedestals topped with post lanterns. Graceful curved limestone steps flanked with bougainvillaea vines lead down to the private patio, complete with a fountain, four sets of french doors, potted plants, and white rose vines. The transition from limestone steps to limestone patio pavers is seamless. The focal point shifts to the left, revealing a recessed entry to the house where an arched oak door with a beveled glass window reflects back onto the steps purposefully. The door is framed by a facade of architectural stone veneer and a recessed balcony with french doors above. All colors and materials used throughout the property integrate beautifully. The carefully orchestrated ambiance of an Italian villa in the rolling hills is complete as you look past the house to dazzling panoramic views.

88 A great personality only begins to describe this grand Mediterranean-style house and property. It shows a lighthearted view to the world by way of a fresco painted on the garage door by the homeowner and her eighty-eight-year-old mother that will stand as a constant reminder of a memorable shared experience. The playfulness continues in the pastel stained concrete stepping-stones that have been molded into the shape of pillows and placed in the lush flower gardens surrounding the house. Everything about the property, including the golden sun-kissed house color, colorful climbing vines, and an abundant array of flowers, speaks volumes about the sunny disposition of the homeowner and how her personality is reflected and shared with the neighborhood.

89 Set back from the street, this captivating and picturesque Spanish Revival home has such a strong focal point that your eye has nowhere to go but directly to the front door. It's reinforced by an elaborately patterned portal surround that adds textural interest to the entry. Landscaping frames the entry path with symmetrically placed trees, boxwood hedges, and potted round shrubs, and abundant seasonal white roses brighten the scheme. Taupe and white house colors act as a sophisticated neutral backdrop to the heavily landscaped garden while the terra-cotta roof tile and red brick path frame it. Black window grilles and railings add a dark contrast to the color plan. There's some whimsy here too, with terra-cotta bunnies hopping around the garden. A little bit of levity adds personality to the property and is always a nice touch.

90 The dynamic focal point of this idyllic Tuscan-style country house divides the property with wide diamond-grid paving that leads to the french door entry. The curved glass and wrought-iron awning and the potted plants at each side reinforce this focus while giving dimension to the flat facade of the house. The expansive courtyard is divided into two distinct sections—a heavily shaded outdoor dining space with decomposed granite pavers on the left and a slightly raised swimming pool area on the right. The private courtyard is placed between the gated entry and the house, using all of the available outdoor space to develop an Italian country-style atmosphere. Climbing rose vines flank the outside walls, framing and softening the entry with coordinating color. Stained trellises and garage doors match the deep colors of the home's doors and windows and work agreeably with the peach house color. This combination is reminiscent of Tibetan colors and contributes to the magic of this enchanting property.

91 What's most striking about this fine Mediterranean home is how well the colors and materials coordinate with the flagstone arches that are original to the house. The paint colors, warm mahogany door, door wreath, and flagstone are soft, muted tones that achieve a subtle sophistication and work in gentle harmony with each other. The long flagstone path offers a seamless surface that flows from the sidewalk, up the steps, and to the entry door. A terracotta roof tile and red Japanese maple tree add contrast and a punch of deep color to the overall scheme of this attractive property.

92 The warm and inviting golden color of this house is complex—it brightens considerably in the sunshine and is more muted in the shade. A lemon tree at the entry adds a partial canopy of bright color that helps to frame the arched black front door and deep door frame that contribute to the sense of entry. Colorful semitropical plants and flowers meander within a stone border and hover close to the house, softening every wall. The quaint balcony, with its eight round flower pots, directs attention upward to the second story and brings color and interest to the corner of this charismatic Mediterranean home.

93 This sophisticated French Mediterranean house has a sunny disposition with a view towards a relaxed lifestyle. The terra-cotta house color, with its strong pink cast, works delightfully with the blue windows and warm white trim. Blue-and-white-striped awnings contribute to the overall lighthearted mood of the place. The house numbers and mailbox, bulbous column caps, gate, and window grilles have a casual elegance that tell you you're about to enter friendly territory. Beyond the fanciful entry gate is a lush semitropical garden complete with large palms and a terra-cotta fountain. The ambiance is breathtaking. A crushed granite pathway leads to the veranda with a seating area where you can sit, relax, and enjoy the atmosphere that's been created here.

94 Here's a great example of how the addition of an unusual flower color can make for a terrific attention grabber. The unusual house colors of this sweet Mediterranean work wonderfully too—they're an offbeat gold with a green cast and taupe that create an appealing combination of balanced color. But it's really the breathtaking deep burgundy tulip color and the well-laid-out gardenscape with similar colors that give this house so much curb appeal. It proves once again that thoughtfully planned landscaping is an important design element that can dramatically enhance house colors and the overall attractiveness of a property.

95 This beautiful Mediterranean-style home is painted a warm white with a golden cast. Oversized terra-cotta planters, Mexican saltillo terra-cotta pavers, a stone wall, lush landscaping, and a wood door add color contrast and texture to the scheme. Open arches in the breezeway frame the plants, flowers, and trees that greatly contribute to the picturesque scene. A rusted wrought-iron light fixture hangs on the elegantly curved arch over the entry columns. It was taken from the interior of the house and retrofitted to use outside. It adds a unique touch that is personal to the homeowners and adds an elegance to the property. Neutral house colors don't have to be bland. Using well-placed accent colors, like those used here, can make the property an eye-catcher with terrific appeal.

96 The neutral field color of this Pueblo-influenced Mediterranean-style house is the backbone for the colorful, textured landscape that is finely balanced on the property. The deep pumpkin color on the eaves and vigas (projecting roof rafters), dark-stained redwood gate, terra-cotta roof tile, and rusty brown front door add a skillfully blended depth of color to the scheme. The house colors balance very well and are quite sophisticated, but it's really the landscaping around the house that makes this property so striking and gives it exceptional curb appeal.

97

Complementary colors red and green always work well together, and these house colors are no exception. The complex, saturated field color of this Mediterranean house changes from a bronzed green to a more muted green with a gold cast, depending on the light. Terra-cotta roof tiles connect to the brick red concrete paving that runs up the steps to a front door of the same color. Embossed medallions under the picture windows have been painted a light yellow to pop out and visually enhance the pattern, while the arched windows are painted a dark green to accentuate the window shape. The home's complementary colors, dark contrast color, and bright highlight color come together as a successfully balanced, sophisticated combination.

98 The surface of this elegant Mediterranean house has been lovingly prepared by gifted artisans to replicate the worn appearance of old homes in Tuscany. The field color is a color-embedded stucco that takes on more depth over time. The trim color was laid on wet and then sponged and stippled to produce a "broken" surface that resembles limestone, a process called scumble combo. The sgrafitto pattern in the upper portion of the house was chalked on with a diamond grid and then handpainted over plaster that had been applied and cured prior to painting. It approximates a raised shield pattern over an incised diamond pattern. A stencil of interior shapes was applied to represent a slightly raised surface and to imitate the look of a faded, sunwashed peach color. Then it was highlighted with drop shadows using watered-down paints and was worked over with a sponge. The process is painstaking, but the result is a work of art.

99 Sunshine and design elements make this brightly colored house extra vibrant and cheery. A range of blue tones are used as color accents on the front door, cobalt planters, backyard table, and in the vivid flowers. Bright white accent paint keeps the color combination fresh. The towering silk tree's blooms were clearly the inspiration for the sherbet house color and match it perfectly. A charming little courtyard, entered through a swinging redwood gate, has a trellised ceiling full of seasonal wisteria blooms and a floor of checkerboard Mexican saltillo pavers that add interest with their graphic pattern. These small details add a personal touch to this tropical-colored Mediterranean charmer.

100 The light terra-cotta field color and soft sage green accents of this pictorial Mediterranean home work beautifully with the darker contrasting colors on the terra-cotta roof tile and pots and the bright terra-cotta painted wrought-iron railings and gate. Lush landscaping with climbing vines, red-and-green-leafed Japanese maple trees, soft ferns, and succulents play an important role in enhancing the property with color, texture, depth, and shadow. By working in unison, color and landscaping have successfully enhanced the overall surroundings and because of it, are all the more pleasing to the eye.

101

If you didn't know any better, you'd swear that you were in a hillside town in Italy, but this Tuscan-style Mediterranean house is half a world away. A mood is set here with the fortressed walls, two bell towers, cantilevered wood-paneled awnings, and loose pea gravel that surrounds the property and is reminiscent of old country backroads. The faded colors of Tuscany—soft gold, sage, and terra-cotta—are placed in focused areas on the house. Much of the warm neutral house color has developed a patina and drip lines that will continue to add more character to the house with time. The spring green market umbrella in the open second-floor patio adds a punch of color that shows how a single item can add color at little cost, even on a distinguished home like this one. Extraordinary panoramic views extend beyond the walls of this magnificent setting.

102 By changing the roofing to terra-cotta tile, adding Mediterranean colors, and replacing the landscaping, this house was dramatically transformed from traditional style to Mediterranean style. Faux finishes were applied to the field color, the front door, and the garage door. Paint was rolled on for the base coat, and then two subsequent coats of different paint colors were applied using a sponge, rag, and deck brush for different effects. The result looks its best when done by a professional faux painter with plenty of experience—otherwise, the look can be splotchy and uneven. Correct application affords the house the look of a worn patina that is usually achieved by natural aging. The saturated colors of this house are balanced and unique, and they work exactly as planned to create the Mediterranean ambiance the homeowners sought.

5 | Modern Color

House Number 125

103 The focus for this metropolitan home is first placed at street level, with rusted steel flower boxes planted with Mexican feather and blue oat grasses. Below are two sets of floating house number plaques with round vented louvers to each side. A secondary focal point becomes apparent when climbing the narrow steps between the two concrete garage structures. It's a visually stimulating journey where architectural lines play against each other. They guide you to two offbeat, acidic yellow/green doors—really the only instance of color on the house except for the striped door mats that coordinate with them. The mats are a wonderful connecting device to the door color and make a big impression, considering the purchase is such a small investment. The architectural blocking of the house is accentuated by four different materials that add texture to the essentially monochromatic color scheme—stained clapboard siding, poured concrete walls, color-embedded stucco walls, and powder-coated aluminum panels. Black windows add a striking contrast. Mahogany guardrails on both the front and back of the house add warmth to the scheme and a strong horizontal line to the minimalist architecture. The backyard has a custom galvanized steel staircase that floats between the garden and the second story, providing a highly creative and functional entry to the upper unit of the building. Loaded with creative ideas for color, texture, and materials, this dynamically designed house puts forward a commanding presence on the urban street it inhabits.

104 Walking down the steps into the private courtyard of this home's colorful premises, you are immediately transformed into a world of autumnal earth tone colors and textures. An unexpected purple front door connects to plants, flowers, and trees in the lush garden and is an exciting addition to the color palette. The terra-cotta stucco wall that runs the width of the garden plays an important role on the property: it stands as a divider between the courtyard and the garages, separating and layering color; it acts as a sculptural element with three square cut-out openings in the wall; and it also intersects the glass-paneled wall through to the inside of the house, giving an illusion that the inside and outside are one space. In the garden, turning around in the other direction, the view is equally inspired. It looks past the grounds of the property to a panoramic view. A triangular fabric tent stretching across the entry provides shade for the house and the courtyard. It also doubles as another interesting sculptural element that divides space on this extraordinary property.

105

The tinted white shade of the light green field color on this house is so subtle that it just registers slightly with pigment. Still, there's enough of it to give it the softest green-gray color that's urbane and elegant in its subtlety. An entry door with horizontal slat openings serves two functions, both literally and figuratively speaking. It allows a peek through the door, revealing a two-level open patio area and astonishing panoramic views, and it opens up the minimalist facade with an architectural point of interest. Contrasting color is added to the scheme with tubular, red house numbers that are placed over the door and the advancing bougainvillaea vine. The vine is a welcome softening device for the clean lines of this contemporary house on the hill.

1070

106 This cool dark gray urban house hangs over the side of the hill like a minimalist sculpture. The perforated COR-TEN rusted garage door and steel panel door warm up the facade with color but architecturally remain cold, hard steel elements, adding an intriguing tension. They're set into a niche that adds dimension to the facade and texture to the austere structure. A white concrete floor passes from the interior to the exterior of the house and transforms into a step-up into the house, adding a spot of bright color. The potted plant by the front door is a nice addition, as it picks up on the color of the rusted steel panels. The sleek stainless steel door knob, house numbers, and doorbell dazzle on this pitch-dark, architecturally dynamic house.

107

The saturated green color of this house blends monochromatically with the light green courtyard walls and complements the red market umbrella and dark brown wood panels. The wood door, gate, garage door, and trellis colors add even more contrasting warmth to the scheme and also help to divide color on the facade of the house. Bright metal finishes on the house numbers, balcony railings, and window frames add a shimmer of light to the scheme, freshening things up. What makes this house especially intriguing is the way in which the house colors are broken up by the shadows cast by the trellis sun shades. Long shadow lines mimic the architectural details on the house—narrow horizontal windows, slats on the front gate, the five-lite paneled front door, tensile strength stainless steel balcony railings, and cut-out openings in the courtyard wall. The shadow lines change with the sun and dance across the facade of the house in moving patterns, lengthening and shortening and finally disappearing as they fade into the night. This home's highly detailed architecture is smart and stylish, and its stimulating and inspired play of light and shadow helps define and highlight the lines of the house to perfection.

108 With its sliding-panel garage doors, this house is reminiscent of a cross between a contemporary barn and an industrial building. Three siding materials (corrugate metal panels, stucco, and clapboard) and three colors have been used on the house to add textural interest to the facade. Blue is the most prominent color. Two additional colors—sage and warm light gray—articulate the architecture further and provide contrast for the scheme. Surrounded by wildflowers, it's a subtle, harmonious collection of color and texture that works very well for this distinctive house in the woods.

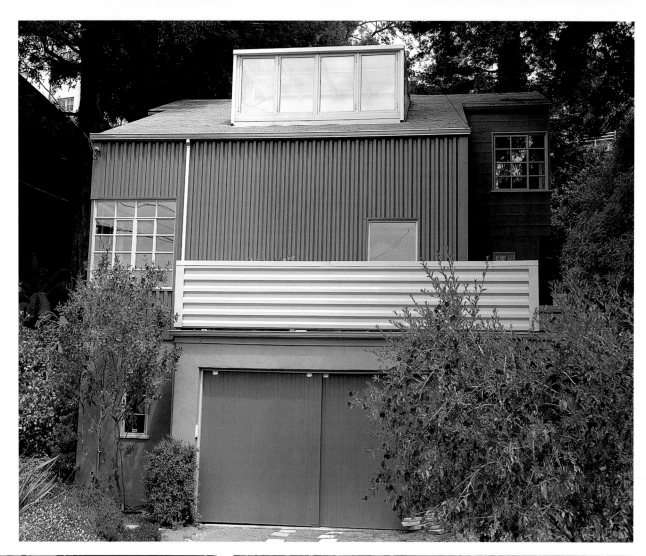

109 A soft neutral field color looks elegant on the classic clean lines of this modern house. Black on the window frames, entry door, railings, square mailbox, and roof shingles provides extreme color contrast that accentuates these details with a dramatic presence. Square-pressed concrete pavers have been custom colored to match the exterior walls and contribute immeasurably to color consistency; a few well-placed pots add polish and help to support a "sense of entry" at the front door; and flat roman window shades with horizontal stays make a strong graphic statement on all of the large picture windows, proving how important interior window coverings are to the exterior of a house. These selections play a significant role in the home's pleasing appearance and cohesive design.

110 The stark, clean lines and use of bold color, space, and light on this house reflect the style of Mexican architect Luis Barragán. Standing outside of the walled-in property, you can catch a glimpse of a purple stucco wall, but what is most apparent is that the subtle warm house color acts as a backdrop to accentuate the home's landscape environment. It's not until you enter through the mahogany swinging gate that you become aware of the blocks of vibrant color visible from the open courtyard area—a recessed wall in violet, an azure blue wall, another violet wall, and an orange ceiling in the breezeway. These colors bring this property its vitality. The open courtyard with its long blue feature wall and water fountain, tipped terra-cotta pots, textured square stone pavers, colorful flowers, and Mexican-style seating combine to create its special take on this "south-of-the-border" modernist home.

111

From the street, through overgrown shrubs and a square trellis structure, you can catch a glimpse of a gleaming structure of corrugated steel. When you enter the courtyard, you begin to understand that there is much more to be revealed about this place. What first appears to be just a monolithic facade is actually a house with lots of interesting color, texture, and details. To the left of the trellised entry area is a large vivid blue picture window and koi pond. Across the courtyard sit two pink Adirondack chairs that are snuggled into the courtyard's landscape environment. It's not until you walk down the driveway and around to the back of the house that you see much more of these colors—pink doors, blue windows, and more of the yellow color-embedded stucco. This avant-garde property has ideas that are fun, inspired, and full of surprises around every corner.

112 The colors and design details of this home have taken the fairly ordinary mid-century apartment building to extraordinary heights. A punchy spring green color on the lower part of the structure helps to keep the focus at ground level. The recessed entry walls have sparingly used a fine, velvety smooth, color-embedded stucco finish that blends with the aluminum frames on the sidelights, garage door, and sconce lights and second-story gray paint color. The sandblasted Azurlite glass offers a cool translucent quality and privacy for the inside. A zippy orange front door adds a great punch of color, and its long vertical glass opening matches the vertical lines of the custom sconce light fixtures on each side of the entry. Conversely, the horizontal frames on the door's sidelights connect with the horizontal garage door frames. Plants on each side of the entry soften it and help to strengthen the focal point. The fashionable urban colors and design ideas used here can be translated to other house styles to accomplish similar dazzling results.

113

The extreme design of this innovative house, with its cantilevered, angled walls and winding grand spiral staircase, divides color into blocks that are dictated by the massing of the architecture. The darker colors protrude and the lighter ones recede into shadow. The green color is picked up on the horizontal banding of the balcony and intersects the house through its visual center. Galvanized steel gutters and aluminum and stainless details in the lighting, railing, front doors, and window frames add lightness and sparkle to this extraordinary house full of twists, turns, and angles.

114

Three monochromatic earth tones create a warm, dimensional palette of color on the three blocks of this modern house. A patina has naturally developed on the stucco that has produced a desirable effect. The stained wood columns at the entry, horizontal railings, and garage door trim add dark contrast to the scheme. Aluminum trellis canopies visually lighten the heavy architecture and generate interest by casting short and long shadows on the facade at different times of the day.

Brushed aluminum house numbers that are recessed into the wall are supported by pins that make the numbers appear to float. Mass planting of one type of flower adds plenty of color and dramatic impact to the property, showing once again that when it comes to landscaping, sometimes less is more. A tremendous amount of attention has been paid to the fine details on this property, and it clearly shows in the home's thoughtfully balanced and harmonious design.

115

This house is of the art moderne style with art deco influences in the gate and etched sidelight windows of the entry door. The identifying features of the style are a flat roof, smooth wall surface, small ledge coping at the roofline, horizontal lines in the walls, and curved corners. The fresh peach house color works well with the contrasting deep red on the windows, gate, and railings. Together, the two are reminiscent of Tibetan colors. Two monochromatic colors used on the house and garden wall effectively add a subtle depth to the scheme by visually shifting two shades of the same color. A sloped rock garden in the courtyard adds a lot of textural interest; though newly planted, it is already well on its way to softening the hard lines of the architecture and is a welcome addition to the property that will only look better with time. The lack of a railing on the gently curving staircase allows it to be an integral part of the garden landscape that almost seems to float up to the gate at street level. What a pleasure it is to see a house of this rare style renovated into such pristine condition.

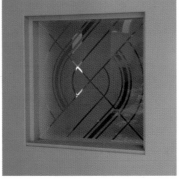

116 A blue house color is sometimes difficult to select because it can end up looking too light or too bright. This is a commendable choice because both the blue and white add warmth while still retaining a refreshing quality. Rather than the more dominating earth tones, it was the saturated blue that was pulled out of the African slate tile on the entry ramp. It was also picked up from the large boulders scattered in the garden. These unexpected color connections work remarkably well. The architecture helps dictate the placement of color; the blue clapboard walls recede, while the angled jutting white stucco portion advances. Dark-stained wood beams at the entry and over the balcony and slate pavers add contrast and warm up the scheme. The garden landscape softens the hard lines of the architecture, adding color and texture. The resulting color combinations are at the same time crisp, clean, warm, and inviting. It's a delicate balance, but one that has been capably achieved on this striking home.

117

This towering home vibrates with three bold colors: red, green, and gold. The three different materials on the cladding—cedar shingles, clapboard, and stucco—help to break up the substantial amount of color with welcome texture. The focus of attention is first placed on the second-story open patio areas with graphically detailed railings and picture windows that provide views of the scenery above neighbors' rooftops. Back at street level, the fanciful wavy lines on the security gate help to offset the straight lines on the house. Ultimately, the crowning glory of this contemporary home is its use of robust color, which is both bold and beautiful.

118

This once-plain mid-century city house has been revitalized with up-to-date materials that make it stand out from a string of similar houses. Slate facing applied to the lower facade adds considerable color and texture to the renovated exterior. It's a terrific selection because it serves as a connecting device that pulls all of the facade colors together. The entry has a re-energized focus, with an oversized etched glass french door with matching sidelights that attract attention and bring light into the house while providing privacy from passersby. Potted plants soften the entry and add a touch of color to the neutral scheme. The balcony railing and etched glass awnings are great ultra-modern additions that add a refined design to the property. Matching stainless steel finishes for all of the smaller details, like the sconce light, house numbers, and doorbell, complement the color scheme and add a bit of sparkle. This is a great example of how selecting the right metal finishes, and keeping them consistent, contributes to the success of the finished product. Finally, the paint color selections on the clapboard, garage door, and trim are outstanding choices that allow the colors to work together rather than fight for attention. For this updated home, "plain" no longer describes the property. It has become a chic and stylish city address.

119

The two buildings on this property, a modern farmhouse and a double garage, are inspired because they're painted different colors—rust for the former and taupe for the latter. The rusty, intricately sculpted iron gate acts as a focal point for the entry to the house through the paved brick courtyard. It serves two purposes, one as a functional entry and the other as a decorative element that injects stimulating interest to the property. It sits aside the garage and is connected to a redwood fence that relates to the main house with its color and tone. The arched vines that grow between the two buildings create a dramatic, moody passageway to a second gated entry to the courtyard. Terra-cotta pots and lush landscaping add softness and color to the grounds between the buildings, enhancing this enchanting setting.

120 This remarkably different stucco house uses alternating concrete blocks that create a horizontal striped pattern for the foundation while establishing robust graphics for the property. A strong focal point is fashioned by the intersection of a grand staircase that leads to the private second-level patio area and bold portal entry to the house. The strong dusty desert house color pulled from the foundation colors helps to visually connect the house and foundation. A dusty red, used sparingly on walls that surround the home's two teal green doors, helps to pinpoint the doors' locations. The home's western exposure to the evening sky influenced this selection of colors—and what could be better inspiration than the setting sun? Color and architecture unite to invent a unique, eclectic combination of modern, Pueblo, and southwestern styles that make this house a standout.

121

Cleverly designed woven galvanized steel doors add a unique and engaging presence to this smart house. Black french doors and stainless steel balcony railings overlooking the streetscape enhance the house with clean architectural lines that are quite cosmopolitan. The warm field color is a welcome addition that works particularly well with the black and cool metal finishes. A massing of fuchsia watsonia flowers bring a welcome "pop" of bright color to the sophisticated neutral scheme of this urban-chic home.

122 This commanding house has great presence on the street. A soft green color that wouldn't overwhelm the property was chosen, and the resulting scheme may be quiet, but it's quite sophisticated and works well. The house sits atop a soft brown brick foundation surrounded by overscaled plants of the same color that help to visually soften the structure. Redwood balcony boards, visible from the street, tie in with the same brown tones and complement the green house color. Together they work to balance and enhance the total color scheme. Galvanized steel stair railings that climb up to the front door and cut back and forth across the facade add a cool gray color and a graphic, linear quality to the architecture. The balcony railings complement the steps and add more horizontal lines that break up the large surface of the house. It's a well-planned scheme that works exceedingly well for this property.

123

Modern and Santa Fe architectural styles have been successfully merged on this strikingly handsome home. Trellis sun shades add strong visual interest by casting long shadows on the facade that change throughout the day. Two colors used for the house and one for the integral colored concrete paving blend together seamlessly to create a unified distribution of color. The color shift adds depth that picks up on the varied sensory qualities and subtle color complexities of a dusty desertscape. Flowers add a welcome bright color to the streetscape and the private patio. One mature palm tree on the property adds a grand scale and a finishing touch to complete the refined southwestern scheme.

124

There are so many well-chosen design elements on this home that it's hard to know where to begin. The tiled step color of this impressive house inspired the three bold shades chosen for the field color—taupe, brick, and gold. Stainless steel horizontal channel reveal lines separate the house into its three blocks of color. Sparkle is added with brightly assorted metal finishes on the canopy, gutter pipes, custom light fixture, house numbers, embossed polka-dot planter box, railing, and mailbox. The front door is cleverly sheltered by a glass-paneled canopy with heavy, cantilevered supports that help make a strong central focal point while adding architectural interest. A cross pattern on the oak and cherry wood door and the corresponding cross on the transom above serve to visually extend the height of the entrance and reinforce the focal point. The small, informal garden helps to soften the architecture and separate the house from the street. A plum tree to the left picks up the color of the brick-colored bay window brilliantly, adding the weight of this color to the left side of the house for an unusual effect. Well-placed color works beautifully throughout this thoughtfully detailed property.

125 This outstanding L-shaped house, built on a natural knoll, makes use of panoramic views from most of the large picture windows. The view of the house is equally lovely. There is a variety of earthtone colors used, from the two different stucco colors and the stained siding, entry door, and trellis sun shades to the powder-coated doors, windows, and railings—all working together in color harmony. The almost white, natural concrete walls, paving, and steps on the lower portion of the house lighten the scheme with the addition of fresh color. This color choice visually connects to the white lawn chairs and interior white walls and furnishings, bringing the inside out and the outside in. The trellis sun shades, located above the windows and doors, shade the windows and cast shadows that throw graphic lines across the house that change with the movement of the sun, adding interest to the facade. The main entry to the house uses these same colors and, in addition to it, pavers that blend with the scheme. There are so many wonderful design details on the property that it's difficult to point them all out. What's most important to understand is that every feature has been purposefully and thoughtfully considered. These elements connect with each other to produce a cohesive color plan and design that's subtle, elegant, and flattering from every direction.

126 This unusual modern house features a barn red color on the round housing, garage doors, and trellis, and the warm, lighter field color blends with it. Red is a difficult color to use in big doses, but because this color is toned and shaded, it works very well. The round house softens the hard lines of the architecture, while the lush landscaping fills in with texture to finish the job. This residence proves that complementary colors don't have to exist on the house alone—here, the red house color successfully complements the green landscaping. Stainless steel, galvanized steel, and anodized aluminum details on the front door, stairway railing, door canopy, house numbers, lighting, and trim bring a cool sparkle to the warm color scheme of this well-designed modern property.

127 This small house, transformed from traditional to modern, is chock-full of creative ideas. The field color is divided into two colors, sage green and gold—one on clapboard, the other on stucco. The rusty red door picks up the color of the roof shingles and two awnings, making an important color connection for the scheme. The entry door's steel and glass awning, with attached house numbers and a stucco portal, adds a dynamic focal point. The "filled in" picture window to the right provides privacy and a sound barrier from the busy city street. An array of smaller narrow windows keeps things private but allows light to enter the house in addition to providing visual interest. The windows are topped by a grid-patterned awning, adding a second canopy design to the house. The light-reflectant metals of the vertical and horizontal recessed aluminum channel reveal lines, mailbox, and porch light supply bright contrast. Finally, plant massing reflects the house colors and adds textural interest to this attractive city dwelling.

128 This spectacular house has a dramatic presence in a setting reminiscent of stacked houses in the hilly seaside towns along the Mediterranean coastline. The house has minimalist qualities that use structure to create pure and simple spaces. The exception to the straight lines of the house is the gently curved colonnade, in a saturated, sun-drenched golden color, that intersects the house. Its protected Douglas fir ceiling has been coated with a clear interior lacquer that is turning it a desirable shade of orange as it ages, adding a depth of color to the scheme. Architecturally, the massing of the house is divided into blocks that are separated by earth tone colors. The clean lines of the architecture and the aging, muted colors of the stucco patina create an interesting tension between old and new, but they work very well together to blend into the natural environment in which the home is nestled. Semitropical plants and trees further the Mediterranean influence and complete the well-conceived and skillfully executed ambiance.

129 The details make this formerly plain house now memorable. The colors are neutral, but the aluminum-framed windows and door, lighting, canopy with etched glass, and house numbers add a metallic glow and bring significant sophistication to the house. Black slate tile steps and walls add a dramatic contrast that brings attention to the home's entry. Overscaled plants in built-in planters add the final dramatic detail that doubles as a softening device between the house and the city street. This may be a small house, but the attention it now draws is huge.

6 | Townhouse Color

House Number 136

130 The fresh pastel green on this home's front door picks up the softest leaf color of the quirky little tree on the sidewalk and provides bright color contrast to the ivory field and white trim colors. The tree has been trimmed to frame both the arched portal entry and the window, bringing attention to both and adding texture to the property. Seasonal pink blooms on the tree bring a delightful addition of color that's most welcome on this enchanting Colonial townhouse.

131 The dark green color on the front door and shutters of this old Colonial townhouse works so agreeably because it's a complementary color to the old red brick. The details that make this house a little bit different are the combination of bright pink flowers and the friendly doormat with matching colors. It's a fun connection and it adds a little bit of levity to this classic home.

132

Painting this stylish Colonial one refined color allows the focus to be on the distinguished architectural details found in the leaded-glass transom and elaborate entablature above the door, paneled shutters, scrolled ironwork in the glass paneled doors, and elegant light fixture. The toned green color also works very well with the old worn white marble on the house, making this well-dressed home elegant, polished, and timeless.

133

This historic urban carriage house has been renovated and returned to its original glory. A very modern update comes with the new overhead carriage house doors. The focal point has effectively been shifted away from the front door to the "garage" doors by the placement of black urns and wall-mounted lanterns on each side and an elaborate balcony railing above. The combination of a deep terra-cotta field color and a cherry stain on the doors is unusual, but works very well together, especially with black details on the house that create a dark contrast for the scheme. The heavy cornice dresses up particularly well in black, and the repetition of color on the windows, balcony, stars, light, and hitching posts reinforces the color and contributes to its dramatic presence on this old city street. This home is a treasure.

134 The art moderne style of architecture is reflected in this smooth-surfaced, flat-roofed house with horizontal banding and streamlined geometry. Its blue multi-framed iron windows, four-light obscure glass door, and transom are the focus of interest for the simple design of the facade. A potted tree adds just a touch of color and texture, which is most welcome at the front door. The aging limestone facing panels have developed a wonderful patina that lends itself very well to the blue trim color. This urban modernist home is a rare find. What a treat!

135 This original Colonial townhouse has classic good looks and colors of impeccable taste. All of the colors are historical reproductions and complement the old red brick beautifully—the door matches it and the gray shutters pull out the color from each brick. Warm white trim is a very appealing choice for these colors and contributes immeasurably to the sophistication of the scheme. The railing, grille work, and lantern are painted black and add a crispness to the scheme. You can't go wrong with this time-honored collection of dignified colors.

136

Loaded with charisma and great personality, this 1843 Colonial row house has taken a leap away from the traditional colors of its time. The soft pastel combination of light green and blue are unusual enough, but it's really the delightful pink door color that takes the scheme to a whole new level.

The potted pink flowers add an especially charming touch by matching the front door color. Because pink is used in such a small dose, it works. It allows the house to retain its special personality among the other townhouses on the street, without going too far. The colors of this old home are definitely unusual, but they look sensational.

137 This four-story 1860s Colonial revival house features an elaborate mansard roof and sophisticated color selections from top to bottom. Lush flowers and plants in window boxes soften the hard brick facade at street level and blend in beautifully with all of the house colors. The heavy paneled black walnut door with beveled glass windows is magnificent and picks up on the warm colors of the red brick facade. Continuity on the exterior of the house is achieved through the use of the same horizontal blind and color selection that blends in for every window. It makes a big difference in the home's overall appearance. All details and colors have been considered carefully on this cosmopolitan townhouse—and it shows.

138

With the exclusion of the front door color, the principle behind the selection of successful house colors such as these is good to remember because it always works: keep it simple. Black and white is a safe combination that will always work well with a red brick facade. It's a natural and it has been done for centuries. The door, then, becomes an opportunity for color. This spring green color is a terrific choice that works with black and white, but is especially effective with the soft red brick because it's a complementary color. What's exciting about this selection is that it gives the house an up-to-date color. The flowers in the window boxes are great connecting devices that pull all of the colors together while providing some texture. The modern view towards color works very well for this Colonial townhouse, and it is a pleasure to behold.

139 A new and improved color selection enhances this 1890s red brick urban townhouse. The dramatic and exciting use of this bold blue for the front door and cornice colors cheers up the house immeasurably. The door knocker was purchased in England as a souvenir and is a good example of how to personalize a home in a small but delightful way. Flat roman shades with horizontal stays add an eclectic appearance with a dash of modern flair to the facade of this distinguished home.

140

This old brick carriage house has been cleverly converted to a modern, hip home with the addition of a few new elements: a Brazilian cedar paneled entry with a concealed door and bright contemporary door hardware, industrial gooseneck reflector lights, black window grilles, and a trendy light green field color selection. These additions enhance and give new life to this transformed urban dwelling.

7 | Traditional Color

House Number **149**

141 This refined ranch-style home uses warm beige and white paint colors that blend beautifully with the naturally weathered cedar shingle roof tiles. The green door is a classic color for this combination that always works well and also happens to pick up the green landscape colors. Interior shutters add a sophistication to the exterior view, too, but what really elevates the property is the show of white tulips in bloom. To grow this amount of tulips is a labor of love because the bulbs need to be removed and replanted annually. The effect is stunning when the sun shines through them, lighting them from behind and making them appear translucent. The effect creates dazzling and memorable curb appeal, and though it's only a seasonal show of color, it's worth the wait when springtime brings them around again.

142 The ambiance of this traditional farmhouse sweeps you away to another place and time, perhaps to the countryside in the south of France. The house is revealed down a long driveway flanked by a shaded canopy of fruitless mulberry trees. Landscaping continues to be a focal point, with Chinese berry trees bordering either side of the entry path. The house color has faded over time to a washed out muslin and blends with the newer, lightly whitewashed shutters and the naturally weathered redwood gates. An elegant French-style settee fits in with these toned-down rustic colors. Even the decomposed crushed granite on the driveway and pathways seems to blend in with the house and its surrounding colors. What has developed is a fashionably worn "wine country" ambiance that lends itself to the look of an enchanted country estate.

143

The dark color of this classic traditional house is complex; it appears dark green in sunlight and almost black in shadow. The color is a dramatic backdrop for the soft pink flowers that run the entire length of the house. The arched portico is painted in a warm white glossy oil-based alkyd, giving it a deep finish that highlights the architecture and brings more attention to the entry. The rich golden-stained oak door, softened by topiary plants on each side and adorned by a wreath with a rusted steel ribbon design, adds the finishing touch for this strong central focal point. The house color is dramatic, but since it's a deep color that recedes, it draws attention to itself in only the most positive light and retains a regal elegance that brings a sense of pride to the homeowners and admiration from neighbors.

144 The brilliant Dutch blue door color is the centerpiece for this house, making the entryway a strong focal point and drawing attention to it with vivid color. The combinations of gray, beige, and green used in different proportions are the secondary focus for color on the house. Two subtle tones, one on the shutter and the other on the frame, enhance the windows with an extra layer of detailing. Lush green landscaping shields the house from street traffic and adds privacy while softening the lines of the house and adding textural interest.

145 This traditional city house with elegant windows, lunettes, arched frames, and refined balconies features a horizontal band of a lighter neutral that divides two subtly different field colors, adding interest to the facade. A warm white has been used on the recessed entry walls to lighten and brighten the space and make it more welcoming. The narrow steps are filled with pink flowers and plants that add color to the neutral scheme while softening the hard lines of the red brick steps and creating a hospitable entry to the house. The flowers and the leaded-glass window are color coordinated and are in view when climbing the steps. The division of color is sophisticated, adding dimensional color and enhanced appeal to this well-dressed home.

146 The dynamic green color of this classic home has a lot of personality and is a great backdrop for the bougainvillaea vines that grow up onto the side of the house and the two red rose trees that frame the entry steps. The red and green colors complement and enhance one another. Luscious, warm white trim on the broken arch pediment and arched windows with elegantly curved mullions enhances the overall appearance of the house. It's a "good white"

that adds the right amount of warmth to the color-saturated scheme. The elegant dark green, almost black, front door is painted with a European oil enamel that provides a rich depth of color you can't achieve with latex paint. A door is the perfect place to use this type of paint, because it keeps the amount used to a minimum for important environmental safety concerns. A colorful flower garden marches up stairs that twist and turn, guiding you to the entry of this distinguished home.

147

This house is a excellent example of how creative expression can make a dynamic personal statement. The traditional style has been made eclectic in its design with the use of contemporary materials and colors—deep green with brown trim and orange accents. Orange paint used sparingly—under the eaves—is a great way to successfully add a bright color without going overboard. The stainless steel house number plaque, light fixtures, railing, door hardware, gate, landscape lighting, and doorbell add contemporary flair and sparkle to the scheme. Etched glass in the front door, sidelights, and garage door windows allows light in while providing privacy and adding style. The back-

yard, accessed through an unusual modern gate, features a minimalist sculptural water feature that intersects the space and creates a calm respite for the senses. One can relax on the modern orange chairs—which pick up the color of the orange eaves, making an undeniably fun connection of color. The deck is made out of Brazilian wood, which adds a rich color to the backyard. The 10'x10' window made from an airplane hangar bifold door contributes a grand scale to the house and connects the inside to the outside by opening up the wall with windows. All of the creative ideas that have been used on this property make this home a standout in its color and material selection, design, and artistic invention.

148 Once set on a larger piece of land, this unique carriage house now inhabits a smaller plot of land surrounded by a concrete jungle. Its previous incarnation probably explains the large "garage" doors at street level, an extra-long driveway, and the old-growth terrain, which are unusual commodities for most urban properties—and what make this place so special. The fresh blue field color is shielded by the shade of a sizeable tree that helps to break up the color of the house from the street while adding texture and color to the property. Metallic paint on the door trim and acanthus leaves on the second-floor columns add a subtle sophistication and a bit of a twinkle to this gracious home and property.

149 The aesthetically pleasing beige with a dash of a green tint used for the field color of this timeless house works particularly well with the home's warm white trim. A painted patterned brick wall and paneled garage door add texture to the facade, while the roof, brick pavers, and front door color work in agreement with each other and add saturated contrasting color to the scheme. This is a refined color combination that works with the existing roof color to create an expertly cultivated scheme.

150 The classic styling of this house offers dramatic contrast, using a bright white trim that pops out against black-stained cedar shingles. We can't see the door color, but this black and white selection leaves the option for an imaginative door color wide open. It's an opportu-nity to use an unexpected color that can add unique style and personality, and in this case, a pleasant surprise as you round the corner to view the entry. The trellis, flowers, and landscap-ing are softening devices that assure an abundance of color for this handsome home.

151 This traditional house mixes it up with Mediterranean features, like terra-cotta roof tiles, window grate, and its fanciful house colors. The mint green field color and purple on the windows, door, and gate brighten up the scheme with its lively color composition used in correct proportions. The brick steps and terra-cotta roof tile complement the green field color and help to ground the offbeat colors of this delightfully eclectic urban home.

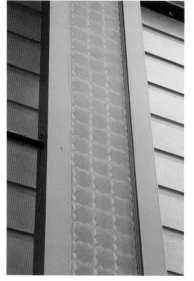

152 An artist free of restrictions of any kind fashioned this painterly creation, an example of design ingenuity gone wild. These colors won't fit into many neighborhoods, but this house is welcome in its neighborhood and fits its place very well. The home's exterior was a painter's canvas, with every part considered independently and also as a unit. The inspirational ideas shown here can be used, whole or in part, for many other styles of houses using many other colors, including more subdued color selections. There is no doubt that the combination of faux finishes, stenciling, and layered patterns was a brilliant accomplishment; the process was complicated, time-consuming, and required an artist's talent. Ten layers of paint were applied to achieve a depth of color and to tone down the electric orange and red base colors. The artist used no precise formulas and adjusted the colors as the layers were applied. The result, though a bit eccentric, is most definitely a unique, three-dimensional work of art and a true labor of love.

153 One view of this small traditional house shows its cherry tree in full bloom in springtime, while the other portrays the property when the tree's bloom is gone. In either case, the tree is a very useful softening device between the house and the street. When the tree is in full bloom, it's a great example of how blossoms can create dramatic impact with their show of magnificent seasonal color. The white accent paint has a slight pink cast that works especially well with the flowers, and all of the colors are very well suited to the subdued and refined silvery sage field color. A stack of round river rocks by the french door adds a calming Zen influence that complements the ambiance created by the Japanese cherry tree and contentedly welcomes visitors to this attractive home.

154 What would otherwise have been just another beige house on the street has become an example of urban chic by the use of a saturated canary yellow paint color used in the recessed entry. The 5-lite lightly etched modern glass door, red-painted house numbers, etched glass windows, stainless steel hanging pendant light fixture, and mailbox give the home vivacity and a modern sophistication. The yellow wall color is successful because it's used in a small amount and in a contained space. Partially hidden from view, it's a great, unexpected delight upon its discovery.

155 The entry to this traditional eclectic house with both Craftsman and Colonial detailing is draped with lush bougainvillaea, which adds intense color interest to the property. The red flowering vine warms up the gray field color, saturated toned blue accent colors on the door and shutters, and crisp white trim, creating a strong focal point for the entry to the house. The white picket fence is a sensory image that evokes a time gone by and creates a picture of "home sweet home" for this charming house.

156 The design of this property has been expanded to include a garage that was transformed into a studio space overlooking the backyard gardens. A bridge connects the house to the studio with a wonderfully designed sculptural railing. The two buildings are different colors and different styles but work together as opposites: the house uses more traditional colors with copper accents, while the cottage has a more contemporary look with a modern, fresh color selection. This is a terrific reuse of space and a dynamic design for what otherwise would have been just another garage sitting at the end of a long driveway. It works to create a compound and expands the property with modern style and panache.

157 Architectural features have been added to this splendid traditional house, giving it new style and flair. The etched glass canopy above the door is art nouveau inspired and is reminiscent of the type of awning that you might find in Paris. The addition of a terrific offbeat shade of green for the front door enhances the entry and draws positive attention to it. It's a great example of how the simple use of one unusual color in a small area can add a lot of personality to a house. The wrought-iron trellis and railings with gold-leaf balls frame the picture window and connect its design to the awning, elevating the style of the house further. An array of flowers around the property brightens up the neutral house with a show of delightful colors, adding the finishing touch that enhances this home's sensational appeal.

158

Here, the style of a traditional house has virtually been transformed by the addition of a massive trellis to the facade and a color selection that shifts the style to a southwestern theme. The dusty house colors and tile pavers fit into the scheme and reinforce the architectural elements with their color. A toned-down red front door and oversized plants are reminiscent of the kind of color and landscaping that you might find in an arid climate. The home's desert theme has merged successfully into a style that is distinctive and has created a unique appeal for the property.

8 | Tudor Color

House Number 166

159

This gorgeous gated Tudor house uses colors that are complex and that work harmoniously with the meticulously crafted landscaping. The old clinker brick, reclaimed from buildings after the 1906 San Francisco earthquake and fire, lends a rustic charm to the dignified architecture. Every side of the house has received an equal amount of attention to the fine points, making each feature on the house as important as the other. Details abound and include leaded-glass windows, copper verdigris gutter pipes, a limestone portico, redwood and wrought-iron gates with limestone column caps, and brick and flagstone pavers. All details work separately and in unison to create this beautifully balanced property of refined color, style, and sophistication.

160 This storybook house has many classic details that contribute to its charm, including the steeply pitched cross gable roof with cedar shingles, Gothic revival leaded-glass casement windows, and tall, narrow grouped windows, half-timbered beams, and dark stained, paneled oak door. All of the paint colors have been pulled directly from the color of the brick facade and work together in perfect harmony. The house is nestled into a site built below street grade and is surrounded by lush foliage and flowering trees that soften the scenery and add even more enchantment to this lovely setting.

161

As beautiful as this painted white brick Tudor may be, it's the roses that give the house its exquisite, eye-catching curb appeal. The flowers are layered for effect: climbing pink rose vines adorn the facade, while a separate white rose garden grows along the outside perimeter wall of the property. The white roses, in all their glory, accentuate the house color and create a monochromatic scheme when viewed from the street. The dark green accent color is enhanced by the greenery of the landscaping, including the low hedge that grows along the sidewalk. French doors open onto the patio, which is made with square concrete pavers placed in a harlequin pattern on the grass—a simple, clever solution for patio flooring. A wide-planked front door, textured brick wall cladding, steeply pitched roof, and grouped leaded-glass windows are typical features of the Tudor style and are represented at their best on this elegantly landscaped house.

162 The color of the plants, trimmed rounded bushes, and flowers have been carefully selected to work in unison with this dignified classic Tudor house. Every detail has been considered in order to create color harmony and a balanced appearance for the entire property. The red brick pavers, facade, and chimney stack and the roof tiles are picked up in the color of plants in the garden and make important color connections. Muted earth tones on the house complement each other and effortlessly blend in with the natural setting. The gardens surrounding the house, from the front yard to the terraced backyard gardens with stone walls and stone pavers, and elegantly detailed railings play a key role in the rich, balanced colors of the successful design and beauty of this picturesque property.

163

The chocolate brown cedar shingles on this Tudor revival pick up the same color of the brick facade, allowing the house to read as one continuous color from top to bottom. The change in materials from the shingles to the old brick to the square pavers that edge the garden adds visual and textural interest. As these colors recede, attention is drawn to the warm white color of the columned entry, leaded-glass window frames, window boxes with colorful flowers, and the half-timber on the gabled roof. Finally, the landscaping, with its lush garden, enlivens the entire scheme with fresh color and texture on this charmingly quaint home.

164 The homeowners of this Tudor discovered the colors that they wanted to use for their house while walking the streets of a small village in southern Germany. They took photographs of the house and then matched them as closely as possible to colors from a paint manufacturer's custom color options. The selections are bold and beautiful and work so well because they follow the criteria for using daring paint colors: the house is small and can tolerate more color than a large home; it's set back and shielded from the street and protected from full view; and it is covered in the shade of a wooded setting that subdues the color intensity. The splendid vibrant colors make a powerful statement, but by fitting all of the criteria, they produce a very favorable outcome on this enchanting house in the woods.

165 A light gray field and darker gray trim color on this quaint Tudor work well, but it's the abundant annual flowers that make it so distinct. The flowers are well placed, providing a show of color from one end of the house to the other. The simple additions of a window box, shutters, and an Adirondack chair enhance the detailing on the house and give it even more charm. This is also a very good example of how the use of color beyond the painted walls of a house can add character that give a property enormous curb appeal.

166

Here's a fine example of how the use of one unusual, unexpected color can elevate the appeal of a house substantially while still retaining the classic look and style of a traditional Tudor. The gold stucco paint brings this house to life, adding a warm sunny glow to the more classic, subdued stone and brown trim colors. This modern color selection provides the house with an updated look that makes it stand out from the rest. White paint on the windows and recessed entry adds a shimmer of light that brightens the scheme, while the setting of old-growth trees and lush landscaping completes the storybook scene.

167 A selection of warm tan and soft green colors have been pulled from the warmest shades of this home's multicolored slate roof tiles. The cool shade of the stamped concrete entry path have been pulled out of the slate tile too. These cool tones sandwich the warm house colors, adding contrast to the scheme. Dormer windows pop out of the roof in five locations and contribute to the considerable charm of this country-style English Tudor, while small white flowers in the garden supply just the right amount of sparkle to this delightful home.

168 This classic Tudor revival home is loaded with charm, with a triple-stacked chimney, steeply sloped slate roof, herringbone-patterned panels, small leaded-glass windows, rough-hewn half-timber, and tipped terra-cotta pots. Peach and taupe field colors are pulled from the multicolored roof tile, making significant color connections. The articulated details are very much like what you might find on an estate in the English countryside, but these colors are fresher and more up-to-date, lending this enchanting home a personality of its own.

169 This captivating Tudor home deserves praise for its adventurous combination of bold, saturated colors. The arched portal features a deep red that calls attention to itself and beckons you to enter. The same color is cleverly picked up on the two-toned shutters, leaving its frame the same color as the half-timber. The old paint and handle set on the door have developed a natural patina over the years that's worth keeping, so the door is protected and kept intact with a clear satin sealant. Its dusty color is mimicked on the natural cedar roof tile, which has also weathered naturally. A fanciful wreath adds a friendly greeting as you enter the house. What is most outstanding about this home, however, is that the robust colors are articulated on every detail to ensure that all of the architectural features on the house are noticed—and they are, winningly.

170 This Tudor home is reminiscent of dwellings found in old English towns and villages, where the houses were built right up to the street. The house colors are a great combination, but it's the placement of red trim details that make it most interesting. Painted in unusual locations, like the inside of the window frames and under the eaves, the red adds an undeniably eye-catching appeal. Using a darker color on the first floor of a house generally makes the house feel grounded, but in this case it's been reversed and actually works very well. The darker color pulls the eye up to the more articulated architectural details above, thus shifting the balance of color successfully on this handsome city home.

171 This stunning house, built on a heavily forested property of old-growth evergreen and deciduous trees, is a blend of Tudor and Norman Revival architectural styles. The faux finish on the stucco was achieved by painting sections of the house with a solid-colored elastomeric base coat and then washing the stucco with multiple coats of a color-tinted sealer. Many layers were applied to achieve a look that matched the existing naturally aged patina. The two-story stucco walls are covered by a thirty-foot-high peaked roof clad in vintage carriage-house slate tiles. The gold Tuscan field color picks up the gold tones in the tiles and brightens the house with its sunny disposition. Elegant architectural detailing is expressed through leaded-glass windows framed with dark green window frames, cast-concrete Gothic arches, rusticated stone walls and paths, a ten-foot-high picture window, verdigris copper rain spouts, and beautiful handcrafted mahogany and leaded-glass doors. With its outstanding architectural details and color, this house is a magnificent example of an inspired medieval English country estate.

172 These are field colors that you might expect to see on a Tudor-style home, but the accent color on the windows and french door in the backyard is what makes these house colors so distinctive. A muted orange picked up from tones in the old clinker brick elevates the house colors to the next level, brightening their somber tone and adding welcome personality to the scheme. The clinker brick matches the tonal qualities of the giant redwood's trunk and blends effortlessly into the picture-perfect setting.

9 | Victorian Color

House Number 193

173 This Victorian dollhouse has taken a leap of faith with its bold use of colors—red, green, and yellow. It was worth the gamble. The colors are divided proportionally and articulate the architecture of the house in all of the right places. Landscaping softens and frames the house and a large old-growth tree casts a long shadow and shelters the house from the sun while softening its dramatically colorful appearance. The old adage "good things come in small packages" certainly applies to this little jewel.

174 This attractive old Victorian, built in the 1860s, has been rejuvenated by using a more contemporary color palette. The cool sage green house color and dark green door and shutters work well as a monochromatic scheme. Screen doors are often an eyesore, but this one integrates beautifully with the existing architecture—and with exemplary results. The white picket fence, trellis, and porch, complete with a rocking chair, are lovely reminders of simpler times.

175

This lovely Victorian has been modernized with eclectic details that make it much more interesting. The black french door with a contemporary handleset, round window in the pediment, and the clean lines of the up/down window shades have updated the facade of the house. The addition of a purple plum tree and potted plant add welcome color and texture. But what really makes this house so special is the choice of the fresh, airy colors that have been used for the facade. They add a subtle sophistication to the scheme that allows the meticulous architecture to speak for itself.

176 This grand Queen Anne uses a simple design strategy that organizes the color on the large house successfully. It starts with a thalo blue field color as the center color. "Georgian Ivory" sandwiches the blue, and the terra-cotta roof color and red brick foundation surround it all. These colors create alternating patterns of light and dark that add contrast to the scheme. Finally, yellow dentils under the cornice add a tiny, bright, dashed line of color. The resulting plan provides harmonious, balanced color for this magnificent Victorian house.

177

The fresh quality of this Eastlake Stick house brightens up the streetscape with a pastel blue that retains a level of sophistication sometimes difficult to achieve with this color. The heavy use of white trim and the decoratively arched pediment at the entry articulate the architectural details while neutralizing the house color so that it doesn't overtake the scheme. A darker blue on the windows, steps, trim, and double entry doors adds a welcome dark contrast. Images of sunshine are repeated in the panels with carved sunbursts at the entry, the unexpected and delightful surprise of a sunlit gold, multidimensional glaze on the vestibule walls, and the gold leaf that sparkles on the smallest details of the house. These colors add warmth and are the perfect complement to the blue scheme of this delightful Victorian house.

178 This charming two-story Victorian cottage is reached by traversing a footbridge with repeating cut-out scroll patterns in the railing panels. The subdued, earthy colors work beautifully with the color of the tree on the lower level that reaches up past the bridge and partially camouflages the house. Though the house colors are drab, drab never looked so good: the muted tones of this monochromatic scheme are sophisticated and unusual. The door hardware, house numbers, and mailbox keep the same muted colors with their toned-down metal finishes. A red etched-glass light pendant and leaded-glass multicolored panel add a bit of color. The glossy oil-based paint used on the door, portal, bridge, gate, windows, and window frames adds an extraordinary mirror finish that brightens the olive tones with its reflective qualities. The sheen highlights these articulated areas and allows them to take center stage so that the house shines—and it does. This house is a gem.

179 The choice of warm neutrals for this elegant Edwardian Victorian is outstanding. The home features almost as much trim as field color, so it's especially important that the colors are balanced properly. Good whites are difficult to achieve with great results, but this one hits the nail right on the head. It's warm and fresh, it blends without losing its identity, and it isn't so bright that the colors lose their equilibrium with each other. The addition of the delicately sculpted railings, matching gate, and hanging light fixture reinforce the black door color without overpowering the house with contrasting color. The garage door color recedes and grounds the house, allowing the eye to shift to the right and focus on the stately entry of this gorgeous home, with its handsome portico and black double entry doors.

180 This picturesque old red brick Victorian house features three different shades of green on the column, column brackets, and shutters, which serves to highlight each of the details to their best advantage. It's a highly developed use of color that adds complexity without overdoing it. There are two roof styles on this house. The slanted metal roofing over the porch is a modern rooftop solution with a practical function that will allow the snow to slide off it in snowy weather; it works well because it picks up the front door and brick color and blends in without drawing too much attention. The slate roof is original to the house, which was built in 1886. Mixing colors and materials together can be overdone, but the selections for this house have achieved results that unify the materials and colors effortlessly.

181

This Victorian country house features a swinging wicker love seat on the porch with cushions that match the house color, small diamond cutouts in the fence, flagstone pavers, and an abundance of white rose bushes and colorful flowers in the garden. The green field color is complex, reading both cool and warm, depending on the sunlight, while the front door is a dark plumbrown that adds contrasting color. Other small details work to accentuate the door color: the mailbox, horizontal window blinds, and red-leafed maple tree colors in the backyard act as connecting devices that unite the colors, making a stronger statement together than alone. The stage is set for a warm, friendly, and welcoming environment.

182 This Victorian uses a historic field color, but the combination of colors are definitely twenty-first century. The deep burgundy-stained doors work very well by adding a rich contrast to the saturated blue house color, proving that a small addition of color can make a big impact. The reproduction door hardware adds a nice touch and works well with the interior wood blind colors that are seen through every window of the house. The blinds are a great example of how important it is to choose window coverings that harmonize with the exterior colors. All coordinating colors and details have been attended to on this newly constructed house, and it is a pleasure to behold.

183 "A house with a sunny disposition" is probably the best way to describe this brightly colored property. At street level a buttery yellow freestanding garage and white picket fence give a hint of what's to come. Through the gate and down a switchback path is a most unusual setting. Here, an eclectic folk-style Colonial house sits a couple of stories down from the street and is completely enclosed and protected from street view. The bright and happy color selection of yellow and holly berry are not only unusual, they're inspired. Matching Adirondack chairs with ottomans beg you to sit, relax, and enjoy the lushly landscaped, private setting in utter peace and quiet.

184 It's often difficult to achieve pastel schemes that are sophisticated, but this one has worked out beautifully. There's a concept at work that makes the difference: the stained red wood steps tone down the turquoise color, and palm trees create a tropical mood that sets the tone for the property and its colors. A leaded-glass window in the front door elevates the home's level of refinement too. This house, with its bright, happy color that's also warm and friendly, has lots of style and is reminiscent of colors that you might find in the Florida Keys.

185 A soft yellow field color defines this modernized Victorian set on a steeply sloped street. Green-painted steps connect to the landscaping of the street by pulling the color up onto the deck and to the entry doors to the house. A sage green accent trim color helps define the architecture on the paneled fascia board, and the addition of french doors modernizes the house and opens it up to a view of the city. The overall feeling around the house, including the lushly landscaped backyard, is fresh and airy. Colorful blossoms and a bright lemon tree add the finishing touch of contrasting color to this exceptionally attractive, pristine property.

186

The deep army green base color of this dignified Queen Anne Victorian visually shortens the height of the four-story building and guides attention to the lightly colored portico and up the steps to the second level entry. The lighter tones and darker shades of the straw color palette on the upper three stories highlight the best of the architectural detailing. Potted plants soften the entry, and the simple addition of a graphic design on the door mat helps pull all of the colors together to create an attractive entry for each unit of this elegant Victorian house.

187 Set back and angled to the street, this Victorian house features gray square cobblestone pavers that wind their way between the curb to the entry of the house, widening into a patio area and adding terrific texture to the property. The antique bronze door knocker, brown-stained interior shutters, terra-cotta planters, and flowers and trees add just the right kind of muted tones to the dusty gray-green house color, while the black color on the doors adds dramatic contrast. Trees separate the house from the street, providing privacy and noise reduction while adding an enticing irregular distribution of sunlight and shade to the property. The atmosphere created with color, light, and texture is sublime.

188 This red brick Victorian with its turned posts, scroll brackets, and intricate architectural details has a lot of character and enticing appeal. The four paint colors are placed so that the best of the details are highlighted—soft coordinating colors on the trim and dark color contrast on the door and shut-ters, all complementing the brick facade and garden landscape. White wicker chairs on the porch brighten the scheme and are reminiscent of a time gone by, begging you to sit and rest a spell. The porch is separated from the street by a small garden filled with blooming flowers that add an ethereal quality and color to this little dollhouse.

189

The warm, sophisticated neutrals and black accents used on this delightful Victorian house are brilliant color selections that blend effortlessly. Deep ruby red-painted steps provide the scheme with a deep contrasting color that's picked up again as an accent on the panels below the cornice, making a great color connection. Heavy turned balusters, articulated gingerbread detailing, a slate roof with coordinating colors, and ornate heavy cast-iron railings elevate the house with a high quality of design and materials. Gold leaf, used sparingly on the iron gate finials and the window colonnettes, adds just the right amount of sparkle as a finishing touch to the discriminating details of this fine home.

190 The colors of this Edwardian Victorian are two saturated toned greens that are divided between the upper and lower levels. But it's the bright orange front door that gives the house its extraordinary presence. This focal point continues to draw attention with its elaborate heavy leaded-glass doors and sidelights, planter boxes flanking the stairs, and rustic brick steps that lead up to the door and connect in color to it. Interestingly, a dining room chandelier has been retrofitted to be used in the recessed entry, creating a unique and completely unexpected addition that adds a dash of whimsy and personal style to this predominantly classic, partly unconstrained, and most definitely captivating home.

191

Achieving a successful pink color on a house is quite an accomplishment. A pink house is in danger of looking like cotton candy if you're not careful, but this one hits the mark. The Stick Victorian is a dollhouse that doesn't overwhelm the architecture or one's senses with its color. The two monochromatic tones of pink on the field and shutter colors are subtle, complex, and sophisticated. Gray for the roof tile and porch grounds the field color with its neutrality, allowing a place to rest the eye, while the outdoor swing seat cushions pull all of the colors together with its floral design. The resulting difficult-to-achieve color combinations work well for this country home. Mission accomplished.

Martha Hart
House
1871

192 The clinker brick that was used in the construction of this finely articulated 1904 Edwardian Victorian was reclaimed from the San Francisco earthquake and fire of 1906 and was added onto the house post-construction. It will tell its story for many years to come. The two updated saturated green colors complement the brick and add tremendous warmth to the scheme. A soft yellow trim hits the spot with just the right amount of contrast to the field color. White marble steps, an elaborate railing, a french door, columns, an amber glass hanging light fixture, door wreath, and a potted plant pack a lot of punch for the small recessed portico entry and add visual strength to this important focal point. Gold leaf on the columns and around the windows adds a twinkle and glow to the dark colors of this charismatic turn-of-the-century home.

193

The refreshing blue house color of this grand Second Empire Victorian is visually broken up by lush green landscaping, large old-growth trees, and an ample amount of white trim that helps to highlight and emphasize the architectural detailing. Original to the house, the hexagonal-shaped slate shingles on the mansard roof are a darker shade of blue that matches the window shutters and helps to create balanced color by deepening the color scheme. White wicker rocking chairs on the porch add a picturesque quality that continues on every corner of this airy, expansive, resplendent property.

194 Inspired by colors in the terrazzo steps that lead to the front door, the deep red, brown, and rich creamy trim colors make an important connection and create a successful blend of color. The plum tree also links to the house colors and helps to reinforce the color scheme. This appealing Victorian home is a very good example of how house color, paving, and landscaping can work together harmoniously to create strong visual impact that generates terrific appeal for the home.

Inspirational Design Ideas

Curb appeal is certainly about using good color, but it also takes into consideration other important aspects that make a house "sing," completing the property's look and giving it polish. Adding a strong focal point, having great landscaping, and using the right details, large or small, will bring the design of the house to a final conclusion in which every corner of the property has been considered. Let's take a look at why these areas of focus are so important.

Sense of Place

> "A sense of place belongs to whoever claims it hardest, remembers it most obsessively, wrenches it from itself, shapes it, renders it, loves it so radically that he remakes it."
> —Joan Didion

"Sense of place" is a subjective idea. It refers to the sentiment surrounding a location, but its meaning differs depending on who is talking about it. It can be a perception or an attitude, an exploration of the meaning of "home," or an observation about what bonds people to a place.

Sense of place concerns more than just the property itself. It also encompasses a meaning and a relevance to the larger community. The area's people, plants, landscape, culture, and history all combine to create a daily rhythm, harmony, and character. Sense of place exudes a community sentiment and creates a sense of attachment and belonging. You know it's present when you feel psychologically comfortable in the location. The house and site fit into the surrounding environment and are not at odds with it. They feel as if they were always meant to be there and were created for the space that they occupy.

Sense of place cannot be described as curb appeal, and yet it has it. It has a lot to do with "fitting" the neighborhood you live in. Look around—does the architecture of your house fit the environment of your property, your street, and the neighborhood? Even if it's different, do the style and the colors blend in? Does the landscaping reflect the local terrain? Is there continuity on the house that expands to include all of the details that have been

used on the property? When you are designing your house, consider these important points so that the results will provide an environment that fits the place where you live.

The Focal Point

A focal point is simply a strong, intentional, concentrated point of interest. It's the place where your attention is naturally directed and where your eye rests easily. Without a focal point, your focus is scattered because the eye sweeps along without finding a place to rest. With a strong focal point, unity, harmony, and balance are created.

A focal point should be the first thing that you see and should show off the best qualities of your house. For the exterior of a house, the focal point is almost always the front door since it acts as a beacon to visitors. The home's place of entry draws attention to itself and guides visitors inside. But secondary focal points can be created as well.

Creating a focal point doesn't take as much effort as you might think. It can be created by simply flanking the front door with interesting potted plants and placing a wreath on the door. At night, lighting can further enhance the focal point by highlighting the area.

ABOVE: "Color as a focal point" describes this view, where cold, hard lines and a narrow set of stairs guide you to the unusual door color and entry to the house.

ABOVE: The view from the front door towards the entry gate is a secondary focal point. The gate captures your attention as the orange-painted ceiling guides you to it with its strong directional color.

ABOVE: The color that surrounds this entry door gives pizzazz to otherwise neutral house colors, adding personality as well as guiding you to the front door. The colors of the Japanese maple tree and stone wall coordinate with the entry, creating continuity between the house color and the surrounding landscape.

RIGHT: This is a reverse focal point. The arch captures and frames the landscape, bringing your attention to the strongest point of interest—the spectacular panoramic view.

ABOVE : The brick path makes a strong and welcome entrance to this house. Flowers and lighting on each side of the path emphasize it. The front door is dark and attracts attention, while the wreath and bookended plants help to reinforce the entry's strong focal point.

ABOVE: The Buddha figure at the end of the garden path gives a visual ending point and a place to rest the eye.

ABOVE : A simple addition of potted hydrangeas reinforces the color of the front door and draws you to the entry with its linear placement.

Landscaping

The importance of good landscaping cannot be overstated. It's as important as the design of the house because it conveys a message that all details have been methodically considered and implemented. It's a good investment too. A good landscape plan can add fifteen percent to the value of your house and can enhance the curb appeal to help sell your house when the time comes. It is essential in creating a sense of place.

Great landscaping blends with the color and design of your house and doesn't overwhelm it. It sets a tone by providing a welcoming atmosphere that reflects your personality and enriches the street with its finished appearance. It creates privacy, subdues noise from the street, and happily welcomes you home after a long day at work. A green lawn makes the house look appealing, but creative approaches are being implemented more and more these days, such as added mounds, terraced landscapes, stone walls, trellises, fences, and rock gardens. Formal flower gardens or a landscape of loosely designed, drought-resistant plants rule today's landscapes. Flowers, distributed in correct proportion and in combination with the right colors, blend with each other and with the house colors to enhance both. The arrangement of plants, flowers, and trees balances out the architecture of the house and softens its hard edges. Great house colors are important, but the landscaping adds the color and the dimensional and textural qualities that help complete the look.

Many of the images in the book may inspire you to create a new or improved garden landscape for your home. A landscape designer, architect, or even an expert at a local garden center may be able to help you identify many of the plants, flowers, and trees from the photographs in this book and determine if they will grow in your area. If not, he or she may be able to suggest appropriate replacements.

The Details

"God is in the details."
Ludwig Mies van der Rohe

Look closer—the details that are used on a house shine and bring life to it. Awnings, canopies, drapery, windows, window grilles, and trellises can add tremendous architectural interest and texture to the facade of the house. Interesting and unusual door hardware, house numbers, and doorbells enhance the personality of the entry area and can add sparkle with their metallic finishes. A path can make a strong visual and textural statement while guiding you around the property. Lighting can add nighttime drama in addition to lighting the path to the front door, highlighting landscaping, and brightening the porch to make the house visible in the dark. Doors, garage doors, gates, and railings can emphasize the architectural details of the house or bring added attention to it by creating a mix of architectural elements and adding an eclectic feel to the place. The door in particular is an important area to emphasize because it's the first thing you see as you arrive and it sets a standard of quality for what you can expect to see upon entering the house. Small unexpected details, like hand-blown glass balls floating in a fountain, concrete pillow stepping-stones, stacked river rocks at the entry, or dried gourds sitting on an entry bench inscribed with a message can add a great deal of personality too. These details add the finishing touches and interest that can take your house from ordinary to extraordinary.

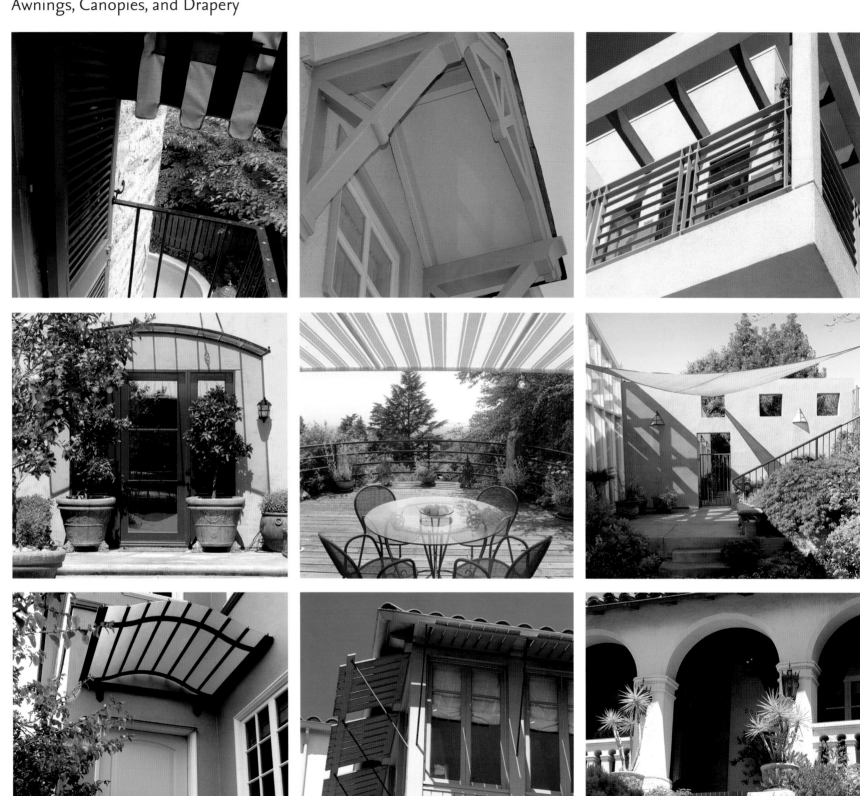

Door Hardware

Doors

Garage Doors

 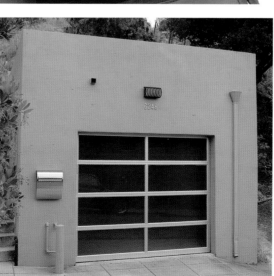 

Gates and Railings

Pavers

Windows and Grilles

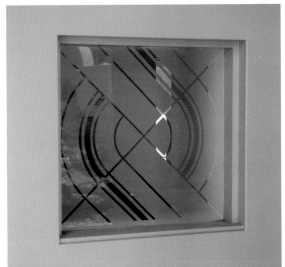

Things to Avoid

1. Don't unnecessarily break up the continuity of your paving surfaces. Use one continual material from the street to the entry unless you purposely mix materials that work together aesthetically. If there is a change, it should be an intentional part of the design. And keep it simple—don't have so many changes in materials that it looks like a patchwork quilt.

   It's common to ignore the color of the pavers, particularly for painted or color-embedded concrete. Too many people paint the concrete a standard gray color, no matter what the color scheme, because they think it looks most like a natural concrete color. (It doesn't.) The color of the pavers should be chosen based on the colors you've selected for the rest of the exterior so that they work together in harmony. Most manufacturers have a selection of standard floor paints that can be used for concrete, and any color can be custom matched to work with your house colors.

2. Just because the front door is wood doesn't mean that it shouldn't be painted. If it's a paint-grade wood, it's probably screaming for color. An exception to this is when you use a quality "architectural grade" wood door, like a solid mahogany or oak that is meant to be stained or left natural (with a protective coating, of course). If it's a paint-grade wood material, go ahead and paint it as was intended by the manufacturer. It will look better and is a great opportunity for a splash of color. Also, consider this: a flat paint-grade door with no details looks like an interior closet door. Investing in a door and door hardware of quality will add class and can dramatically enhance the attractiveness of your home.

3. Don't mix materials for mailboxes, house numbers, door hardware, lighting, doorbells, etc., if you can help it. Stick with one finish, such as brass, black, or stainless steel. You can't always do it, but the key is to keep as many finishes the same as possible—especially when they're right next to each other.

4. Don't use plastic terra-cotta flower pots for display. They're only meant to get your plants or flowers from the store to your house or sink into larger pots. Transplant them into high-quality pots or planter boxes around your house.

   Also, pay attention to how you arrange them. Group them aesthetically; consider balance, visual appeal, and how it will affect the focal point. Remember this simple rule: sometimes less is more.

5. If you have more than one door, or other competing architectural elements, consider placing the focal point at the entry door and have everything else blend with the house colors so that they don't compete with each other. Even if "everything else" is lovely, the old adage holds true here: too much of a good thing is *really* too much.

6. Don't use stone aggregates and artificial turf as a replacement for green landscaping. They'll leave your house cold and lacking in curb appeal.

7. When there is a change of design on your fence, consider keeping the paint color the same for the sake of continuity. Even better, try to match the new fence to the existing one for a seamless look.

8. Consider window coverings as part of the overall exterior design. They are visible and need to be kept tidy and consistent in color and design. This may seem obvious, but it cannot be overstated.

9. Do not use a cyclone or chain-link fence for your entry gate. Instead, use a decorative, quality fence for the entrance to your property. If expense is an issue, economical yet attractive solutions are available. Even a simple wooden fence from your local home supply store would be an improvement over a metal industrial-looking fence.

Color and Product Specifications by House Number

1

Field Paint Color
Manufacturer: Finnaren and Haley Paints
Collection: Authentic Colors of Philadelphia
Color number: 9
Color name: Todd House Yellow

Window, Window Frame, and Portico Paint Color
Manufacturer: Finnaren and Haley Paints
Color number: CW060W
Color name: Sea Cloud

Door Paint Color
Manufacturer: Finnaren and Haley Paints
Color number: AC116N
Color name: Roasted Pepper

Shutter Paint Color
Manufacturer: Finnaren and Haley Paints
Collection: Authentic Colors of Philadelphia
Color number: 27
Color name: Grand Staircase Blue

Asphalt Composition Shingle Roofing
Manufacturer: CertainTeed
Product: Hallmark Shangle
Color name: Bronzed Brown

2

Field Paint Color
Manufacturer: Pittsburgh Paints
Color number: 512-6
Color name: Rattan Palm

Window, Window Frame, Cornice, and Portico Paint Color
Manufacturer: Benjamin Moore
Color number: EXT. RM.
Color name: Lancaster White

Door
Paint Color
Manufacturer: Benjamin Moore
Color number: EXT. RM.
Color name: Black
Doorbell
Manufacturer: Flora & Fauna
Product: Squirrel Doorbell
Product number: WL20075
Material: Solid brass
Finish: Polished verdigris patina

Source: www.houseandgardenaccents.com
House Numbers
Manufacturer: Flora & Fauna
Product: Hand-carved house numbers
Product number: WL20263
Material: Solid brass
Finish: Polished verdigris patina
Note: Available at www.houseandgardenaccents.com

Composition Asphalt Shingle Roofing
Manufacturer: CertainTeed
Product: Presidential Shake
Color name: Weathered Wood

Color Consultant
Rory Boyle
R. Boyle Painting
Pacifica, California

3

Field Paint Colors
Color #1
Manufacturer: Benjamin Moore
Color number: 818
Color name: Watertown
Color #2
Manufacturer: Benjamin Moore
Color number: 826
Color name: Stunning

Window Paint Color
Manufacturer: Benjamin Moore
Color number: 308
Color name: Golden Vista

Window Frame and Trim Paint Color
Manufacturer: Benjamin Moore
Product: Super Spec
Color number: 170 01
Color name: White

Door Paint Color
Manufacturer: Benjamin Moore
Color number: 2085-20
Color name: Pottery Red
Note: My match

4

Field Paint Color
Manufacturer: Benjamin Moore
Color number: 2175-40
Color name: Adobe Dust

Window Paint Color
Manufacturer: Benjamin Moore
Color number: 1305
Color name: Bird of Paradise

Window and Door Frame Paint Color
Manufacturer: Benjamin Moore
Color number: 2047-10
Color name: Forest Green

Door Paint Color
Manufacturer: Benjamin Moore
Color number: 1305
Color name: Bird of Paradise

Screen Door Paint Color
Manufacturer: Benjamin Moore
Color number: 2003-10
Color name: Million Dollar Red
Note: My match

Shutter and Projecting Eave Paint Color
Manufacturer: Benjamin Moore
Color number: 2047-10
Color name: Forest Green

Reveal Lines (Shutter) and Accent (Bracket) Paint Color
Manufacturer: Benjamin Moore
Color number: HC-132
Color name: Harrisburg Green
Note: Both colors used on fascia board, projecting eaves, and trim.

5

Field Paint Color
Manufacturer: Behr
Color name: Custom
Tinting base: 4670
One gallon formula:
  B 1Y45
  C 1Y42
  F 7

Window and Railing Paint Color
Manufacturer: Behr
Color name: Ultra Pure White

Door, Shutter, Portal, Round Vent, and Garage Door Paint Color
Manufacturer: Behr
Color name: Custom "dark forest green"
Deep base: 5340
One gallon formula:
  B 8Y30+1/96
  C 1Y3+1/96
  E 1Y36+1/96

KX 26

Water Fountain
Manufacturer: A. Silvestri Co.
Product: Lion Fountain
Material: Cement
Stain: White-gray
Finish: Marble

Carriage Post Light
Manufacturer: Rejuvenation Hardware
Product: Fulton Carriage Post Mount Light
Product number: N643
Finish: Cast iron
Note: My match. Similar product.

Roof Tile
Material: Cedar shake shingle

Courtyard Pavers
Product: Medium rock aggregate with pattern of 6" square black slate tile
Note: My match

6

Field Color
Clapboard Siding Solid Stain Color
Manufacturer: Benjamin Moore
Color name: Custom "green"
Tinting base: 067-2B
One gallon formula:
  OY 4 x 22
  BR 2 x16

Stone Veneer
Manufacturer: Eldorado Stone
Product: Country Rubble
Color name: Alderidge
Note: My match

Window, Window Frame, and Trim Paint Color
Manufacturer: Benjamin Moore
Color number: OC-95
Color name: Navajo White

Door Paint Color
Manufacturer: Sherwin Williams
Color number: SW6121
Color name: Whole Wheat
Note: My match

Shutter Paint Color
Manufacturer: Benjamin Moore
Color number: HC-64
Color name: Townsend Harbor Brown

Composition Asphalt Shingle Roofing
Manufacturer: CertainTeed
Product: Woodscape Series
Color name: Slate Blend
Note: My match

Landscape Design
Richard & Robert Wilson
Wilson Landscaping
Huntingdon Valley, Pennsylvania

Color Consultant
Thomas Woodend
Medford, New Jersey

7

Field Paint Color
Manufacturer: M.A.B. Paints
Collection: Color Symphony
Color number: 5699D
Color name: Gettysburg

Window, Window Frame, Sidelight, and Door Frame Paint Color
Manufacturer: M.A.B. Paints
Color number: 150
Color name: White

Door Paint Color
Manufacturer: Behr
Color name: Custom
Tinting base: Deep base 5340
One quart formula:
  B 0 1 0
  R 1 3 0 0
  V 1 1 7 0
  Add two tablespoons of black paint (gloss).

Shutter Paint Color
Manufacturer: M.A.B. Paints
Color number: 98229N
Color name: Evening Empress
Note: My match

Replica Plaque
Note: Plaques can be found online at eBay. Search this category: Collectibles/Historical Memorabilia/Firefighting/Signs & Plaques.

Pavers
Material: Red brick

8

Field Paint Color
Manufacturer: Benjamin Moore
Color number: 1497
Color name: Rolling Hills

Window, Window Frame, Portico, Sidelights, and Door Frame Paint Color
Manufacturer: Benjamin Moore
Color number: INT. RM.
Color name: Atrium White
Note: Mix interior color into exterior paint product.

Door Paint Color
Manufacturer: Benjamin Moore
Color number: EXT. RM.
Color name: Cottage Red

Pavers
Material: Rustic red brick

Composition Asphalt Shingle Roofing
Manufacturer: CertainTeed
Product: Landmark TL
Color: Moire Black

Note: My match

Color Consultant
M. B. Jessee Painting and Decorating
Oakland, California

9

Clapboard Siding
Material: Cedar siding
Stain
Manufacturer: Sherwin Williams
Product: Woodscapes
Type: Polyurethane semi-transparent stain
Color name: Brown Bark

Window, Window Frame, and Door Frame Paint Color
Manufacturer: Benjamin Moore
Color number: HC-166
Color name: Kendall Charcoal

Window Paint Color (Cottage)
Manufacturer: Benjamin Moore
Color number: HC-72
Color Name: Branchport Brown
Note: My match. These are metal windows. Use metal primer before painting them.

Door, Screen Door, and Shutter Paint Color
Manufacturer: Benjamin Moore
Color number: HC-124
Color name: Caldwell Green
Note: Window and window frames on the side of the house

Roof Tile
Material: Gray slate

Pavers
Material: Green slate

Wall Lantern at Entry
Manufacturer: Artistic Lighting and Design
Product name: Jefferson
Product number: 704
Material: Solid brass
Color: Charcoal
Note: My match

10

Field Paint Color
Manufacturer: Benjamin Moore
Color Number: AC-1
Color name: Coastal Fog

Window, Window Frame, Sidelights, Cornice, and Portico Paint Color
Manufacturer: Benjamin Moore
Color number: 925
Color name: Ivory White

Door Paint Color
Manufacturer: Benjamin Moore
Color number: 1306
Color name: Habanero Pepper

Shutter Paint Color
Manufacturer: Benjamin Moore
Color number: AC-3
Color name: Texas Leather

Color Consultant
Constance Scott
Art4 Architecture
Berkeley, California

11

Field Window, Window Frame, Portico, and Trim Paint Color
Manufacturer: Benjamin Moore
Color number: 2148-60
Color name: Timid White
Note: My match. Clapboard is vinyl siding from Lowes (Color: Colonial White).

Stone Facade
Material: Pennsylvania Limestone Cobble

Door, Shutter, and Mailbox Paint Color
Manufacturer: Benjamin Moore
Color number: 2062-20
Color name: Gentleman's Gray
Note: Shutters feature the same color as the door and mailbox (though the color has faded considerably).

Garage Door Paint Color
Manufacturer: Benjamin Moore
Color number: 2148-50
Color name: Sandy White
Note: My match

Composition Asphalt Shingle Roofing
Manufacturer: CertainTeed
Product: Landmark Series
Color name: Moire Black

12

Field Stone
Material: Wissahickon schist
Note: Original to old home. Similar stone can be located at: Chestnut Hill Stone, Ltd. Glenside, Pennsylvania

Window, Window Frame, Portico, Sidelights, Door Frame, Storm Door, and Trim Paint Color
Manufacturer: Benjamin Moore
Color number: INT. RM.
Color name: Atrium White
Note: Mix paint color into exterior paint product.

Door and Shutter Paint Color
Manufacturer: Benjamin Moore
Product: EXT. RM.
Color name: Heritage Red

Composition Asphalt Shingle Roofing
Manufacturer: CertainTeed
Product number: CT20
Color name: Nickel Gray (regional color)
Note: All my matches

13

Field and Trellis Paint Color
Manufacturer: Benjamin Moore
Color name: Custom
Tinting base: N105-3B
  OY 1 x 20
  BK 1 x 7
  RD 7.25
  GY 4
  WH 29

Window, Window Frame, and Door Frame Paint Color
Manufacturer: Benjamin Moore
Color number: EXT. RM.
Color name: Lancaster White

Door and Shutter Paint Color
Manufacturer: Benjamin Moore
Color number: EXT. RM.
Color name: Essex Green

Composition Asphalt Shingle Roofing
Manufacturer: Elk
Product: Prestique I—High Definition
Color name: Black

Steps
Material: Red brick

Pavers
Material: Black slate tile

14

Stone Facing
Material: Wissahickon schist
Note: Original to old home. Similar stone can be located at: Chestnut Hill Stone, Ltd. Glenside, Pennsylvania

Window, Window Frame, Sidelights, Canopy, Projecting Eave, and Portal Paint Color
Manufacturer: Benjamin Moore
Color number: OC-95
Color name: Navajo White

Door and Eyebrow Window Trim Paint Color
Manufacturer: Benjamin Moore
Color number: HC-51
Color name: Audubon Russet

Shutter Paint Color
First-Floor Shutter
Manufacturer: Benjamin Moore
Color number: 1523
Color name: Embassy Green
Note: My match
Second-Floor Shutter
Manufacturer: Benjamin Moore
Color number: HC-126
Color name: Avon Green

15

Field Paint Color
Manufacturer: Morwear
Color name: Custom
Tinting base: 4710T
One gallon formula:
  B-2Y6
  C-1Y39

Window, Window Frame, Door Frame, Sidelights, Garage Door, and Portico Paint Color
Manufacturer: Kelly-Moore
Color number: 20
Color name: Western Acoustic

Door Paint Color
Manufacturer: Morwear
Color name: Custom
Tinting base: 7840A
One quart formula:
  B-28
  KX-3
  C-42
  D-6
  E-2Y27
Note: Custom matched to forest green shutter color.

Shutters
Manufacturer: Atlantic Shutter Systems
Product: Authentic Shutters
Type: Raised Panel—Charleston

Color name: Forest Green
Material: Fiberglass

Composition Asphalt Shingle Roofing
Manufacturer: Elk Corporation
Product: Prestique Plus High Definition
Color name: Sablewood

Pavers
Material: Red brick

16

Field Stone Facing
Manufacturer: Delaware Quarries, Inc.
Product: Princeton Stone
Type: Full Veneer

Window, Window Frame, Door Frame, Canopy, Portal, and Lower Shutter Paint Color
Manufacturer: Benjamin Moore
Color number: 927
Color name: White Swan

Door and Upper Shutter Paint Color
Manufacturer: Benjamin Moore
Color number: 2114-10
Color name: Bittersweet Chocolate

Dormer Siding Paint Color
Manufacturer: Benjamin Moore
Color number: 861
Color name: Shale

Composition Asphalt Shingle Roofing
Manufacturer: CertainTeed
Product number: XT30
Color name: Oakwood
Note: All my matches

17

Field Paint Color
Manufacturer: Fuller O'Brien
Color number: 2C21-3
Color name: Armenian Stone

Window, Window Frame, Sidelights, Columns, and Horizontal Molding Paint Color
Manufacturer: Benjamin Moore
Color number: EXT. RM.
Color name: Brilliant White
Note: My match

Door Paint Color
Manufacturer: Behr
Color name: Midnight Dream

Shutter Paint Color
Manufacturer: Benjamin Moore
Color number: HC-130
Color name: Webster Green

Composition Asphalt Shingle Roofing
Manufacturer: CertainTeed
Product: Landmark Series
Color: Granite Gray
Note: My match

18

Field Stone
Name of stone: Wissahickon schist
Note: Original to old home. Similar stone can be located at: Chestnut Hill Stone, Ltd. Glenside, Pennsylvania

Window, Window Frame, Dormer Siding, and Portal Surround Paint Color
Manufacturer: Benjamin Moore
Color number: 919
Color name: Buttermilk

Door, Screen Door, and Shutter Paint Color
Manufacturer: Benjamin Moore
Color number: 2171-10
Color name: Navajo Red

Wrought-Iron Wall Lantern
Manufacturer: English Garden Furniture
Product: New England Wall Lantern
Note: The light fixture on the house is old. This is a similar product.
Note: All my matches

19

Dormer Siding, Portal and Trim Paint Color
Manufacturer: Benjamin Moore
Color number: HC-93
Color name: Carrington Beige

Stone Facade
Material: Wissahickon schist
Note: Old stone. Similar stone can be located at Chestnut Hill Stone, Ltd., Glenside, Pennsylvania
Note: My match

Window, Window Frame, and Trim (at Dormer) Paint Color
Manufacturer: Benjamin Moore
Color number: HC-82
Color name: Bennington Gray

Door and Shutter Paint Color
Manufacturer: Benjamin Moore
Color number: 2053-20
Color name: Dark Teal

Lantern by Entry
Manufacturer: Brass Light Gallery
Product: Carriage lantern with straight arm wall mount
Product number: EX-5106-A10
Material: Aged verdigris patina with clear seeded glass

Roof Tile
Material: Dark gray slate
Note: Original to house

Pavers
Material: Bluestone slate
Note: Original to house

20

Stucco Paint Color
Manufacturer: Kelly-Moore
Color name: Custom
Tinting base: 1240-222
One gallon formula:
  C 4
  F 8
  L 1Y44

Window, Window Frame, Garage Door Frame, Portal, and Trim Paint Color
Manufacturer: Kelly-Moore
Color number: 26
Color name: Oyster

Door Paint Color
Manufacturer: Benjamin Moore

Color name: Custom
Tinting base: N103-4B
One gallon formula:
  OY 3 x 12
  BK 2 x 16
  MA 6 x 24
  WH 1 x 8

Shutter, Horizontal Frieze, Garage Door, Clapboard and Window Box Paint Color
Manufacturer: Kelly-Moore
Color name: Custom
Tinting base: Deep base, 333
One gallon formula:
  B 24
  F 8
  L 2Y28

Frieze Trim Paint Color
Manufacturer: Kelly-Moore
Color number: B40-3
Color name: Pagan

Composition Asphalt Shingle Roofing
Manufacturer: CertainTeed
Product: Presidential TL
Color name: Weathered Wood

Pavers
Material: Flagstone

Color Consultant
Bob Buckter
San Francisco, California

21

Field Paint Color
Manufacturer: Benjamin Moore
Color number: 1537
Color name: River Gorge Gray

Window, Window Frame, Door Frame, Sidelights, Panel, Railing, and Portico Paint Color
Manufacturer: Benjamin Moore
Color number: HC-84
Color name: Elmira White

Door Paint Color
Manufacturer: Benjamin Moore
Color number: EXT. RM.
Color name: Black Forest Green

Quoin Paint Color (Corners of House)
Manufacturer: Benjamin Moore
Color number: 1546
Color name: Gargoyle

Entry Steps
Material: Painted concrete
Paint Color
Manufacturer: Benjamin Moore
Color number: HC103
Color name: Cromwell Gray
Note: Add enough black to turn the color to a medium gray tone.

Medallion Paint Color
Manufacturer: Blue Pearl Metallic Paint
Color name: Tarnished Silver
Note: My match

Composition Asphalt Shingle Roofing
Manufacturer: CertainTeed
Product: Landmark TL Ultimate
Color name: Moire Black
Note: My match

Pavers
Material: Black slate with red brick border

22

Field Paint Color
Manufacturer: Behr
Color name: Custom
Accent base: 9560
One gallon formula:
  B 28+1/96
  C 1Y26+1/96
  R 15+1/96
Note: Painted stone

Door, Window, and Bench Paint Color
Manufacturer: Behr
Color name: Custom
Accent base: 9670
One gallon formula:
  AX 1/96
  E 1Y
  F 5Y

Window Frame, Door Frame, and Shutter Paint Color
Manufacturer: Behr
Color name: Custom
Accent base: 9670
One gallon formula:
  AX 5Y
  B 4Y40+1/96
  F 1Y7+1/96

Composition Asphalt Shingle Roofing
Manufacturer: CertainTeed
Product: Landmark AS
Color name: Burnt Sienna

Landscape Architect
Doug Julian
Julian Design
Doylestown, Pennsylvania
Note: Mailbox matches coordinating house colors.

23

Color-Embedded Stucco Field Color
Manufacturer: LaHabra
Product: Custom
Match to:
Manufacturer: Benjamin Moore
Color number: 1008
Color name: Devonwood Taupe

Window, Window Frame, and Trim Paint Color
Manufacturer: Benjamin Moore
Color name: Custom
Tinting base: N096-1B
One gallon formula:
  OY8
  GY 7
  WH 2x20

Door
Material: Natural mahogany
Protectant
Manufacturer: Penofin
Product: Original Blue Label Oil Wood Finish
Color name: Transparent

Composition Asphalt Shingle Roofing
Manufacturer: CertainTeed
Product number: XT30
Color name: Black

Pavers
Material: Cobblestone
Note: Antique relics from the San Francisco streets after the 1906 earthquake

Color Consultant
Lois Wachner-Solomon
Piedmont, California

24

Field Paint Color
Manufacturer: Glidden
Color number: 50YY 59/117
Color name: Sculpted Stone

Window Frame, Door Frame, and Trim Paint Color
Manufacturer: Morwear
Color name: Cello Blanco

Door, Window, and Railing Paint Color
Manufacturer: Rust-Oleum
Color name: Gloss Black
Note: Oil base paint

Porch Floor Paint Color
Manufacturer: Glidden
Color number: 30YY 17/140
Color name: Stone Quarry

Composition Asphalt Shingle Roofing
Manufacturer: CertainTeed
Product: Landmark TL
Color name: Black
Note: My match

25

Stone Facade
Material: Wissahickon schist
Note: Old stone. Similar stone can be located at:
Chestnut Hill Stone, Ltd.
Glenside, Pennsylvania

Clapboard Siding, Window, Window Frame, Garage Door, Garage Door Frame (Not Shown), French Door, and Trim Paint Color
Manufacturer: Sherwin Williams
Color number: SW6192
Color name: Coastal Plain

Front Door and Shutter Paint Color
Manufacturer: Sherwin Williams
Color name: Custom
Tinting base: Ultra deep
One gallon formula:
  WH 1/128
  B1 30/32
  L1 28/32
  Y3 20/32

Roof Tile
Material: Vermont slate
Note: Original to house. Slate was laid in 1926. Check local distributors for availability in your area.

26

Stone Facade
Material: Wissahickon schist
Note: Old stone. Similar stone can be located at:
Chestnut Hill Stone, Ltd.
Glenside, Pennsylvania

Window, Window Frame, and Garage Frame Paint Color
Manufacturer: Benjamin Moore
Color number: 205
Color name: Simply Irresistible

Front Door, Garage Door, and Shutter Paint Color
Manufacturer: Benjamin Moore
Color number: 207
Color name: Vellum

Roof Tile
Material: Vermont slate
Note: Original to house. Slate was laid in 1926. Check local distributors for availability in your area.
Note: All my matches

27

Field Paint Color
Manufacturer: Benjamin Moore
Color number: HC-124
Color name: Caldwell Green

Door
Manufacturer: Summit Woodworking
Product: 5-lite paint grade door with 3/16" etched reed glass
Paint Color
Manufacturer: Benjamin Moore
Color number: OC-121
Color name: Mountain Peak White

Etched Glass
Manufacturer: Etchings
San Rafael, California

Etched Glass Coating
Manufacturer: Diamon-Fusion International
Note: Hides finger prints and makes etched glass water repellent.

Door Handle Set
Manufacturer: Double Hill Hardware
Product: Manchester
Product number: E 1251P MAN-US10B
Finish: Oil-rubbed bronze

Door Frame, Window, Window Frame, and Trim Paint Color
Manufacturer: Benjamin Moore
Color number: OC-121
Color name: Mountain Peak White

River Rocks and Boulders
Source: Shamrock Materials, Inc.

Railing
Product: Custom wood railing
Materials: Redwood and 3/4" copper pipe

Porch Decking
Material: Redwood

Entry, Steps, and Porch Landing
Material: Treated redwood

28

Field Paint Color
Manufacturer: Pratt & Lambert
Color number: 1144
Color name: Corsican

Door (Not Shown), Shutter, Window, Window Frame, and Trim Paint Color
Manufacturer: Fuller O'Brien
Color number: G-113
Color name: Stone White (old color)
Formula for G-113:

Tinting base: 614-91
One gallon formula:
BLK 0p8
YOX 0p12
OXR 0p1/2

**Composition Asphalt Shingle
Roofing**
Manufacturer: CertainTeed
Product: Landmark
Color name: Moire Black
Note: My match

29

Stucco Field Color
Note: The house features original stucco from 1928, and a deep complex patina has developed over a long period of time with a depth of color that is not repeatable. There are a number of different colors in the stucco. I've matched three color-embedded stucco colors that most closely represent them.

Color-Embedded Stucco Field Color
Manufacturer: LaHabra
Color number and names:
X-524, Alamo (Base 200)—most dominant color
X-580, Sierra Tan (Base 200)
X-25, Saddleback (Base 200)
Note: The stucco has black speckles of sand in it.
Sealant
Manufacturer: VIP Lighthouse Products
Product: Ombrella
Silane/Siloxane
Label: VIP Concentrate
Code: 1550
Chimney
Material: Whitewashed brick
Window and Window Frame Paint Color
Manufacturer: Pratt and Lambert
Color number: 2264
Color name: Flagstaff
Note: My match
Door
Material: Douglas fir (original to 1920s house)
Finish
Source: Rockler Woodworking and Hardware
Product: Rotten Stone
Number: 53892
Note: Rotten stone is a fine powdered rock used as a polishing abrasive in woodworking. Its composition is usually limestone mixed with silica.
Shutter Paint Color
75% of:
Manufacturer: Benjamin Moore
Color number: 2138-40
Color name: Carolina Gull
Note: My match
Entry Light Fixture
Note: The fixture is original to the house. See "English Garden Furniture" in the resource section for similar light fixtures.
Gate to Courtyard
Material: Clear heart redwood

Stain
Manufacturer: Watco
Product: Exterior Oil Finish
Color name: "Original" clear
Roof Tile
Product: Cedar shingles with copper trim at roofline
Pavers
Material: Connecticut Bluestone
Note: The stone shapes are random squares and rectangles. They are available from Graniterock, Watsonville, California, or check with a local stone retailer for availability.

30

Field Paint Color
Manufacturer: Fuller O'Brien
Product: Weather King II
Color number: 3W24-5
Color name: Belmont Brown
Window and Window Frame Paint Color
Manufacturer: Benjamin Moore
Color number: 1559
Color name: Arctic Shadows
Door Paint Color
Manufacturer: Benjamin Moore
Color number: 189
Color name: Morgan Hill Gold
Roof Tile
Material: Terra-cotta clay
Note: The homeowner, Ross Powers of Berkeley, California, is a professional house painter who contributed knowledgeable information about house painting to this book.

31

Field Paint Color
Manufacturer: Kelly-Moore
Color number: KM3613-2
Color name: Sun-Warmed Tile
Door and Window Paint Color
Manufacturer: Kelly-Moore
Color number: KM3964-1
Color name: Beach Bum
Window Frame, Trellised Canopy, Trim, and Picket Fence Paint Color
Manufacturer: Kelly-Moore
Color number: KM3965-2
Color name: Head for the Beach
Composition Asphalt Shingle Roofing
Manufacturer: CertainTeed
Product: Landmark Series
Color name: Driftwood
Note: My match

32

Field Paint Color
Manufacturer: Benjamin Moore
Color number: 2143-70
Color name: Simply White
Door, Window, and Garage Door Paint Color
Manufacturer: Benjamin Moore
Color number: EXT. RM.
Color name: Black Forest Green
Note: Front door is original to the house, which was built in 1928

Gutters and Flashing
Material: Copper
Sconce Lighting
Manufacturer: Arroyo Craftsman
Product: Berkeley 7" Wall Mount
Product number: BB-7W
Finish: Bronze
Note: Similar product. My match.
Roof Tile
Material: Natural heavy cedar shake
Pavers
Manufacturer: Calstone
Product: Quarry Stone
Material: Concrete
Color name: Connecticut Green
Entry Steps
Material: Black slate

33

Stone Facade
Name of stone: Wissahickon schist
Note: Original to old home. Similar stone can be located at: Chestnut Hill Stone, Ltd. Glenside, Pennsylvania
Window, Transom, Door, and Window Frame Paint Color
Manufacturer: M.A.B. Paints
Color name: Custom
Accent base: 048-1971
One gallon formula:
C-1Y24
I-8
L-2Y44
Door, Shutter, and Gate Paint Color
Manufacturer: M.A.B. Paints
Color name: Custom
Alkyd paint
Accent base: 048-1911
One gallon formula:
B-10
E-4Y8
KX-1Y10
T-1Y14
Entry Door Trim Paint Color
Manufacturer: M.A.B. Paints
Color number: 425
Color name: Patriot Red
Note: My match

34

Field Paint Color
Manufacturer: Benjamin Moore
Color name: Custom
Tinting base: N103 1B
OY 2 x 20
BK 20
RD8
Door, Window, and Sidelights Paint Color
Manufacturer: Dunn Edwards
Color name: Custom
Tinting base: W901, U Base
Permasheen 2002
One gallon formula:
4-24
8-2Y18
14-28
13-2
10-11Y

Window Frame, Column, and Trim Paint Color
Manufacturer: Benjamin Moore
Color number: EXT. RM.
Color name: Lancaster White

35

Field Paint Color
Manufacturer: Benjamin Moore
Color number: HC-107
Color name: Gettysburg Gray
Window Paint Color
Manufacturer: Benjamin Moore
Color number: HC-166
Color name: Kendall Charcoal
Window Frame and Door Frame Paint Color
Manufacturer: Benjamin Moore
Color number: OC-32
Color name: Tapestry Beige
Door Paint Color
Manufacturer: Benjamin Moore
Color name: Custom
Tinting base: N096-4B
One gallon formula:
RX 1 x 31 1/4 + 1/8
BK 4 x 8
MA 6x
WH 16
House Plaque
Manufacturer: Canterbury Designs
Product: Domed House Plaque
Product number: 5021
Material: Resin with four leaf clover

36

Field Color
Manufacturer: Sherwin Williams
Color number: SW6389
Color name: Butternut
Door, Window, Window Frame, Sidelights, Railing, Column, and Trim Color
Manufacturer: Sherwin Williams
Color number: SW7006
Color name: Extra White
Note: My match
Door Color
Manufacturer: Sherwin Williams
Color number: SW6258
Color name: Tricorn Black
Finish: Gloss
Note: My match
Shutter and Dormer Paint Color
Manufacturer: Ace Paints
Color number: 46A
Color name: Pawnee
Porch Floor
Material: Grapera Hardwood
Manufacturer: Flood
Wood Finish
Product: Flood Pro Spa-N-Deck 100% Acrylic Wood Finish
Color name: Chestnut
Wrought Iron Gate and Railing Paint Color
Manufacturer: Rust-Oleum
Product: Satin Rust Preventive
Finish: Low Sheen
Color number: 7777 504
Color name: Black
Note: My match

37

Field Paint Color
Manufacturer: Kelly-Moore
Color number: KM600-D
Color name: Brownbridge
Window and Trim Paint Color
Manufacturer: Kelly-Moore
Color number: KM557-M
Color name: Gatehouse
Window Frame Paint Color
Manufacturer: Kelly-Moore
Color number: KM522-D
Color name: Camp Tent
Door and Canopy Paint Color
Manufacturer: Kelly-Moore
Color #1
Color number: KM557-M
Color name: Gatehouse
Color #2
Color number: KM-522-D
Color name: Camp Tent
Composition Asphalt Shingle Roofing
Manufacturer: Elk Premium Building Products
Product: Prestique Plus High Definition
Color name: Weathered Wood
Concrete Paving Paint
Manufacturer: Kelly-Moore
Color number: 1350-195
Color name: Rustic Redwood
Note: Mix into concrete paint product
Steps
Material: Red brick

38

Field and Trellis Column Paint Color
Manufacturer: Benjamin Moore
Color name: Custom
Tinting base: N105-1B
One gallon formula:
OY-24
OG-2
GY-8
Paneled Bay on House and Garage Structure
Material: Cedar
Stain
Manufacturer: Cabot
Product: OVT Solid Stain
Color name: Cape Cod Gray
Note: Exterior gray plywood sheets with 16" on center battens
Garage Doors
Manufacturer: Loewen Doors
Material: Cedar
Finish: Whitewashed
Stain—First Coat
Manufacturer: Cabot
Product: Semi-Solid Stain
Color name: Bark
Stain—Second Coat
Manufacturer: Cabot
Product: Semi-Solid Stain
Number: WH/10X
Color name: Custom White
Note: Allow first coat to dry for a week. Apply second coat heavily and let it dry overnight. The following day, wipe off top coat with rags in the direction of the wood grain. Wipe down areas

that have become too dry with paint thinner and a rag.

Window and Window Frame
Manufacturer: Loewen
Paint Color
Manufacturer: Benjamin Moore
Color name: Custom
Tinting base: 183-3B
One gallon formula:
OY 1 x 15
BB 1 x 10
OG 5
WH 2 x 4
BR 9
Dutch Door
Product: Custom
Material: Knotty alder
Note: Features frameless, uneven planks
Stain
Manufacturer: Penofin
Product: Original Blue Label Oil
Color name: Transparent Cedar
Warehouse Lighting over Garage
Manufacturer: Hi-Lite Manufacturing
Product: Gooseneck Wall Mount
Mounting option: B-1
Material: Galvanized metal
Note: My match
Sconces by Back Door
Manufacturer: English Garden Furniture
Product: The Craftsman
Material: Sheet metal and iron
Color name: Painted black
Composition Asphalt Shingle Roofing
Manufacturer: Elk
Product: Prestique High Definition
Color name: Antique Slate
Paving
Manufacturer: Davis Color
Color name: Mesa Buff
Product: Integral color
Type: Seeded and washed stone aggregate
Architect
Taylor Lombardo
San Francisco and Oakville, California

39

Siding
Material: Cedar shingle
Conditioner
Manufacturer: Sunnyside
Product: Boiled Linseed Oil
Note: Shingles will darken with age.
Door, Window, and Trim Paint Color
Manufacturer: Benjamin Moore
Color name: Tartan Red (old color)
Tinting base: 096-4B
One gallon formula:
RX 2 x 5 1/4
MA 2 x 1 1/2
RD 6 x 3 1/4
WH 24 3/4
Window Frame and Trim Paint Color
Manufacturer: Benjamin Moore

Color number: EXT. RM.
Color name: Essex Green
Note: Colors are reversed on greenhouse windows and window frames.
Entry Pavers
Material: Flagstone
Note: My match

40

Field Paint Color
Manufacturer: Benjamin Moore
Color number: 925
Color name: Ivory White
Window Paint Color
Manufacturer: Benjamin Moore
Color number: 1574
Color name: Rushing River
Door, Shutter, and Window Frame Paint Color
Manufacturer: Benjamin Moore
Color number: 1575
Color name: Rainy Afternoon
Roof Tile
Product: Natural cedar shingle
Note: All my matches

41

Field Paint Color
Manufacturer: Benjamin Moore
Color number: HC-26
Color name: Monroe Bisque
Window, Outer Window Frame, and Trellis Paint Color
Manufacturer: Benjamin Moore
Color number: HC-106
Color name: Crownsville Gray
Door and Inner Window Frame Paint Color
Manufacturer: Benjamin Moore
Color number: 047
Color name: Savannah Clay
Gate Paint Color
Manufacturer: Benjamin Moore
Color number: HC-26
Color name: Monroe Bisque
Pavers at Steps
Source: Echeguren Slate, Inc.
Material: Slate
Color: India Multi Red
Size: 12"x12"

42

Field Paint Color
Manufacturer: Sherwin Williams
Color name: Custom
Tinting Base: 6403-45 203
One gallon formula:
B1-2 OZ.
Y3-58/32
R2-5/32
Window Frame (Not Seen), Door Frame, Garage Door, and Trim Paint Color
Manufacturer: Sherwin Williams
Color number: SW7006
Color name: Extra White
Door Paint Color
Manufacturer: Sherwin Williams
Color name: Custom
Tinting base: 6403-34 140
One quart formula:
Y3-1/32
W1-16/32
B1-5/32

L1-20/32
R3-6/32
R2-3/32
Figurative Sculpture
Manufacturer: Giannini Garden Ornaments, Inc.
Product: Nike di Samotrace
Product number: 874
Material: Concrete
Finish: Antico

43

Field Color
Second-Floor Panel Paint Color
Manufacturer: Ralph Lauren
Color number: GH67
Color name: Irish Splurge
Note: My match. This is an interior color but can be matched to any exterior paint manufacturer. Ralph Lauren makes interior paint only.
First-Floor Color-Embedded Stucco Field Color
Product: Color-embedded stucco
First Coat
Manufacturer: LaHabra
Number: X-475
Color name: Viejo (dominant color)
Second Coat
Manufacturer: LaHabra
Number: X-55
Color name: French Vanilla
Note: Second coat should be added while the first coat is still wet.
Window Frame, Column, Projecting Eave, and All Trim Paint Color
Manufacturer: Kelly Moore
Color number: 14
Color name: Frost
Door Paint Color
Manufacturer: Ralph Lauren
Color number: GH166
Color name: Aquinnah Sunset
Note: This is an interior color but can be matched to any exterior paint manufacturer. Ralph Lauren makes interior paint only.
Porch Ceiling
Material: Redwood
Manufacturer: Superdeck Brand Products
Product: Transparent Exterior Wood Stain
Color number: 1909
Color name: Shasta White
Note: Use as a whitewash on a redwood ceiling.
Gate
Product: Custom
Material: Rusted COR-TEN steel
Swimming Pool Tile
Manufacturer: Portobello America
Product: 3"x3" glazed porcelain tile
Product number: Hard #89403
Color name: Jerusalem Mosaic
Roof Tile
Material: Natural cedar shingles

Pavers
Material: Arizona flagstone
Pattern: Random
Note: Used on the porch and around the pool with ground cover.

44

Cedar Siding Color
Manufacturer: Cabot
Product: Bleaching Oil
Doors and Windows
Manufacturer: JELD-WEN
Doors and Windows
Product: Vinyl Clad Exterior/Wood Interior Windows
Color name: White
Trellis
Material: Solid cedar
Stain
Manufacturer: Benjamin Moore
Product: Semi-Transparent Exterior Stain
Color name: Sea Gull Gray
Composition Asphalt Shingle Roofing
Manufacturer: CertainTeed
Product: Landmark
Color name: Charcoal Black
Paving
Material: Loose gravel
Architect
Matthew Mills
Pinehurst, North Carolina
Designer
Cynthia Kent-Mills
Pinehurst, North Carolina

45

Field Paint Color
Manufacturer: Kelly-Moore
Color number: 26
Color name: Oyster
Window Paint Color
Manufacturer: Benjamin Moore
Color number: EXT. RM.
Color name: Essex Green
Window Frame, Porch Support Column, and Porch Railing Paint Color
Manufacturer: Benjamin Moore
Color name: Custom
Tinting base: N103-3B
One gallon formula:
OY 2 x 8
BK 29
BB 18
YW 4
BR 3
WH 26
Door Paint Color
Manufacturer: Benjamin Moore
Color name: Custom
Tinting Base: 096-3B
Quart formula:
BR 15
OG 2 x 6
Note: This color was matched to the brick steps.
Fence
Material: Untreated redwood
Paving
Entry Path
Material: Flagstone

Steps and Porch
Material: Red brick

46

Field Paint Color
Manufacturer: Benjamin Moore
Color number: 1042
Color name: Caramel Apple
Window, Window Frame, and Trim Paint Color
Manufacturer: Benjamin Moore
Color number: 943
Color name: Spanish White
Note: My match
Door
Material: Douglas fir
Stain
Manufacturer: ZAR
Product: Oil-Based Stain
Number: 110
Color name: Salem Maple
Shutter Paint Color
Manufacturer: Benjamin Moore
Color number: 2120-10
Color name: Jet Black
Note: My match
Fence and Trellis
Material: Redwood
Stain
Manufacturer: Behr
Product name: Premium Weatherproofing Wood Finish
Product number: 500
Color name: Natural Clear
Note: Fence caps are copper.

47

Field Paint Color
Manufacturer: Pratt & Lambert
Color number: 1479
Color name: Hemlock
Window, Window Frame, Garage Door, Flower Box, Trellis, and Trim Paint Color
Manufacturer: Kelly-Moore
Color number: WS27
Color name: Diamond White
Note: My match
Door
Paint Color
Manufacturer: Kelly-Moore
Color number: KM3102-2
Color name: Royal Regatta
Note: My match
Hardware
Manufacturer: Baldwin Hardware
Product: Atlanta Mortise
Product number: 6570-264
Finish: Satin chrome
Slate on Steps
Material: Kota Blue Slate, gauged
Source: Echeguren Slate, San Francisco, California
Architect
Jonathan Feldman, Architect
Lisa Lougee, Designer
Feldman Architecture, LLP
San Francisco, California

48

Field Paint Color
Manufacturer: Benjamin Moore
Color: Custom

Tinting base: N105-4B
One gallon formula:
WH 23
OG 0 x 15
OY 1 x 3
BK 3 x 8
GY 1 x 4

Door, Window, Window Frame, Sidelight, Bracket, and Projecting Eave Paint Color
Manufacturer: Benjamin Moore
Color number: OC-132
Color name: Grand Teton White

Custom Gate
Material: Untreated Western red cedar

Composition Asphalt Shingle Roofing
Manufacturer: CertainTeed
Product: Landmark
Color name: Moire Black
Note: My match

Pavers
Manufacturer: Mt. Moriah Stone
Product: Moriah patio flagstone

49

Color-Embedded Stucco Field Color
Manufacturer: Dryvit Systems, Inc.
Product: Sandpebble DPR
Color Number: 480A
Color name: Lakewood
Base type: MID

Windows
Manufacturer: Sierra Pacific Windows
Product: Aluminum-clad windows with baked-on paint finish
Color name: Brown

Door
Source: Well Hung Doors, Inc.
Product: Custom
Material: Cherry
Stain
Manufacturer: Cabot
Product: Interior Wood Stain
Number: 2019
Color name: Cherrywood
Protective Top Coat
Manufacturer: Cabot
Product: Harbormaster
Material: Oil-based polyurethane
Finish: Satin, 2401
Note: It's okay to use an interior stain color on an exterior door as long as the door is recessed and protected with an exterior protective finish.

Garage Door (Not Shown), Brackets (at Entry Door), and Trellis Paint Color
Manufacturer: Kelly-Moore
Color number: KM522-D
Color name: Camp Tent

Painted Trim
Manufacturer: Sherwin Williams
Color name: Custom "dark brown"
Tinting base: Ultra deep
One gallon formula:
B1 10Y20
R2 63
Y3 16

Short Stucco Wall and Lower Foundation Wall Color
Manufacturer: Dry-Vit Systems, Inc.
Product: Sandpebble DPR
Color number: 478
Color name: Moss
Base type: MID

Roof Tile
Manufacturer: DiBenedetto Roof Tile Company
Product: Elegante Roof Scape
Color name: Slate Brown
Note: This is a cement roof tile. My match.

Pavers
Manufacturer: American Slate Company
Product: 12"x12" slate tile
Color name: China Multicolor
Note: My match

50

Cedar Stain Color
Manufacturer: Amteco
Product: TWP (Total Wood Preservative)
Number: 501C
Color name: Natural Cedar

Window, Columns, Door, Window Frame, and Trim Paint Color
Manufacturer: Benjamin Moore
Color number: EXT. RM.
Color name: Black Forest Green

Door
Manufacturer: Ocean Sash & Door Company
Product: Custom door with clear beveled glass
Paint Color
Manufacturer: Benjamin Moore
Color number: EXT. RM.
Color name: Country Redwood
Hardware
Manufacturer: Rocky Mountain Hardware
Product: Entry Set
Product number: #E423
Knob style: Potato, #K203
Finish: White bronze medium
Mail Slot (in Door)
Manufacturer: Rocky Mountain Hardware
Product: Slot with Two Doors
Product number: #MSD112
Finish: White bronze medium
House Numbers
Manufacturer: Rocky Mountain Hardware
Product number: Model #HN
Finish: White bronze medium

Light Fixture on Porch
Manufacturer: Coe Studios
Product number: HL-EN
Material: Solid Bronze

Porch Paint Color
Manufacturer: Benjamin Moore
Color number: EXT. RM.
Color name: Black Forest Green
Note: Mix into exterior wood floor paint product.

Pavers and Short Wall
Material: Red brick

51

Field Paint Color
Manufacturer: Benjamin Moore
Color number: HC-166
Color name: Kendall Charcoal

Window, Window Frame, Door Frame, Columns, Garage Door, Picket Fence, and Trim Paint Color
Manufacturer: Benjamin Moore
Color number: OC-55
Color name: Paper White

Door
Material: Old oak
Stain
Manufacturer: Cabot
Color name: Cordovan Brown
Note: Use any clear exterior protectant over stain.

Porch Floor Paint Color
Manufacturer: Benjamin Moore
Color number: 2108-30
Color name: Brown Horse

52

Field Paint Color
Manufacturer: Benjamin Moore
Color: Custom
Tinting base: N103-3B
One gallon formula:
YW 1 x 19
BR 2 x 3
WH 2 x 28
BK 2 x 25
GY 26

Window, Window Frame, and Horizontal Molding Paint Color
Manufacturer: Benjamin Moore
Color number: OC-45
Color name: Swiss Coffee

Door
Material: Old oak
Stain
Manufacturer: ZAR
Number: 116
Color name: Cherry

Wreath Relief Paint Color (on Entry Portal)
Manufacturer: Benjamin Moore
Color number: HC-126
Color name: Avon Green

Doorbell
Manufacturer: spOre, Inc.
Product: De-Light Illuminated Doorbell Button
Product number: DBD-W- B
Button color: White (w)
Ring finish: Bronze.

Marching Ants over Bay Window
Source: Target Stores
Material: Metal

53

Field Paint Color
Manufacturer: Benjamin Moore
Color number: 2084-10
Color name: Brick Red

Window Paint Color
Manufacturer: Benjamin Moore
Color number: 2153-50
Color name: Desert Tan

Window Frame, Projecting Eave, Rafter, Garage Door, and Trim Paint Color

Manufacturer: Benjamin Moore
Color number: 2140-20
Color name: Tuscany Green

Door (Not Shown)
Material: Oak
Protectant
Manufacturer: Cabot
Product: Clear Solution
Number: 9100
Color name: Natural
Note: My match

Garden Wall(s) Paint Color
Manufacturer: Benjamin Moore
Color number: 2145-20
Color name: Terrapin Green

Porch Paint
Manufacturer: Benjamin Moore
Color number: 2140-20
Color name: Tuscany Green
Note: Mix into exterior wood floor paint.

Pavers
Material: Arizona Flagstone

Landscape Design and Color Consultant
Lisa Goodman
Goodman Landscape Design
Berkeley, California

54

Field Paint Color
Manufacturer: Kelly-Moore
Color number: Y-40-3
Color name: Smyrna

Window
Material: Aluminum
Note: If you have a wood window, use the same color as the window frame.

Window Frame, Door Frame, Projecting Eave, and Trim Paint Color
Manufacturer: Kelly-Moore
Color number: 23
Color name: Swiss Coffee

Door Paint Color
Manufacturer: Kelly-Moore
Color number: I-27-1
Color name: Guernsey

Handle Set
Manufacturer: Omnia
Product: Waldorf Entry Handle Set
Finish: Brushed chrome

Doorbell
Manufacturer: spOre, Inc.
Product: Square Illuminated Doorbell Button
Product number: DBS-W
Trim finish: Anodized aluminum
Button color: White (w)

House Numbers
Manufacturer: Steel Art
Product: Dimension Letters in Enviro Bold
Material: Stainless Steel
Note: Minor design alteration made by homeowner

55

Field Paint Color
Manufacturer: Kelly-Moore
Color number: F 34-2
Color name: Trocadero

Window, Window Frame, Door Frame, Railing, Column, Projecting Eave, and Clapboard Paint Color
Manufacturer: Kelly-Moore
Color number: N 19-3
Color name: Noble House

Door Paint Color
Manufacturer: Kelly-Moore
Color number: D 10-3
Color name: Tango Red

Architect/Consultant
Andre Ptaszynski
Jensen/Ptaszynski
Lafayette, California

56

Siding
Material: Cedar shingles
Stain
Manufacturer: Penofin
Product: Penetrating Oil
Color name: Transparent Redwood

Door, Door Frame, Window, Window Frame, and Trim Paint Color
Manufacturer: Behr
Color number: 760D-6A
Color name: Spanish Galleon

House Numbers
Manufacturer: Restoration Hardware
Product: House Numbers
Finish: Bronze

Steps, Window Frame (Back of House), and Railing
Material: Redwood
Stain
Manufacturer: Behr
Product: Premium Weatherproofing Wood Finish
Number: 502
Color name: Redwood

Sconce Lighting
Manufacturer: Restoration Hardware
Product: Madera Outdoor Sconce
Glass: Iridescent art glass
Finish: Bronze

Doorbell
Manufacturer: Craftsmen Hardware Company
Product: Pacific Style Bell Button
Product number: C356X-2
Finish: Hammered copper with brass button

Composition Asphalt Shingle Roofing
Manufacturer: Elk Corporation
Product: Prestique Plus High Definition
Color name: Barkwood

57

Field Paint Color
Manufacturer: Sherwin Williams
Collection: Exterior preservation palette
Color number: SW2846
Color name: Roycroft Bronze Green

Door and Window Paint Color
Manufacturer: Sherwin Williams
Collection: Exterior preservation palette
Color number: SW2801
Color name: Rookwood Dark Red

Window Frame and (unless otherwise noted) Trim Paint Color
Manufacturer: Sherwin Williams
Color number: SW7022
Color name: Alpaca

Lower Horizontal Trim and Porch Cap Paint Color
Manufacturer: Sherwin Williams
Color number: SW6199
Color name: Rare Gray

Porch Paint Color
Manufacturer: Sherwin Williams
Product: Treadplex Porch Paint
Color name: Tricorn Black

Porch Ceiling Light Fixture
Manufacturer: Old California Lantern Company
Product: Custom. Based on Westmoreland Place Series.
Metal finish: New Verde
Glass: Gold Iridescent

Composition Asphalt Shingle Roofing
Manufacturer: Tamko Roofing Products
Product name: American Heritage Series
Color name: Black Walnut

58

Field Paint Color
Manufacturer: Benjamin Moore
Color number: EXT. RM.
Color name: Briarwood

Window, Window Frame, Door Frame, and Bracket Paint Color
Manufacturer: Benjamin Moore
Color number: INT. RM.
Color name: China White
Note: Mix interior color into exterior paint product.

Door Paint Color
Manufacturer: Kelly-Moore
Color number: 159
Color name: Sequoia Redwood

Handmade Cement Steps
Formula:
  5 parts river or stucco sand
  1 part cement
  Powdered concrete dye in umber and black
Directions:
Pour formula into wooden frame (use bending plywood), and when still wet, hand-trowel it to shape. Sprinkle powdered concrete dye into the formula to give it texture and to make it resemble stone.
The amount added is arbitrary—add the dye gradually until it reaches the desired look.
Note: The steps have been inspired by the concrete gardens of Harland Hand. Visit www.harlandhandgarden.com for more information.

Threshold and Trim Paint Color
Manufacturer: Benjamin Moore
Color number: HC-69
Color name: Whitall Brown

Pavers on Entry Steps
Source: Import Tile, Berkeley, California
Material: Slate
Product: Kashmir Rose

Composition Asphalt Shingle Roofing
Manufacturer: CertainTeed
Product: Presidential Shake
Color name: Shadow Gray
Note: My match

59

Field Paint Colors
Clapboard (Second Floor)
Manufacturer: Sherwin Williams
Color number: SW2083
Color name: Grist Mill

Color-Embedded Stucco Field Color #1
Manufacturer: LaHabra
Color name: Custom "copper"
Matched to: Pantone 145U
Finish: Semi-smooth

Color-Embedded Stucco Field Color #2
Manufacturer: LaHabra
Product: X-40, Base 200
Color name: Dove Gray
Finish: Semi-smooth

Door and Window
Manufacturer: Builders Door & Window Supply
Material: Clear Douglas fir

Stain
Manufacturer: Sikkens
Product: Cetol 1
Color number: 45
Color name: Mahogany

Finish Coat
Manufacturer: Sikkens
Product: Cetol Door and Window Satin
Finish: Clear
Coats applied: 3
Note: Same stain and finish under eave

Window Frame Paint Color
Manufacturer: Sherwin Williams
Color number: SW2060
Color name: Casa Blanca

Door
Manufacturer: Builders Door & Window Supply
Material: Clear Douglas fir

Stain
Manufacturer: Sikkens
Product: Cetol 1
Color number: 45
Color name: Mahogany

Finish Coat
Manufacturer: Sikkens
Product: Cetol Door and Window Satin
Finish: Clear
Coats applied: 3

Door Handleset
Manufacturer: Schlage
Product: Wakefield
Product number: FA 360 WKF 613
Finish: 613, oil-rubbed bronze

Door Knocker
Manufacturer: Claussen
Sculptural Iron

Product: Dragon/custom
Finish: Bronze

Entry Lighting Fixture
Manufacturer: Kichler Lighting
Product: Seaside Collection
Product number: 9022NI
Finish: Brushed nickel

Handmade Rain Gutter Basin with Granite River Rocks
Material: Concrete
Directions: Shape a sheet of 94 1/4" x 12" bending plywood into a 30" diameter cylinder. Make the form with two 3' x 3' (min.) sheets of 3/4" plywood by cutting a 30" diameter hole in the center of each sheet. Push the cylinder through the holes in both sheets of plywood so that one sheet is around the top and one is around the bottom, making a form that will keep the cylinder shape in place when the concrete is poured into it. Dig a 30" diameter gravel bed below grade where the concrete basin will sit. Place the inlet drain pipe (which sits in the middle of the basin and connects to the drain pipe) before pouring the concrete basin. The inlet pipe will need to be flush with the bottom of the bowl when it's finished, so stuff the pipe with a rag to keep concrete from entering it. Place the form on the gravel bed and around the inlet drain pipe. The top of the form should sit about 6" above the top of the inlet drain pipe. Cut a notch out of the bottom of the cylinder to allow the inlet pipe to connect to the drain pipe. Pour the concrete into the form. As the cement sets (it takes about an hour), trowel it into a bowl shape and stipple with a sponge for texture before it dries completely. Once the concrete has set, remove the form. Wait a day, and then fill the bowl 3–4" deep with 1"-diameter granite river rocks. Hang the rain chain directly above the center of the bowl to allow water to pass through the river rocks, to the inlet drain pipe, and out to the sidewalk through the grated drain pipe.
Note: The rain chain will only work with 2' deep (min.) projecting eaves. There must be a minimum 2-degree slope between the basin and the street for this to work.

Composition Asphalt Shingle Roofing (not seen)
Manufacturer: Elk Corporation
Product name: Prestique I High Definition
Color: Sablewood

60

Field Paint Color
Manufacturer: Fuller O'Brien
Color number: 2C7-6
Color name: Euro Gray

Door, Window, Window Frame, Trellis, Picket Fence, and Trim Paint Color
Manufacturer: Fuller O'Brien
Color number: 1C23-1
Color name: Queen Anne's Lace
Note: My match

Porch Paint Color
Manufacturer: Fuller O'Brien
Product: Porch & Floor Paint
Color number: 2C7-6
Color name: Euro Gray

Plaza Fountain
Manufacturer: A. Silvestri Co.
Product: Plaza Fountain/Lions Head
Color number: 128
Material: Cast stone
Finish: Stone

Stone Facing
Manufacturer: Eldorado Stone
Product: Top Rock—La Quinta
Note: My match

Pavers
Material: Arizona flagstone

61

Color-Embedded Stucco Field Color
Manufacturer: Habite
Color name: Custom
Tinting base: 1240-121
One gallon formula:
  A 14
  I 4 1/2
  L 2

Garage Door, Exposed Rafters, Battered Foundation Paint Color (Rear of House), and Projecting Eaves
Manufacturer: Kelly-Moore
Color name: Custom
Tinting base: 1240-413
One gallon formula:
  B 28
  D 9
  KX 3Y12

Window
Manufacturer: Sierra Pacific Windows
Product: Exterior Aluminum Clad Windows
Material: Anodized Aluminum
Color name: Bronze

Door
Material: Douglas fir

Stain
Manufacturer: Cabot
Product: Semi-Solid Stain
Color name: Foothill
Note: My match

Top Coat
Manufacturer: Cabot
Product: Harbormaster Polyurethane
Finish: 2401, Satin
Note: My match

Door Knocker
Manufacturer: Kwikset
Product: Avalon
Collection: Architecturally Inspired Collection
Finish: Nickel

Entry Pendant Light Fixture
Manufacturer: CX Design
Product: Persia II Pendant
Product number: HLT90

Material: Italian scavo glass diffuser and plated brass hardware
Finish: Antique bronze
Diffuser color: Ice

Wall-Mounted Light Fixture (Back of House)
Manufacturer: Kichler
Product number: 9023
Product name: Seaside
Finish: Olde bronze

Column Caps (Back of House)
Manufacturer: Napa Valley Cast Stone
Material: Cast stone
Note: My match

Pavers
Source: Echeguren Slate
Product: 12"x12" slate tile
Color: African multicolor

Architect
Chris Volkamer
Volkamer Architecture
Oakland, California

62

Field Paint Color
Manufacturer: Benjamin Moore
Color number: 1581
Color name: Millstone Gray

Window, Window Frame, Door Frame, Door Threshold, Sidelights, Trellis, and Trim Paint Color
Manufacturer: Benjamin Moore
Color name: Custom
Tinting base: N103-4B
One gallon formula:
  OY 7 1/2
  BK 5 x 1 1/4
  RD 10 1/2
  WH 3 x 12

Door and Window Trim (at Entry) Paint Color
Manufacturer: Benjamin Moore
Color name: Custom
Tinting base: N096-4B
One quart formula:
  BR 1 x 0
  BK 0 x 3
  MA 1 x 13
  WH 0 x 7

Antique Korean Temple Gate Stain
Manufacturer: Flood
Product number: CWF-UV
Finish: Clear wood

Pavers
Material: Ceramic tile
Product: Mexican Saltillo pavers
Note: Available at most tile shop outlets

63

Field Paint Color
Manufacturer: Benjamin Moore
Color number: 993
Color name: Beachcomber

Window, Window Frame, Trellis, and Trim Paint Color
Manufacturer: Benjamin Moore
Color number: EXT. RM.
Color name: Lancaster White

Door Paint Color
Manufacturer: Benjamin Moore
Color number: EXT. RM.

Color name: Cottage Red

Hanging Light Fixture
Source: Moravian Book Shop,
Bethlehem, Pennsylvania
Product: Lighted Moravian Star
Color number: CCUMS18
Material: Vinyl
Size: 18" diameter

Terra-Cotta Pavers and Steps
Source: Country Floors
Note: My match

Color Consultant
Eileen Connery Design
Novato, California

Landscape Architect
Bradley Burke
San Francisco, California

64

Field Paint Color
Manufacturer: Benjamin Moore
Color name: Custom
Tinting base: 183-3B
Five gallon formula:
OY 21.5
TG 1/4
BK 1x27
OG 30
GY 11 1/2
WH 25

Window, Window Frame, Door Frame, Projecting Eave, and Trim Paint Color
Manufacturer: Benjamin Moore
Color name: Custom
Tinting base: N103-1B
Five gallon formula:
OY 27.5
OG 2.5
GY 5x5
WH 3x20

Door
Product: Custom
Material: Pine

Protectant
Manufacturer: Watco
Finish: Natural Oil

Stucco Garden Wall
Manufacturer: Quikrete
Product: Finish Coat Stucco
Color name: Uncolored

Wall Cap
Material: Redwood

Stain
Manufacturer: Cabot
Product: Clear Solution
Color name: Natural

Sconce (on Garden Wall at Entry)
Manufacturer: Arroyo Craftsman
Product: Huntington Sconce with Roof and Double T Bar Overlay
Product number: #HS-10
Metal finish: Bronze (B2)
Glass: Gold white iridescent (GW)

Pavers
Material: Natural flagstone

65

Painted Stucco Paint Color (Lower)
Manufacturer: Pratt & Lambert
Product: Elastomeric Paint
Color name: Custom

Tinting base: Z6093
One gallon formula:
OY 3x23
BK 26
RD 11
GY 16

Shingle Siding
Material: Redwood

Stain
Manufacturer: Cabot
Product: Clear Solution
Color name: Natural

Door, Windows, Window Frame, and Trim Paint Color
Manufacturer: Benjamin Moore
Color number: EXT. RM.
Color: Essex Green
Note: Front door is leaded glass (as well as some of the other windows).

Pavers (in Breezeway)
Manufacturer: GMS Global, Inc.
Product: 18" x 18" Indian Slate
Color name: India Kota Brown
Note: Slate color is my match.

Pavers (Steps)
Material: Red brick

66

Color-Embedded Stucco Field Color
Manufacturer: LaHabra
Color Name: Mesa Verde
Number: X-215
Note: Base 100
Note: My match

Window, Window Frame, Door Frame, Garage Door Frame, and Trim Paint Color
Manufacturer: Benjamin Moore
Color name: Custom
Tinting base: N096-2B
One gallon formula:
BK-1x6
RX-4
OY-2x
YW-4

Door Paint Color
Manufacturer: Benjamin Moore
Color name: Custom
Tinting base: N096-3B
One quart formula:
OY-5
TG-1
RX-11
BK-1

Garage Door, Projecting Eave, Exposed Rafter, and Column Paint Color
Manufacturer: Sherwin Williams
Color name: Custom
Tinting base: SW1160
One gallon formula:
AA-2Y24
EE-28
F-4
GG-6
II-Y18
MM-6
LL-2Y

Door Hardware and Door Knocker
Manufacturer: Period Brass
Product: Kingston
Handle product number: 5710
Knocker product number: 7638

Four Ceramic Tiles at Entry
Manufacturer: Richards and Sterling
Product: Urbino Verde

Light Fixtures
Manufacturer: Arroyo Craftsman
Product names and numbers:
Monterey, MH-24 (pendant);
Monterey, MC-17 (column wall mount fixture); and Evergreen, EW-12 (flush wall mount fixture)
Finish: Verdigris
Glass: Opaque White

Colored Concrete Paving
Manufacturer: Davis Colors
Product number: 160
Color name: Sunset Rose
Note: Path and driveway color

Color Consultant
Debra Cibilich
Debra Cibilich Design
San Francisco, California

Architectural Designer
Philip Perkins
Philip O. Perkins Design
Oakland, California

67

Field Paint Color
Manufacturer: Benjamin Moore
Color number: HC-42
Color name: Roxbury Caramel

Window, Bracket (at Roof Line), and Trim Paint Color (Front of House)
Manufacturer: Benjamin Moore
Color number: 1561
Color name: Castle Peak Gray

Window Frame, Projecting Eave, Column Cap, and Trim Paint Color (Front of House)
Manufacturer: Benjamin Moore
Color number: 986
Color name: Smoky Ash

Column and Stair Riser Paint Color
Manufacturer: Benjamin Moore
Color number: 1197
Color name: Pumice Stone

Porch Floor Paint
Manufacturer: Dunn Edwards
Product: Tuff Floor
Color number: W810-12-1
Color name: Brick

Interior Designer/Color Consultant
Lou Ann Bauer
Bauer Interior Design
San Francisco, California

68

Siding
Material: Western red cedar

Stain
Manufacturer: FSC Coatings
Product: TWP (Total Wood Protectant)
Number: TWP501
Color name: 501 Natural

Window, Window Frames, Projecting Eave, Balcony Railing, and all Black Trim Paint Color
Manufacturer: Sherwin Williams
Color number: SW6258

Color name: Tricorn Black
Note: All of these paint colors are on the front of the house.

Door
Manufacturer: Liberty Valley Doors
Product: Custom
Material: Stain-grade fir
Designer: Veverka Architects, San Francisco, California

Stain
Manufacturer: Sherwin Williams
Product: Wood Classic Stain
Number: SW3109
Color name: Bright Cherry

Window Bay Panel, Dentil, Stucco Planter Box with Inset Tile, and Short Wall (by Garage Door) Paint Color
Manufacturer: Sherwin Williams
Color number: SW3022
Color name: Black Alder

Ceiling at Entry Paint Color
Manufacturer: Sherwin Williams
Collection: Exterior Historical Color
Color number: SW2821
Color name: Downing Stone

Garage Door, Planter Box, and Stucco (Back of House) Paint Color
Manufacturer: Sherwin Williams
Color number: SW3045
Color: Russet Brown

Windows (Back of House)
Manufacturer: Blomberg Window Systems
Product: Windowwall Series
Material: Aluminum windows with thermosetting acrylic finish
Color: Black

Slate Steps
Material: Brazilian Black Cleft Slate
Source: Echeguren Slate, San Francisco, California

Ceramic Planters on Balcony
Manufacturer: Asia Trade Imports
Product: Glazed Ceramic planters
Color name: Black

Door Hardware
Manufacturer: Sun Valley Bronze
Product: Handle x Lever Mortise Lock Entry Set
Product number: CS-901 with L-106 Square lever
Finish: S3, Silicon Bronze

Color Consultant
Kittredge Opal
Kentfield, California

Architect
Jerry Veverka
Veverka Architects
San Francisco, California

69

Field Paint Color
Manufacturer: Benjamin Moore
Product number: EXT. RM.
Color name: Charleston Brown
Finish: flat

Window Paint Color
Manufacturer: Benjamin Moore

Product number: EXT. RM.
Color name: Tudor Brown
Finish: Semi-Gloss

Window Frame Paint Color
Manufacturer: Benjamin Moore
Color number: OC-17
Color name: White Dove
Note: My match

Door Paint Color
Manufacturer: Benjamin Moore
Color number: 1309
Color name: Moroccan Red

Pavers
Material: Oversized red brick

70

Field Paint Color
Manufacturer: Kelly-Moore
Color number: KM510-D
Color name: Table Mountain

Foundation Wall
Material: Red brick

Window Paint Color
Manufacturer: Kelly-Moore
Color number: AC-86N
Color name: Rich Earth

Window Frame and Trim Paint Color
Manufacturer: Kelly-Moore
Color number: 230
Color name: Graystone

Door
Material: Fir

Finish
Manufacturer: Varathane
Product: Natural Oil Finish

Hanging Light Fixture
Manufacturer: Arroyo Craftsman
Product: Mission 7" Hanging Pendant
Product number: MH-7
Finish: Verdigris patina
Glass: Gold-white iridescent

Composition Asphalt Shingle Roofing
Manufacturer: CertainTeed
Product: Landmark Series
Color name: Terra Cotta
Note: My match

Concrete Paving
Manufacturer: Davis Colors
Product: Premium Ready Mixed Color
Number: 160
Color name: Brick Red
Note: My match. The concrete paving is old and original to the house.

71

Field Paint Color
Manufacturer: Fuller O'Brien
Color number: G96
Color name: Huckster

Door, Door Frame, Side Lights, Window, Window Frame, Projecting Eave, and Trim Paint Color
Manufacturer: Fuller O'Brien
Color name: Custom
Tinting base: 664-91
One gallon formula:
Add four drops of umber to the tinting base to warm up the color.

Recessed Entry Paint Color
Manufacturer: Fuller O'Brien
Color number: B63
Color name: Maverick

Stone Columns (at Gate)
Source: American Soil Products
Material: River-washed stone
Color name: Montana Gold

72

Field Paint Color
Manufacturer: Benjamin Moore
Color number: INT. RM.
Color name: Linen White
Note: Mix interior color into exterior paint product.

Window Paint Color
Manufacturer: Benjamin Moore
Color number: 1627
Color name: Manor Blue

Door
Manufacturer: 4th Street Woodworking Co.
Product: Custom
Material: Mahogany
Note: Designed by Goodman Landscape Design, Berkeley, California

Stain
Manufacturer: Cabot
Product: Clear Solution
Color name: Natural

Window Glass
Source: Stained Glass Garden, Inc.
Glass: Amber art glass

Wrought-Iron Sculptural Element on Window, Metal Straps, and Mail Slot
Manufacturer: Claussen Sculptural Iron, Oakland, California
Product: Custom

Ceramic Tile
Manufacturer: Country Floors, Inc.
Collection: Maroc
Color number: Colorway #9
Note: Used around the doors and water fountain.

Front Gate with Light Fixture
Manufacturer: Claussen Sculptural Iron, Oakland, California
Product: Custom
Material: Wrought iron

Half-Timber, Beams, Threshold, and Balcony Paint Color
Manufacturer: Benjamin Moore
Color number: EXT. RM.
Color name: Tudor Brown

Planters
Product: Glazed ceramic pots
Color: Blue
Source: AW Pottery

Roof Tile
Material: Terra-cotta clay

Pavers
Source: American Soil Products
Product: Arizona sandstone
Material: Flagstone
Color name: Peach/Orange

Mailbox
Manufacturer: Smith & Hawken
Product: Brass and copper mail-box

Landscape Architect
Lisa Goodman
Goodman Landscape Design
Berkeley, California

73

Field and Trellis Arch Paint Color
Manufacturer: Kelly-Moore
Color number: KM-480-D
Color name: Kiwi Winter

Window and Finial Paint Color
Manufacturer: Benjamin Moore
Color number: HC-5
Color name: Weston Flax

Door
Material: Natural mahogany
Stain
Manufacturer: Cabot Wood Care
Product: Clear Solution
Color name: Natural
Note: My match

Garage Door and Entry Gate Paint Color
Manufacturer: Benjamin Moore
Color number: EXT. RM.
Color name: Country Redwood

Roof Tile
Material: Terra-cotta clay

Garden Wall and Pavers
Material: Old red brick

74

Faux Finish Field Paint Color
Base Coat
Manufacturer: Benjamin Moore
Color number: OC-104
Color name: Antique Lace
Note: Paint two coats for the base.

First Coat—Faux Finish
Manufacturer: Pratt & Lambert
Color number: 2075
Color name: Peach
Directions: Mix six parts Floetrol paint conditioner (available at paint stores) with one part water to achieve a translucent quality. Add a bit of raw umber pigment to the glaze. Apply a heavier coat of this faux finish with brushes.
Note: Color is my match.

Second Coat—Feathered Faux Finish
Manufacturer: Pratt & Lambert
Color number: 2081
Color name: Ginger Whip
Directions: Mix six parts Floetrol paint conditioner (available at paint stores) with one part water to achieve a translucent quality. Add a bit of raw umber pigment to the glaze. Overlap the two faux finish paint colors while the first coat is still wet with a feather brush, sea sponge, and/or 100% terry cloth rag to achieve the desired look. Apply this last color lightly.

Faux Finish Door, Gutter Pipes, and Railing Paint Color
Manufacturer: Benjamin Moore
Color name: Custom Verdigris
Base Coat
Mix together the following

products:
Manufacturer: Benjamin Moore
Product: Moorgard, Metal and Trim Paint
Color number: 363-60
Color name: Bronze Tone
Size: One quart
and
Manufacturer: McCloskey
Product: Special Effects Metallic Glaze
Color name: Copper
Size: One pint
Note: Apply and let dry completely.

Top Coat
Manufacturer: Benjamin Moore
Tinting base: N103-4B
One quart formula:
OY 2.5
WH 24
TG 28
Directions: Water down top coat to a workable consistency. Apply multiple coats to achieve the desired effect, allowing the base coat to come through where desired. To prep, use exterior primer on metal railings.

Window, Window Frame, and Broken Pediment Portal Paint Color
Manufacturer: Benjamin Moore
Color number: OC-104
Color name: Antique Lace
Note: My match

Trim and Quoins (Corner Caps) Paint Color
Base Coat
Manufacturer: Pratt & Lambert
Color number: 2075
Color name: Peach
Note: Apply two coats for the base.

First Coat—Faux Finish
Manufacturer: Pratt & Lambert
Color number: 2082
Color name: Buccaneer
Note: Mix six parts Floetrol paint conditioner (available at paint stores) with one part water to achieve a translucent quality.

Second Coat—Faux Finish
Manufacturer: Pratt & Lambert
Color number: 2077
Color name: Koala
Directions: Mix six parts Floetrol paint conditioner (available at paint stores) with one part water to achieve a translucent quality. Overlap the two faux finish paint colors with a feather brush, sea sponge, and/or 100% terry cloth rag to achieve the desired look.

Concrete Steps Paint Color
Manufacturer: Benjamin Moore
Color number: 2109-40
Color name: Smoke Oyster
Note: Mix into concrete paint product.

Wood Bench
Manufacturer: Smith & Hawken
Product: Lutyens Bench
Material: Teak

Paving
Material: Flagstone

Roof Tile
Material: Terra-cotta clay

Faux Painter Artist/Specialist
Joshua McCullough
Martinez, California

75

Lime-Washed Stucco Field Color
Color name: Custom
Application Specialist
Patrick Bonnemann
Decorative Paint/Lime Wash
Process Specialist
Mill Valley, California

Window
Manufacturer: Blomberg Window Systems
Color name: Spruce Green
Note: Color is my match.

Painted Gate and Grille Work
Manufacturer: Rust-Oleum
Number: 7730
Color name: Teal
Finish: Satin
Note: My match

Window and Door Surrounds
Manufacturer: Napa Valley Cast Stone Products
Material: Cast Stone
Color name: Tuscan Yellow
Number: 32W

Painted Projecting Eave and Garage Door
Manufacturer: Benjamin Moore
Color number: 192
Color name: Key West Ivory

Architect
Fran Halperin
Halperin & Christ
San Rafael, CA

76

Field Paint Colors
Painted Stucco (Upper)
Manufacturer: Sherwin Williams
Color number: SW2336
Color name: Pyramid Gold
Painted Brick (Lower)
Manufacturer: Sherwin Williams
Color number: SW2224
Color name: Caper

Door, Window, and Garage Door Paint Color
Manufacturer: Sherwin Williams
Color number: SW2307
Color name: Red Barn

Window Frame and Trim Paint Color
Manufacturer: Sherwin Williams
Color number: SW6372
Color name: Inviting Ivory

Door Knocker
Manufacturer: Bianchi Lamberto, Florence, Italy
Product: Reproduction
Material: Bronze

Roof Tile
Material: Terra-cotta clay

Paving
Material: Old terrazzo

77

Field Paint Color
Manufacturer: Benjamin Moore

Color number: HC-43
Color name: Tyler Taupe

Door, Window, Sill, and Shutter Paint Color
Manufacturer: Benjamin Moore
Color number: HC-106
Color name: Crownville Grey

Garage Door
Material: Cedar
Protectant
Manufacturer: TWP (Total Wood Protectant)
Product: TWP 200 Series
Finish: Natural

Ceramic Tile at Garage Door
Note: This product has been discontinued. Similar tile can be found at:
Manufacturer: Kibak Tile
Source: Ann Sacks
or
Manufacturer: The Maroc Collection
Source: Country Floors

Pavers
Material: Arizona flagstone
Note: My match

Gate and Wall Light Fixtures
Manufacturer: Edgar Harris, Petaluma, California
Product: Custom
Material: Black wrought iron

78

Field Paint Color
Manufacturer: Sherwin Williams
Color number: SW6060
Color name: Moroccan Brown

Door, Window, and Window Frame Paint Color
Manufacturer: Kelly-Moore
Color number: 14
Color name: Frost

Entry Door Frame Paint Color
Manufacturer: Kelly-Moore
Color number: KM3842-1
Color name: Burbank Aura

Column Caps and Trim Paint Color
Manufacturer: Kelly-Moore
Color number: KM4196-1
Color name: Beach Party

Ornamental Column Finials
Manufacturer: Silvestri
Product: Fruit Basket Post Finials
Material: Concrete

Ornamental Railings
Manufacturer: Olszewski Iron Design
Material: Painted wrought iron
Note: Designed by: Mark Becker, Oakland, California
Paint Color
Manufacturer: Rust-Oleum
Product: Gloss Protective Enamel
Color name: Anodized Bronze

House Number Plaque
Manufacturer: Armador Memorial
Product: Custom
Material: White marble
Note: The plaque was made by a cemetery headstone company using their stone and one of their own font types.

Square Marble Pavers
Manufacturer: Richards and Sterling
Source: Italics, Emeryville, California
Product: Botticino
Material: Italian white marble
Size: 12" x 12" tile

Cobalt Blue Pots at Entry
Manufacturer: AW Pottery
Product: Mekong Collection, Xeo Pot (Size A: 26 1/2")
Product number: 556
Color name: Cobalt Blue

Architectural Designer
Mark Becker
Mark Becker, Inc.
Oakland, California

79

Field Paint Color
Manufacturer: Sherwin Williams
Color number: SW2334
Color name: Luxuriant Gold

Portico Surround Paint Color
Manufacturer: Sherwin Williams
Color number: SW2321
Color name: Bonfire

Cornice Paint Color
Manufacturer: Sherwin Williams
Color number: SW2815
Color name: Renwick Olive

Projecting Eave Paint Color
Manufacturer: Sherwin Williams
Color number: SW2450
Color name: Aged Ivory
Note: My match

Window Paint Color
Manufacturer: Glidden
Color name: Custom
Tinting base: HD 6813, Base 3
One gallon formula:
  B 3-14-0
  E 4-44-0
  KX 0-46-0
  T 2-36-0

Window Frame Paint Color
Manufacturer: Behr
Color name: Custom
Tinting base: Deep base, 9340
One gallon formula:
  I 1Y31
  T 9Y27
  V 4Y38

Door
Material: Mahogany
Protectant
Manufacturer: ZAR
Product: Exterior Water Based Polyurethane
Finish: Satin

Exposed Rafters
Material: Redwood
Protectant
Manufacturer: Penofin
Product: Original Blue Label Oil Wood Finish
Color name: Sierra

Stone on Chimney
Material: Northbrae Rhyolite
Note: The stone is original to the 1920s house. It is an acidic volcanic rock found in Northern California. Napa basalt is a common replacement stone. Available at American Soil

Products.
Roof Tile
Material: Terra-cotta clay
Color Consultant
Jody Suden
Jody Suden Color Design
London, England

80

Field Paint Color
Manufacturer: Kelly-Moore
Color number: 26
Color name: Oyster
Note: The color was painted on the lower brick portion of the house too. It has been partially exposed by flicking off dry paint with a wire brush attached to an electric drill.

Window and Window Frame Paint Color
Manufacturer: Benjamin Moore
Color number: 516
Color name: Ivy League

Shutter, Balcony, Bracket, and Trellis Stain
Manufacturer: Benjamin Moore
Product: Solid Siding Stain
Color name: Cordovan Brown
Tinting base: N089-4B
One gallon formula:
  OY 0 x16
  RX 1 x 4
  BK 6 x 12
  WH 0 x 16
Notes: This color is discontinued but is still available upon request. Some areas are lighter than others because they were painted at different times and have faded with age.

Roof Tile
Material: Terra-cotta clay
Pavers
Material: Flagstone

81

Field Paint Color
Manufacturer: Benjamin Moore
Color number: 2154-40
Color name: York Harbor Yellow

Window, Window Frame, Trellis, and Trim Paint Color
Manufacturer: Benjamin Moore
Color number: OC-121
Color name: Mountain Peak White
Note: My match

Door and Shutter Paint Color
Manufacturer: Benjamin Moore
Color number: 2043-10
Color name: Absolute Green

Roof Tile
Material: Terra-cotta clay

82

Color-Embedded Stucco Field Color
Manufacturer: LaHabra
Product: Custom
Product number: 31005, base 200

French Door, Door Frame, Window, Window Frame, Garage Door, and Trim Paint Color
Manufacturer: ICI
Color number: 1674
Color name: Deep Onyx

Door
Manufacturer: Golden Gate Door & Window
Product: Custom
Material: Natural mahogany

Varnish
Manufacturer: Valspar Brands
Product: McCloskey Man O'War Spar Marine Varnish
Color name: Clear
Finish: Satin

Handle Set
Manufacturer: Baldwin
Product: Concord Mortise Trim, Estate Lock
Product number: 6571.102
Finish: Oil Rubbed Bronze
Note: My match

Lighting (by French Doors)
Manufacturer: Minka Group
Product: Arlington
Finish: Black with seeded glass
Product Number: 8732-04

Railing
Manufacturer: TGW Metals, Inc., Alameda, CA
Product: Custom
Material: Wrought iron
Note: Designed by:
Charlot D. Malin
Troon Pacific, Inc.
San Francisco, California

Paint Color
Manufacturer: ICI
Color number: 1674
Color name: Deep Onyx
Note: Prime with an exterior rust preventative product.

Planter Box
Source: The Magazine
Product: Paolo Rizatto Pots
Material: Plastic
Color name: Black

Pavers, Steps and Risers, Moldings, and Bench at Entry
Manufacturer: Napa Valley Cast Stone
Finish: Medium Etch
Product number: SRX-100 (steps and risers)
Color number: 46W

Designer/Color Consultant and Developer
Charlot D. Malin, Designer
Gregory Malin, Developer
Troon Pacific, Inc.
San Francisco, California

Architect
Babac Doane
Doane and Doane Architects
Lafayette, California

83

Color-Embedded Stucco Field Color
Manufacturer: LaHabra
Number: X9975 30/M
Color name: Custom "terra-cotta"

Window, Window Frame, Garage Door, and Trim Paint Color
Manufacturer: Benjamin Moore
Color number: HC-134
Color name: Tarrytown Green
Note: My match

Door
Material: Oak
Protectant
Manufacturer: ZAR
Product: Exterior Polyurethane
Finish: Satin

Entry Gate Metal Straps
Manufacturer: Eandi Metal Works, Inc.
Product: Custom
Material: Wrought iron

Entry Columns
Manufacturer: Architectural Facades Unlimited
Product: Custom external non-structural columns with round base and capital segments
Material: Precast concrete
Finish: Sandblasted travertine (hand-packed, colored cement that mimics travertine)

House Number Plaque
Manufacturer: Vietri
Product: First Stones
Material: Hand-painted ceramic tile
Note: This item has been discontinued, but Vietri is considering returning it to the line. May possibly be available by special order.

Chairs
Manufacturer: Treillage
Product: Iron Garden Chair
Product number: HIMJR005
Note: My match. This is a similar product. This chair has been discontinued.

Roof Tile
Manufacturer: United States Tile Company
Product: Mission and "S" tiles
Material: Terra-cotta
Color name: El Camino Blend

Pavers
Manufacturer: Import Tile Co.
Product: 12" x 12" Saltillo Mexican Pavers, unsorted
Note: Used with 1" x 1" glazed accent tiles

84

Field Paint Color
Manufacturer: Pratt & Lambert
Color number: 2211
Color name: Yucca Green

Door, Window, Window Frame, Entry Ceiling, Cornice, and Trim Paint Color
Manufacturer: Pratt & Lambert
Color number: 1739
Color name: Shantung

Sconce Light Fixture (at Entry)
Manufacturer: 20th Century Lighting, Inc.
Product: Capri II
Product number: 1120 B
Finish: Worn Blackened Paint

Dome Light Fixture (in Recessed Entry)
Manufacturer: Murray's Iron Works
Product name: Segovia
Finish: Wrought iron with faux honey onyx alabaster
Note: Custom size

Ceramic Tile Mural (in Recessed Entry)
Manufacturer: Kibak Tile
Product: Custom pattern
Source: Ann Sacks

Pavers and Paving
Material: Red brick and concrete with exposed aggregate

Gutters
Material: Copper

Roof Tile
Material: United States Tile Company
Product: Traditional Mission "S" Style Clay Tile
Material: Terra-cotta tile
Color name: Viejo Blend
Note: My match

Gate and Railing
Material: Wrought iron
Paint Color
Manufacturer: Rust-Oleum
Product: Gloss Protective Enamel
Finish: Satin
Color: Black
Note: My match. Use exterior protective primer undercoat.

Architect
Duncan McLeod
Rupel, Geiszler & McLeod
San Francisco, California

85

Field Paint Color
Manufacturer: Fuller O'Brien
Color name: Custom
Tinting base: 663-91
One gallon formula:
  BLK-OP4
  YOX-OP8
  OXR-OP1

Window, Window Frame, and Gutter Paint Color (Second Floor)
Manufacturer: Benjamin Moore
Color number: 1225
Color name: Abbey Brown
Note: My match

Front Door
Material: Oak
Sealer
Manufacturer: Penofin
Product: Original Blue Label Oil Wood Finish Penetrating Sealer
Color name: Clear
Note: My match

French Doors (off of Deck)
Manufacturer: Fuller O'Brien
Color name: Custom
Tinting base: 663-91
One gallon formula:
  BLK-OP4
  YOX-OP8
  OXR-OP1

Entry Steps
Manufacturer: Country Floors
Product: 12"x12" terra-cotta tile

Note: My match

Wall Mounted Light Fixture (Back of House)
Material: Cast aluminum
Manufacturer: RAB Lighting, Inc.
Product: HID Bracket
Note: My match. This is a similar product.

Roof Tile
Material: Terra-cotta clay

Pavers
Manufacturer: Gavin Historical Bricks
Product: Antique granite cobblestone
Color name: Gray
Note: My match

86

Field Paint Color
Manufacturer: Kelly-Moore
Color number: 4069-2
Color name: Southwest Sand

Window and Window Frame Paint Color
Manufacturer: Kelly-Moore
Color number: 14
Color name: Frost

Projecting Eave, Window, and Portal Surround Paint Color
Manufacturer: Kelly-Moore
Mix together the following:
1 part:
Color number: 4069
Color name: Southwest Sand
1 part:
Color number: 4070
Color name: Brighton Beach

Door
Material: Old fir
Stain
Manufacturer: Varathane
Product: Premium Wood Stain
Number: 269
Color name: Dark Walnut
Protectant
Manufacturer: Spar
Product: Exterior Varnish
Number: 16375
Color name: Rich Amber
Finish: Gloss
Hardware
Manufacturer: Baldwin Brass
Product: Barclay Mortise Trim Set
Product number: 6554.102
Finish: Oil Rubbed Bronze

Roof Tile
Material: Terra-cotta clay

Pavers
Material: Red brick laid in chevron pattern

Wrought-Iron Railing
Manufacturer: Kelly-Moore
Product: Rust Inhibitor
Number: 1700-16
Color name: Galaxy Black

Color Consultant
Rich DeMartini
DeMartini Arnott Painting Company
San Francisco, California

87

Field Paint Color
Manufacturer: Benjamin Moore
Color name: Custom
Tinting base: N185 3B
Five gallon formula:
OY 9x27
BB 27 1/2
OG 3x14
BB 27.5
BK 5

Window and French Door Paint Color
Manufacturer: Benjamin Moore
Color number: EXT. RM.
Color name: Essex Green

Window Surround and Horizontal Trim Paint Color
Manufacturer: Benjamin Moore
Color name: Custom
Tinting base: 170-2B
One gallon formula:
MA 9.5
TG 5.75
GY 11.25

Door
Manufacturer: Rustica Arts
Product: Custom Nogales with 1 1/2" beveled glass
Material: Hand-hewn oak
Forge ironwork: Clavos nails and brackets in rust finish
Stain
Product: Danish Rubbing Oil
Color name: Antique Cedar
Note: This is a 6- to 7-step process with sanding and steel-wooling between coats.

Projecting Eave
Material: Douglas Fir
Stain
Manufacturer: Cabot
Product: Clear Solution
Color name: Heartwood

Trim (at Balcony over Front Door) Paint Color
Manufacturer: Benjamin Moore
Color number: 2108-40
Color name: Stardust

All Light Fixtures
Manufacturer: Olszewski Iron Design
Product: Custom
Material: Wrought iron
Designed by: Mark Becker, Mark Becker, Inc., Oakland, California

Roof Tile
Material: Terra-cotta clay

Pavers (Steps and Patio Tile)
Source: Alpha Granite and Marble, Inc.
Product: Scabas tumbled limestone tile

Stone Veneer
Manufacturer: El Dorado Stone
Product: Field Ledge, Veneto style

Architectural Designer
Mark Becker
Mark Becker, Inc.
Oakland, California

88

Field Paint Color
Manufacturer: VIP Lighthouse Products
Product: VIP Elastomeric paint
Color name: Custom
Tinting base: 81-20, deep base
Match to:
Manufacturer: Benjamin Moore
One gallon formula:
YW 1 x 16
OY 2 x 16
BK 8
OG 20
BB 1/2
WH 3 x

Window Paint Color
Manufacturer: Benjamin Moore
Color number: 949
Color name: Sparkling Wine

Window Frame, Projecting Eave, and Bracket Paint Color
Manufacturer: Benjamin Moore
Color name: Custom "soft green"
Tinting base: N103-3B
One gallon formula:
OY 4 x 21 1/2
GY 14
BK 1 x 24
OG 1
WH 4

Railings and Balcony Paint Color
Material: Wrought iron
Paint
Manufacturer: Benjamin Moore
Color number: 2115-10
Color name: Appalachian Brown
Note: Use exterior rust preventative primer undercoat.

Pillow Stepping-Stones
Manufacturer: Omega Salvage, Berkeley, California
Product: Tuffits
Material: Concrete
Note: Pillows come in a range of styles and colors.

Balustrades
Manufacturer: Architectural Facades Limited
Product: Style II
Material: Pre-cast stone
Note: My match

Roof Tile
Manufacturer: US Tile
Product: Traditional Mission "S" Profile
Material: Terra-cotta clay
Color name: Viejo Blend
Note: My match

89

Field Paint Color
Manufacturer: Benjamin Moore
Color name: Custom
Tinting base: N103 2B
Five gallon formula:
OY 12 x 12
BK 5 x 2
OG 2 x 8
GY 3 x 24

Window and Window Frame Paint Color
Manufacturer: Morwear
Color name: Custom

Product: 3001 Hi-Hide Semigloss, White-Base
One gallon formula:
OY 6
FT 1
GY 6
YW 3

Door
Material: Oak
Protectant
Manufacturer: Minwax
Product: Helmsman Spar Urethane
Finish: Satin
Note: My match

Embossed Portal Surround Paint Color
Manufacturer: Benjamin Moore
Color number: 928
Color name: Feather Bed

Wrought-Iron Grille Paint Color
Manufacturer: Rust-Oleum
Number: 777 504
Color name: Satin Black
Note: My match. Use an exterior primer undercoat.

Roof Tile
Material: Terra-cotta clay

Pavers
Material: Red brick
Pattern: Basket weave

90

Color-Embedded Stucco Field Color
Manufacturer: LaHabra
Number: X-71 (Base 100)
Color name: Miami Peach
Note: My match

Window
Manufacturer: Sierra Pacific Windows
Product: Aluminum Clad Windows
Color name: Harvest Cranberry

Door
Manufacturer: Sierra Pacific Windows
Product: Aluminum Clad Doors
Color name: Harvest Cranberry
Hardware
Manufacturer: Sierra Pacific Windows
Product: Capri
Finish: Polished chrome

Garage Door
Material: Redwood
Stain
Manufacturer: Cabot
Product: Clear Solution
Color name: Pacific Redwood

Gate and Glass Awning over Door
Manufacturer: John White Service
Material: Hand-forged steel/glass
Stock parts by: King Architectural Metals
Note: Designed by Alan Koster, San Francisco, California

Wall-Mounted Lanterns at Entry to House
Manufacturer: Progress Lighting
Product: Santa Barbara Wall Mounted Lantern

Product number: P5941-31
Type: Cast
Finish: Black with etched, seeded, hand-blown glass

Wall-Mounted Lights Outside of Entry Gate
Manufacturer: Kichler
Product: Seaside Outdoor Wall 1 Lt. Incandescent
Product number: 9021BK
Material: Aluminum
Finish: Black
Note: My match

Roofing
Manufacturer: McElroy Metal
Product: Maxi-Rib Exposed Fastener Panels
Material: Galvanized Steel
Note: My match. This is a similar product. The product on the house is a natural galvanized steel that has tarnished over time to a light gray color.

Paving in Courtyard
Type: Decomposed granite

Climbing Roses at Entry
Name: Climbing Peace

Architect
Alan Koster
San Francisco, California

91

Field Paint Color
Manufacturer: VIP Lighthouse Products
Product: VIP Elastomeric paint
Color name: Custom
Match to:
Manufacturer: Benjamin Moore
Color number: AC-4 + 25% darker
Color name: Yosemite Sand

Window Paint Color
Manufacturer: Benjamin Moore
Color number: 1230 + 25% darker
Color name: Oregon Trail

Window Frame Paint Color
Manufacturer: Benjamin Moore
Color number: HC-47
Color name: Brooklyn Beige

Door
Material: Mahogany
Stain
Manufacturer: Minwax
Number: 2716
Color name: Dark Walnut

Railing
Material: Wrought iron
Paint Color
Manufacturer: Benjamin Moore
Product: Ironclad Latex, Low Lustre Metal & Wood Enamel
Color number: C163-60
Color name: Bronzetone 60

Roof Tile
Manufacturer: Redland Clay Tile
Product: Baja Mission Sandcast, 4300 Series
Material: Terra-cotta clay
Color name: Old Hacienda Blend
Note: My match

Pavers
Material: Flagstone

Color Consulting
Susan Bottorf and Art Chinn
Garner Chinn 8
Oakland, California

92

Field Paint Color
Manufacturer: Benjamin Moore
Color number: 2153-40
Color name: Cork

Window, Balcony, and Door Frame Paint Color
Manufacturer: Benjamin Moore
Color number: OC-94
Color name: Windswept
Note: Use a metal exterior primer undercoat for balcony railing. Color is my match.

Door Paint Color
Manufacturer: Benjamin Moore
Color number: 2133-10
Color name: Onyx
Note: My match

Entry Steps
Material: Old brick

Roof Tile
Material: Terra-cotta clay

93

Field Paint Color
Manufacturer: Morwear
Color name: Custom
Tinting base: 6820
Five gallon formula:
B 4 x 18
C 7 x 39
F 5 x 45

Window Paint Color
Manufacturer: Benjamin Moore
Color number: 711
Color name: Boca Raton Blue

Window Surround, Column Finial, and Trim Paint Color
Manufacturer: Benjamin Moore
Color name: Custom
Tinting base: N096-1B
One gallon formula:
OY-28
BK-4
GY-18

Door
Manufacturer: Rustica Arts
Product: Custom
Material: Alderwood
Stain: Country Alder

Front Gate
Source: Habité—Antiques
Material: Painted wrought iron
Note: Antique from France

Paint Color
Manufacturer: Benjamin Moore
Product: Ironclad Latex, Low Lustre Metal & Wood Enamel
Color name: Custom
Tinting base: N096-1B
One gallon formula:
OY-28
BK-4
GY-18

Fancy Grille Work on Windows
Designer and Manufacturer: Olszewski Iron Design
Material: Wrought iron
Product: Custom

Paint Color
Manufacturer: Benjamin Moore
Product: Ironclad Latex, Low Lustre Metal & Wood Enamel
Color name: Custom
Tinting base: C163-1B
One gallon formula:
OY-28
BK-4
GY-18
Note: Design was inspired by the antique front gate.

Garage Doors and Projecting Eave
Material: Cedar plank and Douglas fir

Stain
Manufacturer: Cabot
Product: Clear Solution
Color name: Heartwood

Mailbox
Manufacturer: Christine Rotolo/Rotolo Design
Product: Custom
Material: Wrought iron

Paint
Manufacturer: Benjamin Moore
Product: Ironclad Latex, Low Lustre Metal & Wood Enamel
Tinting base: C163-1B
One gallon formula:
OY-28
BK-4
GY-18

Roof Tile
Manufacturer: Redland Clay Tile
Product: Mission Sandcast, 4300 Series
Color name: Old Saltillo SC Blend

Pavers at Entry
Manufacturer: Pave Tile & Stone
Product: Farmhouse Provencal Handmade Parrefeuille
Size: 9" x 15"
Color name: Terra Cotta
Note: My match. The tile has been discontinued. This is a similar product.

Awning
Manufacturer: Sunbrella
Product: Scallop Pattern Fabric
Product number: 4785

Paving
Source: American Soil
Rock type: Gold pathway crushed granite

Hanging Light Fixture at Entry
Source: Foster & Gwin Antiques
Product: Eighteenth-century Spanish light fixture
Finish: Wrought iron

Architectural Designer
Mark Becker
Mark Becker, Inc.
Oakland, California

94

Field Paint Color
Manufacturer: Benjamin Moore
Color name: Custom
Tinting base: N185-2B
One gallon formula:
YW 2X16
OG 28
BK 12.25
TG 1

Door, Window, Window Frames, and Garage Door Paint Color
Manufacturer: Benjamin Moore
Color number: 2111-40
Color name: Taos Taupe

Tulips
Name: Queen of the Night

Roof Tile
Material: Terra-cotta clay

Paving
Manufacturer: American Soil Products
Product: Arizona Sandstone

95

Field Paint Color
Manufacturer: Benjamin Moore
Color number: EXT. RM.
Color name: Montgomery White

Window, Window Frame, and Shutter Paint Color
Manufacturer: Benjamin Moore
Color number: 947
Color name: Navajo White

Door

Stain
Manufacturer: Cabot
Product: Semi-Transparent Stain
Color name: Mission Brown

Protectant
Manufacturer: Minwax
Product: Helmsman Spar Urethane
Finish: Satin
Note: My match

Roof Tile
Manufacturer: Redland Clay Tile
Product: Mission 2000 Series
Color name: Old Sedona Blend
Note: My match

Pavers
Material: Mexican saltillo tile pavers
Note: Natural, sealed clay tiles are readily available at most tile outlets. Colors run from yellow to a subtle reddish orange

96

Field Paint Color
Manufacturer: Benjamin Moore
Color number: 1039
Color name: Stone House

Window, Window Frame, and Trim Paint Color
Manufacturer: Benjamin Moore
Color number: 1044
Color name: Lighthouse Landing

Door Paint Color
Manufacturer: Pratt & Lambert
Color number: 1927
Color name: Maroon Rust

Projecting Eave, Roof Rafters, and Beam (Viga) Paint Color
Manufacturer: Benjamin Moore
Color number: HC-40
Color name: Greenfield Pumpkin

Gate
Material: Redwood

Stain
Manufacturer: Cabot
Product: Clear Solution
Color name: Pacific Redwood
Note: My match

Roof Tile
Manufacturer: Redland Clay Tile
Product: Mission 2000 Series
Color name: Old Hacienda Blend
Note: My match

Pavers
Material: Connecticut Blue Flagstone

Color Consultant
David vanDommelen
vanDommelen Colorworks
San Francisco, California

Landscape Designer
Enchanting Planting
Orinda, California

97

Field Paint Color
Manufacturer: Benjamin Moore
Color number: HC-89
Color name: Northampton Putty

Window and Wrought Iron Railing Paint Color
Manufacturer: Benjamin Moore
Color number: 2137-30
Color name: Durango
Note: Use exterior metal primer undercoat for railing.

Window Frame Paint Color
Manufacturer: ICI
Color number: 654
Color name: Ivory Cream

Door Paint Color
Manufacturer: Benjamin Moore
Color number: EXT. RM.
Color name: Country Redwood

Path and Driveway Paint
Manufacturer: Insl-X
Product: Hot-Trax
Name: Latex Satin Concrete Floor Paint
Color name: Tile Red

Roof Tile
Material: Terra-cotta clay

98

Color-Embedded Stucco Field Color
Manufacturer: LaHabra
Product: Custom
Match to:
Manufacturer: Benjamin Moore
Color number: 1145
Color name: Creamy Custard

Window Paint Color
Manufacturer: Benjamin Moore
Color number: 1245
Color name: Sequoia

Window Frame and Cornice Paint Color
Manufacturer: Benjamin Moore
Mix together:
70%
Color number: HC-108
Color name: Sandy Hook Gray
and
30%

Manufacturer: Benjamin Moore
Color number: HC-35
Color name: Powell Buff
Directions: These colors are brushed on wet and then sponged to approximate the look of limestone.

Door
Material: Philippine mahogany

Protectant
Manufacturer: Varathane
Product: Diamond Spar Urethane
Finish: Water-based
Note: My match

Sgrafitto (on the Stucco Walls between Second Story Windows)
One-Inch Outline of Diamond Pattern over Plaster
Manufacturer: Benjamin Moore
Color number: 1227
Color name: Nutmeg

Diamond Interior
Manufacturer: Benjamin Moore
Color number: 110
Color name: Starfish
Note: Thin paint 40% with water.

Stencil Raised Pattern
Manufacturer: Benjamin Moore
Color number: HC-108
Color name: Sandy Hook Gray

Overwash on Raised Pattern
Manufacturer: Benjamin Moore
Color number: 220
Color name: Yellow Bisque
Directions: Thin paint 40% with water. Highlight about 20% of diamond pattern, some only partially.

Drop Shadow
Manufacturer: Benjamin Moore
Color number: 1194
Color name: Mexican Tile
Directions: Enrich the diamond surround of the raised pattern to create a drop shadow.
Fade some of the drop shadow with:
Manufacturer: Benjamin Moore
Color number: HC-55
Color name: Winthrop Peach
Directions: Thin both paints 40% with water. Sgrafitto is a decoration that's achieved by cutting away parts of the surface layer. It is done to approximate a raised shield pattern over an incised diamond pattern. This sgrafitto pattern was adapted to appear to simulate the fade in the path of the sun.

Steps, Railing, and Portal Surround
Material: Limestone

Roof Tile
Material: Terra-cotta clay tile

Specialty Painter and Sgraffito Artist
Elisa Stancil
Stancil Studios
San Francisco, California

99

Field Paint Color
Manufacturer: Benjamin Moore
Color number: 2015-50

Color name: Funky Fruit
Window, Window Frame, and Door Frame Paint Color
Manufacturer: Benjamin Moore
Color number: OC-69
Color name: White Opulence
Note: My match

Door Paint Color
Manufacturer: Benjamin Moore
Color number: 1665
Color name: Mozart Blue
Note: My match

Swinging Gate
Material: Untreated redwood

Pavers
Material: Mexican saltillo pavers with accent tiles
Source: Country Floors
Note: My match

Roof Tile
Material: Terra-cotta clay

100

Field Paint Color
Manufacturer: Fuller O'Brien
Color name: Custom
Tinting base: 668-91
  BLK OP1+
  YOX 4P 35+
  OXR OP27

Window, Window Frame, Garage Door, Balcony, French Door, and Accent Paint Color
Manufacturer: Benjamin Moore
Color name: Custom
Tinting base: N096-2B
One gallon formula:
  OY 1 x 24
  BK 22
  TG 3
  GY 5
  WH 2x

Wrought Iron Railing and Gate Paint Color
Manufacturer: Benjamin Moore
Color number: 041
Color name: Spoonful of Sugar
Finish: Glossy
Note: Use exterior metal primer undercoat.

Concrete Step Paint Color
Manufacturer: Benjamin Moore
Color name: Custom
Tinting base: 122-01
One quart formula:
  OY 22
  BK 5
  OG 1
  TG 2
  GY 9

Roof Tile
Material: Terra-cotta clay

101

Field Paint Color
Manufacturer: Kelly-Moore
Product: Elastomeric paint
Color name: Custom
Tinting base: 1128-100
One gallon formula:
  C 3Y24
  L 2
  M 1
  R 17

Window and Window Frame Paint Color
Manufacturer: Kelly-Moore
Collection: Architectural Colors
Color number: K35-3
Color name: Palmetto Green

Door
Product: Custom
Material: Douglas fir
Protective Coating
Manufacturer: Sikkens
Product: Cetrol 23 Plus System
Number: 077
Finish: Satin
Color name: Cedar
Note: My match

Sconce Lighting Fixture
Manufacturer: Arroyo Craftsman
Product: Berkeley
Product number: BB-7WGW-BZ
Finish: Bronze metal finish
Glass: Gold white iridescent
Note: My match

Paneling (around Windows), Trellis, and Projecting Eave Paint Color
Manufacturer: Kelly-Moore
Collection: Architectural Colors
Color number: H15-3
Color name: Roman Ochre

Wood-Paneled Awning and Flower Box Paint Color
Manufacturer: Kelly-Moore
Collection: Architectural Colors
Color number: E 10-3
Color name: Autumn Oak

Market Umbrella
Manufacturer: Pottery Barn
Product: Market Umbrella
Product number: 377337
Material: Polyester canvas
Color name: Lime
Note: My match

Roofing
Material: Terra-cotta clay

Paving
Driveway
Material: Black crushed gravel
Patio
Material: Multicolored round pea gravel
Slate at Entry
Manufacturer: American Slate Company
Color number: TCD128
Color name: Desert Beige
Note: My match

102

Faux Field Paint Color
Base Coat
Manufacturer: Benjamin Moore
Color number: 50% of 2155-40
Color name: Semolina
Faux Finish—Second Coat
Manufacturer: Benjamin Moore
Color number: AC-12
Color name: Copper Mountain
Instructions: Mix six parts Floetrol paint conditioner (available at paint stores) with one part water and mix into paint to achieve a translucent quality.
Faux Feather Finish—Third Coat
Manufacturer: Benjamin Moore

Color number: HC-75
Color name: Maryville Brown
Instructions: Repeat instructions above, then overlap the two faux finish glaze colors with a feather brush, sea sponge, and/or 100% terry cloth rag to achieve the desired look.

Window and Window Frame Paint Color
Manufacturer: Benjamin Moore
Mix together the following:
One part color number HC-64
Color name: Townsend Harbor Brown
and
One part color number HC-61
Color name: New London Burgundy

Faux Door and Garage Door Paint Color
Manufacturer: Benjamin Moore
Product: Mooregard Metal and Trim Paint, one quart
Base Coat
Mix together the following:
Manufacturer: Benjamin Moore
Product: Mooregard Metal and Trim Paint, one quart
Color number: 363-60
Color name: Bronze Tone
and
Manufacturer: McCloskey
Product: Special Effects Metallic Glaze, one pint
Color name: Copper
Note: Apply and let dry.
Top Coat
Manufacturer: Benjamin Moore
Tinting base: N103-4B
One quart formula:
  OY 2.5
  WH24
  TG28
Instructions: Water down top coat to a workable consistency. Add a bit of raw umber to the glaze. Apply multiple coats to achieve the desired effect, allowing the base coat to come through where desired.

Railing Paint Color
Manufacturer: Benjamin Moore
Product: Low Lustre Metal and Wood Enamel
Color number: C163-60
Color Name: Bronze
Note: My match

Pavers
Manufacturer: American Slate Company
Product: Slate
Color name: Rajah

Roof Tile
Manufacturer: MonierLifetile
Product: Concrete Roof Tile
Product number: 2VACS 6169
Color name: Villa Casa Grande Blend C/T

Faux Painting Artist/Specialist
Joshua McCullough
Martinez, California

103

Horizontal Clapboard Siding Color (Left Side)
Manufacturer: Cabot
Product: Semi-Solid Stain
Color name: Bluestone

Powder Coated Aluminum Panel at Bay Windows (Left Side)
Manufacturer: NIC Industries
Coating: Prismatic Powder
Epoxy finish: Wrinkle
Color number: EWS 516
Color name: Ash Grey

Color-Embedded Stucco Wall (Right Side)
Manufacturer: LaHabra
Product number: 215-3xxx (add three times the color additive to stock color)
Color name: Mesa Verde
Note: The colors and materials on the clapboard siding, powder coated aluminum panel, and color-embedded stucco are in the same location on the front and back of the house.

French Doors and Windows
Manufacturer: Bonelli Windows and Doors
French Doors
Product: Bonelli Series 1000 Swing Door
Material: Anodized Aluminum
Finish: Anodized Bronze
Windows
Product: Bonelli Series 700 Projected Windows
Material: Anodized Aluminum
Finish: Anodized Bronze

Garage Structure
Material: Natural-colored poured concrete

Garage Door Paint Color
Manufacturer: Sherwin Williams
Color number: SW2118
Color name: Gunmetal Gray

Entry Door Paint Color
Manufacturer: Benjamin Moore
Color number: 397
Color name: Chamomile

Vent Louver
Manufacturer: Seiho
Product: Custom Louver
Model: SX
Material: Water jet-cut stainless steel
Designed by: Zack/deVito Architecture
Note: These are the round vents to the left and right of the house number plate.

Oval House Number Plate
Product: Custom
Material: Stainless Steel
Designed by: Zack DeVito Architecture

Guardrails above Garage
Product: Custom
Materials: Red balou mahogany and naturally rusted COR-TEN steel
Note: Designed by Zack/deVito Architecture

Mahogany Protectant
Manufacturer: Cabot
Product: Clear Solution
Color name: Natural

Planter Boxes above Garage and Guardrails at Windows
Product: Custom design
Material: Naturally rusted COR-TEN steel
Designed by: Zack/deVito Architecture

Decking
Material: Yellow balou mahogany
Wood Protectant
Manufacturer: Cabot
Product: Clear Solution
Color name: Natural

Floating Staircase in Backyard
Material: Galvanized steel
Note: Designed by Zack/deVito Architecture
Paint
Manufacturer: Rust-Oleum
Product: High performance enamel spray paint
Color number: 7715
Color name: Aluminum
Note: Stairs are part galvanized steel, part Rust-Oleum spray paint

Striped Entry Mat
Manufacturer: Chilewich
Note: Colors and designs change seasonally.

Architecture
Jim Zack
Zack/deVito Architecture
San Francisco, California

104

Color-Embedded Stucco Field Color (Seen on Garage Walls)
Manufacturer: LaHabra
Number: X-79 (Base 100)
Color name: Villa

Accent Wall Paint Color (with Three Square Cut-Outs)
Manufacturer: Benjamin Moore
Number: 104
Color name: Sienna Clay
Note: My match

Window Frame Paint Color
Mix equal parts of the following products:
Manufacturer: Benjamin Moore
Color number: 158
Color name: Pineapple Orange
and
Manufacturer: Benjamin Moore
Color number: 159
Color name: Peach Crisp
Note: My match

Door Paint Color
Manufacturer: Kelly-Moore
Color number: AC42-N
Color name: Real Purple

Garage Door Paint Color
Overall Color
Manufacturer: Kelly-Moore
Color number: AC13N
Color name: Pigskin
Frame
Mix equal parts of the following products:
Manufacturer: Benjamin Moore
Color number: 158
Color name: Pineapple Orange
and
Manufacturer: Benjamin Moore
Color number: 159

Color name: Peach Crisp
Note: My match

Gates and Railing Paint Color
Manufacturer: Kelly-Moore
Color number: AC86-N
Color name: Rich Earth
Note: Use exterior rust preventative paint primer

Triangular Shade Sails
Manufacturer: Coolaroo
Product: Triangle Shade Sails
Product number: HS-23
Color name: Desert Sand
Note: This is a breathable UV exterior-approved fabric.

Paving
Manufacturer: Superdeck Brand Products
Product: "Mason's Select" Transparent Concrete Stain
Product number: 50
Color name: Sandstone

105

Field, Garage Door, and Trim Paint Color
Manufacturer: Fuller O'Brien
Color name: Custom
Tinting base: 664-91
Five gallon formula:
BLK 9p26 1/2
YOX 3p33
OXR 12 1/2

Door, Door Frame, Window, Window Frame, and Trellis Paint Color
Manufacturer: Fuller O'Brien
Color name: Custom
Tinting base: 202-25
One gallon formula:
BLK 3 1/2
YOX 4
OXR 1/2
Designer: Hanns Kainz, Hanns Kainz & Associates Architects, San Francisco, California
Note: Door is paint grade wood. Color is my match.

Porch Paint Color
Manufacturer: Behr
Product: Premium Plus Exterior Porch and Floor Paint
Color number: PPF-02
Color name: Patio Green

Light Fixture
Manufacturer: Louis Poulsen
Product: Nyhaun Maxi Wall
Material: Powder-coated aluminum
Color name: White

House Numbers
Manufacturer: Hewi USA
Product number: 987.03
Material: Weather-resistant nylon
Color name: Ruby Red -#33

Architect
Hanns Kainz
Hanns Kainz & Associates
San Francisco, California

106

Field Paint Color
Manufacturer: Behr
Color number: 750F-6
Color name: Sled

Door, Sidelight, and Garage Door
Manufacturer: Bayshore Metals, San Francisco, California
Product: Custom
Material: Naturally rusted COR-TEN steel
Note: Garage door has a perforated dot pattern.

Steel Fastener for Door and Garage Door COR-TEN Steel Panels
Manufacturer: Harrison & Bonini, San Francisco, California
Note: Garage and door are attached to a wood frame with these fasteners.

House Numbers
Manufacturer: www.custom-housenumbers.com
Font: Neutra
Material: Stainless steel

Doorbell (Not Shown)
Manufacturer: spOre, Inc.
Product: Square Illuminated Doorbell Button
Product number: #dbs-w
Color name: White
Finish: Anodized aluminum and rubber button
Note: My match

Architect
Russ Beaudin & Emma Kim
Twelve 13 Architecture
Oakland, California

107

Color-Embedded Stucco Field Color
Manufacturer: Parex
Finish: Medium dash texture
Color name: Match to:
Manufacturer: Dunn Edwards
Color number: DE227
Color name: Rowdy Green

Color-Embedded Stucco Short Wall Color
Manufacturer: Parex
Finish: Medium dash texture
Color name: Match to:
Manufacturer: Dunn Edwards
Color number: DE225
Color name: Easy Going
Note: Gutters and downspouts are also this paint color.

Window
Manufacturer: Bonelli Enterprises
Product number: 700 Series
Finish: Anodized clear aluminum

Door
Manufacturer: Simpson Door Company
Product: Five-lite exterior french door
Product number: 7105
Materials: Tempered clear glass and vertical grain Douglas fir

Sealer
Manufacturer: Penofin
Product: Original Blue Label Oil Wood Finish Penetrating Sealer
Color name: Clear

Door Hardware
Manufacturer: Baldwin Hardware Corporation
Product: Chicago Mortise Trim

Handleset, Estate, Lock
Product number: 6563.264
Finish: Satin chrome

Bay Window Siding
Material: Painted 6" V-groove redwood siding, paint grade
Color name: Match to the following:
Manufacturer: Ralph Lauren
Product number: TH49
Color name: Venetian Red, flat finish
Note: Match Ralph Lauren paint to a manufacturer with an exterior paint product. Ralph Lauren produces interior paint only.

Trellis, Gate, and Garage Door
Material: Resawn red cedar
Sealer
Manufacturer: Penofin
Product: Original Blue Label Oil Wood Finish Penetrating Sealer
Color name: Clear

Balcony Railing (at Side of House)
Product: Custom
Finish
Manufacturer: Tiger DryLac, U.S.A., Inc.
Product: Powder Coating in Metallics
Product number: 39/90000
Color name: Silver
Note: Designed by Robert Nebolon, Architect

House Numbers
Manufacturer: Matthews International Corporation
Product: Projected Mount Design in 6" sans serif font
Product number: M70
Color name: Dark Brown
Material: Cast aluminum

Front Gate
Material: Resawn red cedar
Sealer
Manufacturer: Penofin
Product: Original Blue Label Oil Wood Finish Penetrating Sealer
Color name: Clear

Pavers (Front Yard)
Material: Arizona flagstone

Architect
Robert Nebolon
Berkeley, California

108

Field Paint Colors
Corrugated Steel Panel
Manufacturer: ASC Profiles
Product: 2 1/2" Corrugated Wall Panel
Finish: Duratech 500
Color name: Tahoe Blue
Stucco Paint Color
Manufacturer: Benjamin Moore
Color number: AC-18
Color name: Smoky Mountain
Railing
Manufacturer: ASC Profiles/AEP Span
Product: Corrugated Wall Panel
Finish: Duratech 500
Color name: Parchment
Window
Manufacturer: Bonelli Doors and Windows

Finish: Powder Coat
Color number: RAL 7032
Note: Matches railing color

Gutter and Trim Paint Color
Manufacturer: Fuller O'Brien
Product: Western Exterior Colors Collection
Color number: 86
Color name: Keystone
Note: Matches railing color

Garage Door
Note: Custom-match paint color to ASC Profiles, Tahoe Blue.

109

Field Paint Color
Manufacturer: Kelly-Moore
Product: Kel-Seal Acrylic Terpolymer Coating System
Color name: Custom
Tinting base: 1128-100
One gallon formula:
L 1Y
Note: This paint is for stucco surfaces only

Window Color
Manufacturer: Fleetwood Windows and Doors
Product: Norwood Series 3000 anodized aluminum windows
Color name: Black

Door, Railings, and Mailbox Paint Color
Manufacturer: Rust-Oleum
Product: Oil-Based Protective Enamel
Color number: 7777
Color name: Satin Black
Note: Use an exterior primer on railing and mailbox (under house numbers).

Window Covering
Manufacturer: Castec, Inc.
Product: Flat Roman Shades
Product number: 101 Pacifica
Color: Natural
Material: Unbleached 100% Natural Cotton Duck

Composition Asphalt Shingle Roofing
Manufacturer: CertainTeed
Product: LandmarkTL
Color name: Charcoal Black
Note: My match

Paving
Manufacturer: Sunny Brook Pressed Concrete Company
Product: 24" x 24" squares
Product number: 4000D
Color name: Custom
Note: Custom color matched to interior carpet.

110

Field Paint Color
Manufacturer: Sherwin Williams
Color number: SW2191
Color name: Ligonier Tan

Blue "Feature Wall" Paint Color
Manufacturer: Benjamin Moore
Color number: 2068-30
Color name: Scandinavian Blue

Purple Accent Wall Paint Color
Manufacturer: Benjamin Moore
Color number: 2074-20

Color name: Summer Plum

Breezeway Ceiling Paint Color
Manufacturer: Benjamin Moore
Color number: 2168-20
Color name: Pumpkin Cream
Note: My match

Entry Gate into Courtyard
Product: Custom
Manufacturer: Olson Bros., El Sobrante, California
Material: Mahogany and stainless steel
Finish
Manufacturer: Cabot
Product: Clear Solution
Color: Natural

Metal Edge of Gate
Manufacturer: Dennis Luedeman, Oakland, California
Note: Designed by Andrew Fischer, Regan Bice Architects, Berkeley, California

Garage Door
Product: Custom
Manufacturer: Olson Bros., El Sobrante, California
Material: Mahogany
Finish
Manufacturer: Cabot
Product: Clear Solution
Color: Natural

Hanging Light Fixture
Manufacturer: Louis Paulsen
Product: Orbiter Maxi Pendant
Finish: Natural painted aluminum

House Numbers
Manufacturer: Dennis Luedeman, Oakland, California
Product: Back-Lit House Number Plate
Finish: Stainless steel
Note: Designed by Debra Conteras, Regan Bice Architects, Berkeley, California

Color Consultant
Jill Pilaroscia
The Colour Studio
San Francisco, California

Architect
Regan Bice
Regan Bice Architects
Berkeley, California

Landscape Architect
David Bigham
Berkeley, California

111

Color-Embedded Stucco Field Color
Manufacturer: LaHabra
Color name: Custom
Match to the following:
Manufacturer: Benjamin Moore
Color number: 2159-50
Color name: Wheatfield

Siding
Manufactuer: US Steel Corporation
Product: Galvalume
Panel type: Standard corrugated
Material: Galvanized metal and aluminum

Window
Manufacturer: Milgard Windows
Material: Vinyl

Manufacturer's custom color:
High Sierra Blue
Note: Color has been discontinued. Match to:
Manufacturer: Benjamin Moore
Color number: 2066-10
Color name: Blue
Note: My match

Front Door
Product: Custom
Material: Birch
Manufacturer: ZAR
Finish: Exterior oil-based polyurethane
Finish: Satin
Note: Color has yellowed over time.
Designed by: Stephen Swearengen, Oakland, California

Door Hardware
Manufacturer: Schlage
Product: Century
Finish name: Bright Chrome
Finish number: 625
Note: This model has been redesigned and features a different door handle.

Trellis
Material: Pressure treated Douglas fir

Light Fixture at Entry
Manufacturer: RAB Lighting
Product: Vaporproof Ceiling Lighting Pendant
Material: Die cast aluminum
Color: Natural
Lamp: Incandescent
Note: Similar product

French Doors, Adirondack Chairs, and Garage Door Paint Color
Manufacturer: Benjamin Moore
Color number: 1306
Color name: Habanero Pepper
Note: My match

Pavers in Courtyard
Material: Concrete square pavers

Architect
Stephen Swearengen
El Cerrito, California

112

Color-Embedded Stucco Field Color (Lower Portion)
Manufacturer: LaHabra
Number: X31649
Color name: Custom
Tinting base: 299
Finish: Float
This is a color match to the following:
Manufacturer: ICI
Color number: 874
Color name: Cypress

Field Paint Color (Upper Portion)
Manufacturer: ICI
Color number: 646
Color name: Silver Cloud

Color-Embedded Stucco (Wall and Ceiling in Recessed Entry)
Manufacturer: LaHabra
Product number: X-16 (Base 200)
Color name: Silver Gray
Finish: Santa Barbara Mission

Flooring in Entry
Material: Terrazzo
Colors: Black, white, and gray
Note: Flooring is original to the house.

Door Paint Color
Manufacturer: ICI
Color number: 274
Color name: Canyon Stone

Garage Doors
Manufacturer: BP Glass Garage Doors
Product: Aluminum and glass sectional garage doors
Product number: BP-350
Materials: Aluminum alloy and sandblasted Azurlite glass
Note: My match. This is a similar product.

Garage Frame Paint Color
Manufacturer: ICI
Color number: 878
Color name: Olive Branch

Sidelights
Manufacturer: BP Glass Garage Doors
Product: Custom

House Numbers
Manufacturer: www.custom-housenumbers.com
Product: Neutraface
Finish: Stainless steel
Note: All colors and materials are my matches.

113

Color-Embedded Stucco Field Colors
Manufacturer: Parex Stucco
Name: All custom to match the following:

Color #1
Manufacturer: ICI
Color number: 872
Color name: Virginia Vine

Color #2
Manufacturer: Ralph Lauren
Color number: UL20
Color name: Chrome
Note: Match to an exterior paint. Ralph Lauren produces interior paint only.

Color #3
Manufacturer: Ralph Lauren
Color number: TH14
Color name: Orion Grey
Note: Match to an exterior paint. Ralph Lauren produces interior paint only.

Window
Manufacturer: Bonelli Enterprises
Finish: Clear anodized aluminum

Door
Manufacturer: Bonelli Enterprises
Finish: Clear anodized aluminum

Architectural Glass
Manufacturer: Bendheim Glass
Product: Thread
Note: Glass encapsulates Japanese rice paper between two pieces of clear laminated glass. Fiber is a random pattern.

Wall Mounted Light Fixture
Manufacturer: Kichler
Product: Outdoor Bracket 1 Lt. Incandescent
Product number: 6040NI
Finish: Brushed nickel
Note: My match. This is a similar product.

Slate on Wall
Manufacturer: Echeguren Slate, San Francisco, California
Product: 12"x24" slate
Color name: Indian Autumn

Architect
Alexandra Marynetz and Arnold Mammarella
Origins Design Network
Oakland, California

114

Color-Embedded Stucco Field Color #1 (Lightest Field Color, Right Lower Box)
Manufacturer: LaHabra
Number: 81094
Color name: Custom
Match to:
Manufacturer: Benjamin Moore
Color number: HC-105
Color name: Rockport Gray

Color #2 (Medium Field Color, Left Box)
Manufacturer: LaHabra
Number: 30986
Color name: Custom
Match to:
Manufacturer: Benjamin Moore
Color number: HC-104
Color name: Copley Gray

Color #3 (Darkest Field Color, Right Upper Box)
Manufacturer: LaHabra
Number: 31116
Color name: Custom
Match to:
Manufacturer: Benjamin Moore
Color number: HC-103
Color name: Cromwell Gray

Window
Manufacturer: Blomberg Window Systems
Product: Architectural grade aluminum windows
Color name: Black Walnut

Entry Column and Railing
Material: Redwood

Stain
Manufacturer: Benjamin Moore
Product: Solid Color Stain
Color number: 297
Color name: Golden Honey

Plywood Garage Door Paint
Manufacturer: Benjamin Moore
Color number: HC-105
Color name: Rockport Gray

Vertical Strips
Material: Galvanized steel

Horizontal Slats
Material: Mangaris (an Asian hardwood)

Stain
Manufacturer: Cabot
Product: Australian Timber Oil
Number: 9457
Color name: Amberwood

Window Trellis
Materials: Redwood with galvanized steel trim and hanging hardware

Trellis Awning Stain
Manufacturer: Benjamin Moore
Product: Solid Color Exterior Stain
Product number: #C080
Color: Sea Gull Gray

House Numbers
Manufacturer: Gemini Incorporated
Product: Gemini Letters, Custom
Finish: Cast brushed aluminum

Architect
Baird Wheatley
Baird Wheatley Design
Leucadia, California

115

Color-Embedded Stucco Field Colors
Color #1 (House Color)
Manufacturer: Dryvit
Color number: 398A
Color name: Power Tan
Color #2 (Courtyard Wall)
Manufacturer: Dryvit
Color number: 399
Color name: Coffee Milk

Window
Window manufacturer: Bonelli Doors and Windows
Powder coat color number: 3011
Color name: Tiger Rail

Door
Material: Mahogany
Oil Finish
Manufacturer: Cabot
Product: Australian Timber Oil
Color name: Natural
Note: The etched tempered glass in sidelights was adapted from a design in Art Deco Designs & Motifs by Marcia Loeb, Dover Publications, 1972.

Garage Door
Match to:
Manufacturer: Dryvit
Color number: 399
Color name: Coffee Milk

Porcelain Pavers
Manufacturer: Colorlands
Product: Darkland

House Numbers
Manufacturer: Weston Letters
Style: Deep Ribbon
Color name: Black Anodized

Gate
Manufacturer: Mexico City Ironworks, San Francisco, California
Material: Painted galvanized iron
Note: Designed by Theresa Zaro of Rayner Landscaping
Paint
Manufacturer: Kelly-Moore
Product: Rust-Oleum Water Base Colorants
Color name: Custom
Tinting base: 3707
One gallon formula:
  B 2

F y24
J 10
K 6y
W 2
Note: Check for Kelly-Moore stores that have Rust-Oleum Tint Stations. This color can also be matched to Bonelli Door and Windows, color name: Tiger Rail, 3011.

Architect
Mac Morrison
Lanier-Sherrill-Morrison Architects
San Francisco, California

Landscape Architect
Theresa Zaro
Rayner Landscaping
Novato, California

116

Field Paint Colors
Clapboard Siding Paint Color
Manufacturer: Sherwin Williams
Color number: SW1209
Color name: Seahawk
Note: My match

Stucco Paint Color
Manufacturer: Benjamin Moore
Color number: OC-95
Color name: Navajo White

Door and Window Paint Color
Manufacturer: Benjamin Moore
Color number: OC-95
Color name: Navajo White

Trellis
Material: Cedar
Stain
Manufacturer: Cabot
Product: Semi-Solid Stain
Color name: Mission Brown
Note: My match. Trellis at entry has etched laminated glass panels above.

Railing Paint Color
Manufacturer: Benjamin Moore
Color number: 2127-50
Color name: Pike's Peak Gray
Note: My match. Simulates aluminum color. Use exterior metal primer undercoat.

House Numbers
Source: The Magazine
Product: Corbu
Material: Aluminum

Pavers
Manufacturer: American Slate Company
Product: African Multicolor

117

Field Paint Colors
Color #1 (Red)
Manufacturer: Kelly-Moore
Color number: AC213-5
Color name: High Society
Color #2 (Gold)
Manufacturer: Kelly-Moore
Color number: KM3576-5
Color name: Mandarin Grove

Window
Manufacturer: All Weather Architectural Aluminum
Product: 3000 Series
Color Name: White Powder Coat

Note: My match

Window Frame, Garage Door, Railing, Sconce Light Fixture, and Trim Paint Color
Manufacturer: Kelly-Moore
Color number: 150
Color name: Mallard Green

Door Paint Color (on balcony)
Manufacturer: Kelly-Moore
Color number: KM3576-5
Color name: Mandarin Grove

118

Clapboard Siding, Square Cut-Out Stucco Wing Wall, and Garage Door Paint Color
Manufacturer: Kelly-Moore
Color number: KM702D
Color name: Muddy Creek

Slate Facing
Source: Floor + Stone Depot, San Francisco, California
Material: Malachite
Product number: SLATIL 005

Door, Door Frame, and Window Frame Paint Color
Manufacturer: Kelly-Moore
Color number: 14
Color name: Frost
Note: Windows are standard white powder coated aluminum frame windows. If your windows are wood frames, paint this color.

Planters
Manufacturer: Frontgate Catalogue
Product: Washed Zinc Planters
Material: Fiberglass resin
Note: From catalogue dated November 2004

Illuminated Doorbell
Manufacturer: spOre, Inc.
Product: De-light
Product number: dbd-w
Color name: White
Finish: Anodized aluminum and rubber button

House Numbers
Manufacturer: spOre, Inc.
Product: "Plane" Two Panel Light Box
Finish: Stainless steel

Glass Awning and Balcony Railing
Material: Stainless steel
Design: Mary Revelli, One Off Design, San Francisco, California

Sconce Lighting
Manufacturer: Kichler Lighting
Product number: 6040NI
Finish: Brushed nickel

119

Field Paint Color
Manufacturer: Fuller O'Brien
Color number: 2W15-3
Color name: Tavern Taupe
Note: All trim colors are the same.

Detached Garage Paint Color
Manufacturer: Fuller O'Brien
Product: Weather King II Flat
Color number: 3WA25-4
Color name: Cabernet

Window
Manufacturer: All Weather Architectural Aluminum
Product: 3000 Series Aluminum Casement Windows
Finish: Anodized bronze
Note: My match. This is a similar product.

Fence
Material: Natural untreated redwood

Sculpted Rusted Iron Gate
Designer and manufacturer: Jack Chandler & Associates, Napa, California

Composition Asphalt Shingle Roofing
Manufacturer: CertainTeed
Product: Landmark Premium
Color name: Graphite
Note: My match

120

Field, Portico, and Round Balcony Paint Color
Manufacturer: Benjamin Moore
Color number: 1102
Color name: Boardwalk

Accent Paint Color (around Entry Doors)
Manufacturer: ICI
Color number: 168
Color name: Scenic Rose

Door Paint Color
Manufacturer: Benjamin Moore
Color number: 679
Color name: Olympus Green
Note: Matches Tiger Drylac powder-coated window color.

Windows
Manufacturer: All-Weather Architectural Aluminum
Product: 3000 Series
Material: Aluminum

Color
Manufacturer: Tiger Drylac, U.S.A., Inc.
Product: Powder Coated Color
Product number: RAL6004

Wall Caps
Manufacturer: Napa Valley Cast Stone
Product number: 45C
Material: Cast stone

Concrete Block #1
Manufacturer: Basalite/Dixion
Number: D-521
Color name: Gold
Finish: Light sand blast
Dimension: 8"x8"x16"

Concrete Block #2
Manufacturer: Basalite/Dixion
Product number: D-364
Color name: Terracotta
Finish: Light sand blast
Dimension: 8"x4"x16"

Garage Door and Trellis Wood Stain
Manufacturer: Cabot
Product: Custom Solid Color Stain
OY-4x16
BK-24
BB-8x
WH-14

Note: Matched to Tiger Drylac powder coated window color.

Roofing
Manufacturer: NCI Building Components
Product: Kynar Royal 12" standing seam metal roofing
Product number: K-70
Color name: Stone Gray

Architect
Richard Christiani
Christiani Johnson Architects
San Francisco, California

121

Field Paint Color
Manufacturer: Benjamin Moore
Product: Elastomeric paint
Color name: Custom
Tinting base: 056-01
Five gallon formula:
OY 8 x 9
YW 20
BK 1 x 18
OG 1 x 29

French Door
Manufacturer: Marvin Doors
Product: Outswing, paint grade wood french doors

Paint Color
Manufacturer: Benjamin Moore
Color number: 2132-10
Color name: Black

Garage Door and Trim Paint Color
Manufacturer: Benjamin Moore
Color number: 2132-10
Color name: Black

Railing
Product: Custom
Material: Stainless Steel

Custom "Woven" Doors and Balcony Trim Detail
Manufacturer: Ace Iron, Inc.
Product: Custom
Material: Galvanized steel

Architect:
Gerry Tierney
Kava Massih Architects
Berkeley, California

122

Field Paint Color
Manufacturer: Kelly-Moore
Product: 1128, elastomeric paint/gallon size
75% of:
Color number: KM711-L
Color name: Powdered Graphite

Door, Window, Garage Door, and Trim Paint Color
Manufacturer: Benjamin Moore
Color number: OC-117
Color name: Simply White
Note: My match

123

Color-Embedded Stucco Field Color #1
Manufacturer: Parex/LaHabra
Product: Color-embedded stucco with elastomeric finish coat and medium dash texture
Colors: Oriental Gold

Color-Embedded Stucco Field Color #2
Manufacturer: Parex/LaHabra
Product: Color-embedded stucco with elastomeric finish coat and medium dash texture
Color: Cashmere

Doors and Windows
Manufacturer: Bonelli Doors and Windows
Product: 700 Series
Material: Anodized aluminum
Finish: Bronze

Concrete Driveway and Steps
Manufacturer: Davis Colors
Number: 5084
Material: Integral colored concrete
Formula: Three pounds of 5084 per 94-pound sack of concrete
Note: Steps are prefabricated concrete.

Trellis
Material: Hand-selected, pressure-treated, brown variety Douglas fir
Finish: Unstained

House Numbers
Manufacturer: Matthew, Inc.
Product: 6" Projecting Mount Design
Font: Sans serif
Material: Painted cast aluminum
Color name: Dark Brown

Exterior Light Fixtures
Material: Terra-cotta
Note: Sprayed with the stucco finish to match adjacent wall color and texture

Architect
Robert Nebolon
Berkeley, California

124

Field Paint Colors
  Lower Portion and around Door
  Manufacturer: Benjamin Moore
  Color number: 2137-30
  Color name: Durango
  Upper Portion
  Manufacturer: Benjamin Moore
  Color number: 1099
  Color name: Byzantine Gold
  Bay Window
  Manufacturer: Benjamin Moore
  Color number: 2005-10
  Color name: Red Rock

Window
Manufacturer: Sierra Pacific Windows
Product: Aluminum-Clad Windows with Dual-Pane Clear Glass

Finish
Exterior: Black
Interior: Natural Douglas fir

Door
Manufacturer: JC Cabinets & Doors
Product: Custom

Frame
Material: Book matched riff cut red oak

Panel
Material: Natural cherry

Wood Preservative
Manufacturer: Valspar
Product: Premium Oil Modified Clear Wood Preservative
Note: Preservative is my match.

Metal cross strip
Material: Dark bronze aluminum

Door Hardware
Manufacturer: Baldwin Hardware
Product: New York Mortise Trim Handleset
Product number: 6562.264
Finish: Satin chrome

Steps and Landing
Material: Laminate slate
Manufacturer: Witex
Product: Casa Tiles Plus
Product number: S110CTC
Color name: Pacific Slate Rust
Note: This is an interior product that is not recommended for exterior use except in temperate climates. Check with a professional before using this product.

House Numbers
Manufacturer: www.customhousenumbers.com
Product: 4" High Neutraface
Material: Water jet-cut Brushed aluminum

Hand Rail
Designer and manufacturer: Michael Wentworth, Architectural Metal Work and Design
Product: Custom
Material: Powder-coated steel railing
Color name: Black

Canopy and Gutter Pipes
Designer and manufacturer: Michael Wentworth, Architectural Metal Work and Design
Product: Custom
Materials: Mill finished brushed aluminum and 5/16" clear tempered glass

Color Consultant
Claudia Ellinghaus
The EsGrow Garden & Staging Company
Oakland, California

Architect
Phillip O. Perkins
Phillip O. Perkins Architectural Design
Oakland, California

125

Color-Embedded Stucco Field Colors
Manufacturer: Parex
Product: Color-embedded stucco with elastomeric finish coat and medium dash texture
Custom match to:
Color #1
Manufacturer: Fuller O'Brien
Color number: 2W13-5
Color name: Pepper Spice
Color #2
Manufacturer: Fuller O'Brien
Color number: 2W12-5
Color name: Old Cedar
Note: This is also used under

the eaves with a smooth finish.

Concrete Walls, Paving, and Steps
Material: Natural uncolored concrete

Entry Door, All Wood Siding/Wood Fascia Boards, and Trellis Sun Shades
Material: Resawn red cedar
Stain
Manufacturer: Cabot
Product: Semi-Solid Oil Base Stain
Number: 6138
Color name: Bark
Note: Custom plantation shutter entry door designed by Robert Nebolon, Architect, Berkeley, California

Door Pull at Entry Door
Manufacturer: Forms and Surfaces
Product: Calypso
Product number: CLD 1222
Finish: Oil-rubbed bronze
Finish number: US10B

Custom Cantilevered Awning at Entry
Underside
Product: Aluminum with Low Voltage Marine Lights
Frame Color
Manufacturer: Tiger Drylac U.S.A., Inc.
Product: Powder-Coated Color
Number: RAL-8002
Color name: Red-Brown
Designer: Robert Nebolon, Architect, Berkeley, California

Window
Manufacturer: All-Weather Architectural Aluminum
Product number: Series 3000
Material: Aluminum
Powder-Coated Color
Manufacturer: Tiger Drylac U.S.A., Inc.
Number: RAL-8002
Color name: Red-Brown

French Doors at Patio
Manufacturer: Bonelli Enterprises
Material: Aluminum
Color
Manufacturer: Tiger Drylac U.S.A., Inc.
Product: Powder Coated Color
Product number: RAL-8002
Color name: Red-Brown

House Numbers
Manufacturer: Matthews International Corporation
Product: 6" high Projected Mount Design
Font: Sans serif
Material: Painted cast aluminum
Color name: Dark Brown
Color number: M70

Metal Guard Rail
Designer: Robert Nebolon, Architect, Berkeley, California
Powder Coat Color
Manufacturer: Tiger Drylac, U.S.A., Inc.
Product: Powder Coated Color
Product number: RAL-8002
Color name: Red-Brown

Flagstone Pavers at Front Door Entry
Source: Bouquet Canyon Stone Company
Product: Bouquet Canyon Flagstone

Slate on Balconies
Source: Echeguren Slate
Material: Indian Copper Slate

"Floating" Wedge Wall Sconce
Manufacturer: Shaper Lighting
Product number: Model 682
Color name: Solid Bronze
Note: Sconce has weathered naturally to a dark brown color.

Roofing
Manufacturer: AEP Span
Product: Pre-Finished Metal Standing Seam
Color name: Weathered Copper (not real copper)
Note: Gutters and flashing are same finish

Architect
Robert Nebolon
Berkeley, California

Landscape Architects
Julie Calandra
Wake and Bake Landscape
Oakland, California
and
Kristin Personett
Indigo Design
Oakland, California

126

Field Paint Colors
Garage Wall
Manufacturer: VIP Lighthouse Products
Product: VIP Elastomeric Paint
Match to:
Manufacturer: Dunn Edwards
Color number: SP338
Color name: Seal Point
Wall (on Lower Level) Paint Color
Manufacturer: VIP Lighthouse Products
Product: VIP Elastomeric Paint
Match to:
Manufacturer: Dunn Edwards
Color number: SP2460
Color name: Mesquite Toe
Door
Manufacturer: Blomberg Window Systems
Material: Anodized aluminum
Hardware
Manufacturer: Baldwin Hardware Corporation
Product: Estate Lever
Product number: 5115.264
Finish: Satin Chrome
Door Canopy (Lower Level)
Manufacturer: Michael Wentworth, Berkeley, California
Product: Custom
Material: Galvanized steel
Garage Door, Round House, Trellis, and Canopy Stain Color (Lower Level)
Manufacturer: Cabot
Product: Semi-Transparent Stain
Color name: Barn Red

Railing
Designer and Manufacturer: Michael Wentworth, Berkeley, California
Product: Custom
Material: Anodized aluminum

127

Field Paint Colors
Clapboard
Manufacturer: Benjamin Moore
Color number: HC-124
Color name: Caldwell Green
Stucco
Manufacturer: Benjamin Moore
Color number: 2156-40
Color name: August Morning
Window Frame Paint Color
Manufacturer: Benjamin Moore
Color number: 2143-70
Color name: Simply White
Door Paint Color
Manufacturer: Benjamin Moore
Color name: 2104-10
Color name: Pancake Syrup
Color-Embedded Stucco Portal and Window
Manufacturer: LaHabra
Number: X-40
Color name: Dove Grey (Base 200)
Mailbox
Manufacturer: Mahvelous Mailboxes
Product: Swedish Post
Finish: Satin Steel
Note: This is a similar product.
Light Fixture
Manufacturer: R.A.B. Lighting
Product: Vapor Proof Light, Wall Bracket Fixture
Note: This is a similar product.
Composition Asphalt Shingle Roofing
Manufacturer: CertainTeed
Product number: XT-25
Color name: Brick Red
Note: All my matches

128

Color-Embedded Stucco Field Colors
Color #1
Manufacturer: LaHabra
Number: X10182
Color name: Yellow
Color #2
Manufacturer: LaHabra
Number: X30080
Color name: Lighter "green"
Color #3
Manufacturer: LaHabra
Number: X80194
Color name: Darker "green"
Window
Manufacturer: All Weather Architectural Aluminum
Color name: White Powder Coat
Note: My match
Door Paint Color at Colonnade (Right)
Manufacturer: Benjamin Moore
Color number: EXT. RM.
Color name: Black Forest Green

French Doors off Terrace at Colonnade
Material: Douglas fir
Varnish
Manufacturer: Valspar Corporation
Product: McCloskey Man O'War Marine Spar Varnish
Color name: Clear
Finish: Satin
Garage Doors
Manufacturer: Amarr
Product: 12' tall commercial doors
Model number: 5642
Material: Painted galvanized steel
Color name: Gloss White
Note: My match. This is a similar product.
Warehouse Gooseneck Lighting
Manufacturers: Baselite Corp., Hi-Lite Manufacturing Co., or LSI Industries
Color name: White
Note: My matches. These are manufacturers who make similar products.
Composition Asphalt Shingle Roofing
Manufacturer: CertainTeed
Product number: XT25
Color name: Oakwood
Note: My match
Architect
Chris Volkamer
Volkamer Architecture
Oakland, California

129

Color-Embedded Stucco Field Color
Manufacturer: Dryvit Systems, Inc.
Number: 105
Color name: Suede
Window
Manufacturer: Blomberg Window Systems
Product: Casement windows
Finish: Double glazed aluminum powder coat with a clear anodized finish
Garage Door, Garage Door Frame, and Trim Paint Color
Match to:
Manufacturer: Dryvit
Color number: 105
Color name: Suede
Door
Manufacturer: Blomberg Window Systems
Finish: Double glazed aluminum powder coat with a clear anodized finish
Type: French door, narrow stile, swing in, with 2"x4" framing
Product: 8700 Series
Door Lever
Manufacturer: Omnia Industries, Inc.
Product: Lever latchset and lockset
Product number: 368
Finish: Polished chrome plate
Finish number: US26

Canopy
Manufacturer: Blank and Cables, Inc.
Product: Custom
Material: White laminated glass and metal
Designer: Veverka Architects, San Francisco, California
Sconce Lighting
Manufacturer: Kichler Lighting
Product: Outdoor, Bracket 1 Lt. Incandescent
Product number: 6040 NI
Finish: Brushed nickel
Patio and Floor Slate Tile
Source: Echeguren Slate
Color name: Vermont Black Slate
Architect
Jerry Veverka
Veverka Architects
San Francisco, California

130

Painted Brick Color
Manufacturer: Benjamin Moore
Color number: 241
Color name: Jonesboro Cream
Window and Portal Paint Color
Manufacturer: Benjamin Moore
Color number: OC-130
Color name: Cloud White
Door Paint Color
Manufacturer: Benjamin Moore
Color number: 487
Color name: Liberty Park
Note: All my matches

131

Facade
Material: Old red brick
Window, Window Frame, Door Frame, and Transom Paint Color
Manufacturer: Benjamin Moore
Color number: 942
Color name: Marble White
Door and Shutter Paint Color
Manufacturer: Benjamin Moore
Color number: 1582
Color name: Deep River
Note: All my matches
Steps
Material: Old white marble

132

Facade
Materials: Old red brick
Door, Door Frame, Window, Window Frame, Transom, Shutter, and Flower Box Paint Color
Manufacturer: Benjamin Moore
Color number: 1580
Color name: Intrigue
Note: My match
Steps, Foundation, Lintel, and Sill
Material: Old white marble

133

Painted Brick Color
Manufacturer: Duron (Division of Sherwin Williams Paint)
Color name: Custom

Tinting base: Deep base
One gallon formula:
B 1Y10
C 2Y43
F 2Y20
W 24

Window, Window Frame, Cornice, Balcony Railing, Hitching Post, and Stars Paint Color
Manufacturer: Benjamin Moore
Color number: 2120-10
Color name: Jet Black
Notes: My match. Balcony railing should receive an exterior rust-preventive, metal primer undercoat.

Garage Door
Manufacturer: Ranch House Doors
Product: Custom carriage house overhead door
Product number: RHD-413
Material: Cedar

Stain
Manufacturer: Wood Kote
Product: Jel'd Stain
Number: 204
Color name: Cherry

Hardware
Manufacturer: Ranch House Doors
Hardware numbers: Hinge #1 and Handle #9

Lighting
Manufacturer: Progress Lighting
Product: Wellbourne wall-mount lantern with clear beveled glass
Product number: P5886-31
Finish: Textured black

Urn Planters
Source: Urban Gardener
Product: Urn with handles
Material: Cast iron
Note: My match. Urns of this style are readily available at many garden centers.

134

Facade
Material: Limestone panels

4-Lite Door and Window Paint Color
Manufacturer: Finnaren and Haley Paints
Color number: AC076
Color name: Harbour Blue

135

Facade and Steps
Material: Old red brick

Window, Window Frame, Transom, and Door Frame Paint Color
Manufacturer: Finnaren and Haley Paints
Collection: Authentic Colors of Historic Philadelphia
Color name: Franklin White

Door Paint Color
Manufacturer: Finnaren and Haley Paints
Collection: Victorian Colors
Color name: Tiburon

Shutter Paint Color
Manufacturer: Finnaren and Haley Paints
Collection: Authentic Colors of Historic Philadelphia
Color name: Flintlock Gray

Light Fixture
Manufacturer: English Garden Furniture
Product: New England Wall Lantern
Finish: Black
Note: My match. This is a similar product.

136

Painted Brick Color
Manufacturer: Sherwin Williams
Color number: SW2368
Color name: Carpenter's Lace

Window, Window Frame, Transom, Lintel, Sill, and Shutter Paint Color
Manufacturer: Sherwin Williams
Color number: SW2254
Color name: Wilmington

Storm Door Paint Color
Manufacturer: Lowe's
Product: American Traditions Paint
Color name: Elizabeth Pink

Door Paint Color
Manufacturer: Lowe's
Product: American Traditions Paint
Color name: Harvest Sun

137

Facade
Materials: Old red brick

Window
Manufacturer: Marvin Windows
Product: Double-hung aluminum-clad windows
Color name: Pebble Gray

Window Frame Color
Manufacturer: Benjamin Moore
Color name: Custom
Note: Match to:
Manufacturer: Marvin Windows
Color name: Pebble Gray

Door
Manufacturer: Fiorella Woodworking
Product: Custom
Material: Solid black walnut

Stain
Manufacturer: Mohawk
Product: Wiping stain
Number: M545-207
Color name: Medium Brown

Varnish
Manufacturer: Benjamin Moore
Product number: 407
Product: Clear Varnish
Finish: Low-Lustre

Arched Portal, Shutters, Fanlight, Cornice, and Trim
Manufacturer: Finnaren & Haley
Color number: 8546-N
Color name: Sable Night

Door Hardware
Manufacturer: Baldwin Hardware Corporation

Collection: Estate Knob
Product number: 5000.260
Material: Polished chrome

Lintel, Sill, Foundation, and Steps
Material: Old white marble

Roof tile
Material: Gray Slate. Original to the old house.

138

Facade
Materials: Old red brick

Window, Window Frame, Lintel, Sill, Transom, and Door Frame Paint Color
Manufacturer: Benjamin Moore
Color number: OC-122
Color name: Cotton Balls

Door and Storm Door Paint Color
Manufacturer: Benjamin Moore
Color number: 482
Color name: Misted Ferns

Shutter and Flower Box Paint Color
Manufacturer: Benjamin Moore
Color number: 2120-10
Color name: Jet Black

Steps
Material: Old white marble
Note: All my matches

139

Facade
Materials: Old red brick

Door and Cornice Paint Color
Manufacturer: Benjamin Moore
Color name: Custom "blue"
Tinting base: N096-4B
One gallon formula:
BB 3 x 12
WH 20
RD 14
MA 2 x 1

Window
Manufacturer: Marvin Windows and Doors
Product: Color clad aluminum extruded windows
Type: Double hung
Color: Ebony
Note: My match

Window Covering
Manufacturer: Castec, Inc.
Product: Flat Roman Shades
Product number: 101 Pacifica
Material: Natural cotton duck
Note: My match

Lintel, Sill, Foundation, and Steps
Material: Old white marble

140

Field Paint Colors
First Story
Manufacturer: Benjamin Moore
Color number: 460
Color name: Herb Bouquet
Second Story
Manufacturer: Benjamin Moore
Color number: 514
Color name: Flowering Herbs
Window
Manufacturer: Milgard Windows
Product Classic series vinyl window

dow
Type: Double hung
Color name: White

Door
Material: Brazilian Cedar
Finish
Manufacturer: Watco
Product: Exterior Wood Finish (Oil Based)
Color name: Cedar

Gooseneck Light Fixtures
Manufacturer: LSI Industries
Product: Abolite Angled Reflector
Product number: AD-150
Material: Galvanized steel

Gooseneck Bracket
Finish: Painted natural aluminum
Note: This is a similar product.
Note: All my matches

141

Field Paint Color
Manufacturer: ICI
Color number: 611
Color name: Sea Gull Grey

Window, Window Frame, Door Frame, Sidelights, and Ceiling (in Entry) Paint Color
Manufacturer: ICI
Color number: 659
Color name: Prism White
Finish: Gloss

Door Paint Color
Manufacturer: ICI
Color number: 1178
Color name: Tavern Green

Roof Tile
Material: Natural cedar shingle
Note: All my matches

142

Field Paint Color
Manufacturer: Benjamin Moore
Color number: HC-28
Color name: Shelbourne Buff

Door, Window, Window Frame, and Trim Paint Color
Manufacturer: Benjamin Moore
Color number: OC-124
Color name: Alpine White
Note: My match

Whitewashed Shutters
Material: Whitewashed fir

First-Coat Stain
Manufacturer: Cabot
Product: Semi-Solid Stain
Color name: Bark

Second-Coat Stain
Manufacturer: Cabot
Product: Semi-Solid Stain
Number: WH/10X
Color name: Custom White
Note: The first coat should be left to dry for one week. The second coat is then applied heavily and left to dry overnight. The following day, the stained top coat is wiped off with rags in the direction of the grain of the wood. Areas that are too dry should be wiped down with a rag soaked with with paint thinner. My match.

Planter
Manufacturer: www.plantcontainers.com
Product: Taper Square Ceramic Planter
Product number: IRTS -17
Material: Ironstone
Color name: Espresso
Note: My match. This is a similar product.

Paver
Material: Decomposed crushed granite

143

Field Paint Color
Manufacturer: Benjamin Moore
Color name: Custom
Tinting base: N105-4B
One gallon formula:
OY 22
BK 6 x 16
TG 2 x 18
YW 10
WH 8

Window, Window Frame, and Cornice Paint Color
Manufacturer: Benjamin Moore
Color name: Custom
Tinting base: 309-4B
One gallon formula:
OY 22
BK 6 x 28
TG 2 x 28
YW 18
WH 30

Door
Material: Oak

Stain
Manufacturer: Cabot
Product: Semi-Solid Stain
Color name: Spanish Moss

Sealer
Manufacturer: Penofin
Product: Original Blue Label Oil Wood Finish Penetrating Sealer
Color Name: Clear
Note: My match

Portal Paint Color
Manufacturer: Benjamin Moore
Product: Oil-Based Alkyd Paint
Color number: OC-95
Color name: Navajo White

Steps
Material: Red brick
Note: Also foundation wall

Roof Tile
Type: Natural Cedar Shingles

144

Field Paint Color
Manufacturer: Benjamin Moore
Color number: 1537
Color name: River Gorge Gray

Window and Window Frame Paint Color
Manufacturer: Benjamin Moore
Color number: HC-83
Color name: Grant Beige

Door Paint Color
Manufacturer: Benjamin Moore
Color number: 2067-30
Color name: Twilight Blue

Quoin (on Corners of House) Paint Color
Mix together the following:

3 pints of:
Manufacturer: Benjamin Moore
Color number: 1537
Color name: River Gorge Gray
1 pint of:
Manufacturer: Benjamin Moore
Color number: HC-83
Color name: Grant Beige

Two Tone Shutter Paint Color
Shutter
Manufacturer: Benjamin Moore
Color number: 1.5X HC-83
Color name: Grant Beige
Shutter Frame
Manufacturer: Benjamin Moore
Color number: HC-83
Color name: Grant Beige

Garage Paint Color (Not Shown)
Mix together the following:
1 pint of:
Manufacturer: Benjamin Moore
Color number: 1537
Color name: River Gorge Gray
and
1 pint of:
Manufacturer: Benjamin Moore
Color number: HC-83
Color name: Grant Beige

Composition Asphalt Shingle
Manufacturer: CertainTeed
Product: Presidential Shake
Color name: Weathered Wood
Note: My match

Color Consultant
David vanDommelen
vanDommelen Colorworks
San Francisco, California

145

Field Paint Colors
Upper
Manufacturer: Benjamin Moore
Color number: HC-101
Color name: Hampshire Gray
Lower (Including Garage Doors)
Manufacturer: Benjamin Moore
Color number: HC-100
Color name: Gloucester Sage

Window, Window Frame, and Recessed Entry Paint Color
Manufacturer: Benjamin Moore
Color name: Linen White

Door (Not Seen in Photo) and Balcony Paint Color
Manufacturer: Benjamin Moore
Color number: 2139-10
Color name: River Rock
Note: Use exterior protective undercoat metal primer for wrought iron balcony railings.

Horizontal Accent Trim and Lunette Paint Colors
Manufacturer: Benjamin Moore
Color number: HC-102
Color name: Clarksville Gray
Note: Lunettes are the half-circle spaces above the french windows.

Color Consultant
Garry Bratman
Raleigh, North Carolina

146

Field Paint Color
Manufacturer: Benjamin Moore
Color number: HC-109
Color name: Sussex Green

Portico, Window, Window Frame, Lunette, and Garage Door (Not Shown) Paint Color
Manufacturer: Benjamin Moore
Color number: OC-95
Color name: Navajo White

Door Paint Color
Manufacturer: Fine Paints of Europe
Product: Exterior Hollandlac Traditional Oil Paint
Color name: Custom
Finish: Hollandlac Brilliant
Mix together:
2/3 Black, #0029
1/3 Coach Green, #3088
Note: Fine Paints of Europe colors

Railing Paint Color
Manufacturer: Benjamin Moore
Color number: 2120-10
Color name: Jet Black
Note: My match. Use exterior protective undercoat metal primer.

147

Field Paint Color
Manufacturer: Benjamin Moore
Color number: 2139-20
Color name: Dakota Woods Green

Door, Garage Door, Window, and Window Frame Paint Color
Manufacturer: Benjamin Moore
Color number: 2111-40
Color name: Taos Taupe

Projecting Eave Paint Color
Manufacturer: Benjamin Moore
Color number: 2168-10
Color name: Fall Harvest

Doorbell
Manufacturer: spOre, Inc.
Product: Square Illuminated Doorbell Button
Product number: dbs-a
Button color: Amber
Material: Anodized aluminum and rubber button

Door Handle Set
Manufacturer: Double Hill Hardware
Product: Euro-Style Handle Set/Manchester
Product number: Series E1200, US-26
Finish: Brushed chrome

Sconce Lights (over Garage Doors)
Manufacturer: Hubbardton Forge
Product: Outdoor Sconce, Banded
Product number: 30-5892
Material: Aluminum
Finish: Natural Iron
Glass: White art glass
Note: My match

House Number Plaque
Product: Custom

Font: Hercules
Finish: Stainless Steel

Custom Airplane Hangar Window
Manufacturer: Schweiss
Product: 10'x10' Bi-Fold Doors

Backyard Decking
Material: Brazilian hardwood

Composition Asphalt Shingle Roofing
Manufacturer: CertainTeed
Product: Landmark Premium
Color name: Graphite

Outdoor Dining Chairs
Material: Fiberglass-infused polypropylene
Manufacturer: Design Within Reach
Product name: Air Chair
Color name: Orange

Landscape Architect
Jeff Miller
Miller Company
San Francisco, California

148

Field Paint Color
Manufacturer: Kelly-Moore
Color number: 211
Color name: Delta Blue

Door, Window, Window Frame, and Trim Paint Color
Manufacturer: Kelly Moore
Color number: 14
Color name: Frost

Metallic Door Trim
Manufacturer: Modern Masters, Inc.
Product: Metallic Paint
Product number: ME 289
Color name: Brass
Note: My match

149

Field and Garage Door Paint Color
Manufacturer: ICI
Color number: 598
Color name: Great Desert

Window, Window Frame, and Portico Paint Color
Manufacturer: Benjamin Moore
Color number: OC-95
Color name: Navajo White

Door Paint Color
Manufacturer: ICI
Color number: 60
Color name: Aberdeen Place

Composition Asphalt Shingle Roofing
Manufacturer: CertainTeed
Product: Landmark Series
Color name: Terra Cotta
Note: My match

Design and Color Consultant
Susan Bottorf and Art Chinn
Garner Chinn 8
Oakland, California

150

Cedar Shingle Stain Color
Manufacturer: Cabot
Product: Semi-Solid Stain
Color name: Black
Note: My match

Cornice Paint Color
Manufacturer: Benjamin Moore
Color Number: EXT. RM.
Color name: Black

Window and Window Frame Color
Manufacturer: Benjamin Moore
Color number: OC-121
Color name: Mountain Peak White
Note: My match

151

Field Paint Color
Manufacturer: Benjamin Moore
Color number: 445
Color name: Greenwich Village

Door, Window, Gate, and Garage Door Paint Color
Manufacturer: Benjamin Moore
Color number: 1428
Color name: Wood Violet
Note: Use exterior metal primer undercoat on metal gate.

Window Frame and Arched Entry Paint Color
Manufacturer: Benjamin Moore
Color number: 211
Color name: Fresh Air

Roof Tile
Material: Terra-cotta clay

Pavers
Material: Red brick

152

Upper Field Paint Colors
Clapboard Basecoat
Manufacturer: Fuller O'Brien
Color number: 5W9-6
Color name: Fiery Orange
Clapboard Reveal Lines and Circular Window Frame Paint Color
Manufacturer: Fuller O'Brien
Color number: 4WA24-3
Color name: Canyon Red
Overcoat for Clapboard, Reveal Lines, and Circular Window Frame (Next 5–10 Coats of Paint)
Instructions: To apply, start with Fiery Orange and add Canyon Red and water to each subsequent coat of glaze to thin it out. For each coat, the mixture is stippled or brushed on in small sections with a specialist stippling brush, moving quickly to keep the formula wet before rolling or brushing out an adjacent area. Working in two-foot-diameter areas keeps the color consistent and smooth.

Lower Field Paint Color
Brick Basecoat
Manufacturer: Sherwin Williams
Color number: 5WA22-6
Color name: Ebony Brown
Overcoat (Rolled Lightly over the Ebony Brown)
Manufacturer: Fuller O'Brien
Color name: Shadow Olive

Stenciled Wall at Entry
Base Coat
Manufacturer: Sherwin Williams
Color number: 4WA24-3
Color name: Canyon Red

Stencil
Manufacturer: Fuller O'Brien
Color number: 5WA22
Color name: Ebony Brown
Instructions: Stenciling is achieved by cutting out a pattern with a craft knife into a thick, flexible plastic sheet. Run a dry roller of paint over the template to stencil.

Stenciled Floor at Entry
Colors
Manufacturer: Fuller O'Brien
Color number: 5WA22-6
Color name: Ebony Brown
and
Manufacturer: Fuller O'Brien
Color number: 1W23-5
Color name: Spanish Moon

Whitewash
Manufacturer: Cabot
Product: Semi-Solid Stain
Color number: WH/10X
Color name: Custom White

Instructions: Stenciling is achieved by cutting out a pattern with a craft knife into a thick plastic sheet to make a pattern. Run a dry roller of Ebony Brown paint over the template to stencil. Water down the Spanish Moon paint color, apply with a brush around stenciled pattern, and soften with a sponge. When dry (wait at least a day), whitewash the finished product by applying one coat lightly and wiping off stain with rags before it dries to a transparent film.
Note: My match and instructions.

Hand-Painted Panel at Balcony
Note: All house colors were used to paint the design.

Door, Window, and Window Frame Paint Color
Manufacturer: Fuller O'Brien
Color number: 5WA22-6
Color name: Ebony Brown

Balcony and Stair Railing
Manufacturer: Triangle Coatings, Inc.
Product: Metallic Surfacer
Finish: Iron

Wrought Iron Railing Top Coat
Manufacturer: Triangle Coatings, Inc.
Product: Antiquing Solution
Color: Rust

Brick Steps
Manufacturer: Minwax
Color: Red Oak Stain
Note: This product deepens and glazes the red brick.

153

Field Paint Color
Mix together the following:
50% of:
Manufacturer: Pratt & Lambert
Color number: 2252
Color name: Whale
and
50% of:
Manufacturer: Pratt & Lambert
Color number: 2253

Color name: Zinc

Window, Window Frame, Door Frame, Gate, and Gutter Paint Color
Manufacturer: Benjamin Moore
Color name: INT. RM.
Color name: Atrium White
Note: Mix interior color into exterior paint product.

Door
Material: Original old oak

Planter
Product: Zinc Garden Ornaments Square Planter Box
Product number: Z6
Source: Authentic Provence
Note: My match

Cherry Tree
Type: Akebono Flowering Cherry; also referred to as "Daybreak"

154

Field Paint Color
Manufacturer: Benjamin Moore
Color number: HC-80
Color name: Bleeker Beige

Window, Window Frame, and Cornice Paint Color
Manufacturer: Benjamin Moore
Color number: HC-81
Color name: Manchester Tan

Door and Recessed Entry Paint Color
Manufacturer: Pratt & Lambert
Color number: 1750
Color name: Canary Yellow

Door
Manufacturer: Simpson Door Co.
Material: Douglas fir
Product: 5-Lite Door, View Saver Single Glazing
Product number: 1505
Glass: Lightly etched
Note: My match

Stenciled House Numbers Paint Color
Manufacturer: Benjamin Moore
Product number: 2002-10
Color name: Vermillion
Finish: Gloss
Note: My match. Ask to deepen the color at paint store.

Mailbox
Manufacturer: www.mailboxes.com
Product: Standard—vertical style
Product number: 4520
Material: Stainless steel

Pendant Light Fixture
Manufacturer: Sonneman
Product: Ventilator Ceiling Pendant
Product number: SON-3110
Material: Stainless steel and etched glass
Note: This light fixture may not be UL approved for all exterior locations.
This is a option that is UL approved:
Manufacturer: Louis Poulsen
Product: Nyhavn Maxi Pendant, Outdoor
Finish: Natural aluminum

Note: My match

Design and Color Consultant
Stephen Moore
Stephen Moore Interior Design
San Francisco, California

155

Field Paint Color
Manufacturer: Kelly-Moore
Color name: Custom
Tinting base: 1240-222
One gallon formula:
B Y-16
C Y40
I 10
L 2Y24

Window, Window Frame, Door Frame, Sidelight, Cornice, and Picket Fence Paint Color
Manufacturer: Kelly-Moore
Color number: 45
Color name: White Swan

Door and Shutter Paint Color
Manufacturer: Benjamin Moore
Color name: Custom
Tinting base: N096-4B
One gallon formula:
RX 1 x 15
BB 3 x 24
TG 3 x 12
WH 4 x 2
BK 1 x 18
YW 11 1/2
OG 6

Pavers
Material: Gray Flagstone

156

House
Field Paint Color
Manufacturer: Kelly-Moore
Color number: KM696-D
Color name: Madison Avenue

Window, Window Frame, Cornice, Portico, and Trim Paint Color
Manufacturer: Benjamin Moore
Color number: INT. RM.
Color name: Linen White
Note: Mix interior color into exterior paint product.

Door Paint Color
Manufacturer: Benjamin Moore
Color number: 1267
Color name: Ruby Dusk

Square Red Dot Door Mat
Source: Ikea

Studio
Color-Embedded Stucco Field Color (First Floor)
Manufacturer: LaHabra
Number: X-73 (Base 100)
Color name: Shell
Note: My match

Field Paint Color (Second Floor)
Manufacturer: Kelly-Moore
Color number: KM996-M
Color name: Hawaiian Luau

Door Paint Color (First Floor)
Manufacturer: Benjamin Moore
Color number: 2152-70
Color name: Mayonnaise
Note: my match

Door Paint Color (Second Floor)
50% of:
Manufacturer: Benjamin Moore
Color number: 1537
Color name: River Gorge Gray
Note: My match

Garage Door
Manufacturer: Amarr Garage Doors
Product: Heritage, Prairie Style
Color name: Almond

Trim Paint Color (House and Studio)
Manufacturer: Benjamin Moore
Product number: INT. RM.
Color name: Linen White
Note: Mix interior color into exterior paint product.

Sculptural Railing and Bridge
Designer and Manufacturer: Kyle Reicher/Metal Artist
Product: Custom
Materials: Steel rebar and Pau Lope Brazilian hardwood (Ipe)
Paint Color
Manufacturer: Benjamin Moore
Product: Ready Mixed "Iron Clad" Low Lustre Metal and Wood Enamel
Color name: Deep Bronze
Note: Available in quart size only.

Porch, Porch Steps, and Bridge Floor Boards
Material: Pau Lope Brazilian hardwood (Ipe)
Protective Coat
Manufacturer: Cabot
Product: Australian Timber Oil
Color name: Natural

Mailbox
Manufacturer: Smith & Hawken
Product: Small copper wall-mounted mailbox
Product number: #671487

Wall Plaque in Garden
Manufacturer: Fly Creek Studio
Product: Drawings in Clay—Incised Tablet Panels
Material: Ceramic or acrylic modified plaster with iron oxide pigment

Composition Asphalt Shingle Roofing
Manufacturer: CertainTeed
Product: Landmark TL
Color name: Weathered Wood

157

Field Paint Color
Manufacturer: Benjamin Moore
Color number: HC-107
Color name: Gettysburg Gray

Window, Window Frame, and Projecting Eave Paint Color
Manufacturer: Benjamin Moore
Color number: OC-95
Color name: Navajo White

Door Paint Color
Manufacturer: Martin Senour
Color number: 323-6
Color name: Carpathian Green

Horizontal Trim (at Cornice and below Second Story Window) and Foundation Paint Color
Manufacturer: Benjamin Moore
Color number: HC-100
Color name: Gloucester Sage

Crown Molding Paint Color (on Projecting Eaves)
Manufacturer: Benjamin Moore
Color number: 2072-20
Color name: Black Raspberry

Trellis, Railings, and Awning
Manufacturer: Nueva Castilla
Material: Wrought iron (awning also made with etched glass)
Paint Color
Manufacturer: Benjamin Moore
Color number: 2072-10
Color name: Dark Basalt
Note: Use rust preventive primer for trellis and railings.
Designer
Penelope Di Paoli, Design Planning, San Francisco, California

Pavers
Material: Red brick
Designer
Penelope Di Paoli
Design Planning
San Francisco, California

158

Field and Window Paint Color
Manufacturer: Benjamin Moore
Color number: 1054
Color name: Sherwood Tan

Window Frame and Trellis Paint Color
Manufacturer: Benjamin Moore
Color number: 1000
Color name: Northwood Brown

Door Paint Color
Manufacturer: Benjamin Moore
Color number: 1308
Color name: Red Parrot

Pavers and Paving
Materials: Concrete paving and half bricks
Half Bricks (Brick and Path)
Manufacturer: McNear Brick & Block
Product: Splits
Color name: Sepia
Note: Bricks can be applied onto the existing concrete.

Designer and Color Consultant
John Wheatman
John Wheatman Associates
San Francisco, California

Landscape Designer
Jay Thayer
San Francisco, California

159

Stucco Paint Color
Manufacturer: Benjamin Moore
Color name: Custom
Tinting base: N105-2B
One gallon formula:
OY 1 x 4
BK 10
GY 24
BR 9
RX 2

OG 3/4
TG 1/2

Brick Facade, Chimney Stack, and Gate Support Pedestals
Material: Old clinker brick

Metal Window (and Frames Where Applicable) Paint Color
Manufacturer: Benjamin Moore
Color name: Custom "lighter green"
Tinting base: N096-3B
One gallon formula:
OY 2X28
RX 2 1/4
BK 2X15
WH 3X16
TG 10
BB 5
MA 1
Note: Prep with exterior metal primer product.

Portal Surround
Material: Limestone

Half-Timber, Wrought Iron Gate, and French Doors (in Courtyard) Paint Color
Manufacturer: Benjamin Moore
Color number: HC-69
Color name: Whitall Brown
Note: Prep wrought iron gates with exterior metal primer product.

Garage Door, Bay Window (and Window Between), and Two-Story Window (in Courtyard) Paint Color
Manufacturer: Benjamin Moore
Color name: Custom "darker green"
Tinting base: 333-3B
One quart formula:
BK 27
BR .25
OY 1 x 2
TG 1.50

Roof Tile
Material: Natural cedar shingles

160

Brick Facade
Material: Antique reclaimed brick
Source: Gavin Historical Brick
Product name: Old colonial brick
Note: My match

Stucco Paint Color
Manufacturer: Benjamin Moore
Color name: Custom
Tinting base: N103-2B
One gallon formula:
OY 2x
BK 1 x 2
RX 0 x 4 1/4
GY 0 x 18

Window Paint Color
Manufacturer: Benjamin Moore
Color number: EXT. RM.
Color name: Country Redwood

Door
Material: Oak
Stain
Manufacturer: Cabot
Product: Semi-Solid Stain
Color name: Oak Brown
Protectant

Manufacturer: Cabot
Product: Harbor Master
Polyurethane
Finish: Satin
Note: My match

Half-Timber and Trim Paint Color
Manufacturer: Benjamin Moore
Color name: Custom
Tinting base: N096-3B
One gallon formula:
OY 3 x 12
RD 0 x 24
BK 2 x 12

Roof Tile
Material: Natural cedar shingles

161

Painted Brick Field Color
Manufacturer: Sherwin Williams
Color number: SW7008
Color name: Alabaster

Entry Door, French Door (off of Patio), and Window Frame Paint Color
Manufacturer: Sherwin Williams
Color number: SW6216
Color name: Jasper
Note: All are leaded glass windows.

Entry Light Fixture
Manufacturer: English Garden Furniture, San Rafael, California
Note: Similar product. My match.

Roof Tile
Material: Natural cedar shake

Pavers (Patio)
Material: Square concrete stepping-stones

Pavers (Entry and Steps)
Material: Antique reclaimed brick
Available from: Gavin Historical Brick
Note: Check for local sources. Brick has been used as a border for the diamond pattern concrete path. My match.

162

Stucco Paint Color
Manufacturer: Benjamin Moore
Color name: Custom
Tinting base: N105 3B
One gallon formula:
GY 31
OY 1 x 20
OG 1 x
BK 20

Chimney Brick
Source: Gavin Historical Brick
Product name: Old Crandic Depot Brick
Note: My match

Window and Half-Timber Frame Paint Color
Manufacturer: Benjamin Moore
Color number: 1477
Color name: Deep Creek
Note: Leaded-glass windows.

Door
Material: Old oak

Stain
Manufacturer: ZAR
Product: Oil-based wood stain
Color Name: Rosewood 124

Cast Stone Portal Surround and Picture Window Trim Paint Color
Manufacturer: Benjamin Moore
Color number: 1123
Color name: Palm Desert Tan
Note: Painted on faux stone

Entry Paver
Material: Red brick

Railing
Material: Wrought iron

Paint Color
Manufacturer: Benjamin Moore
Color number: 1477
Color name: Deep Creek
Note: Use exterior rust preventive undercoat primer.

Composition Asphalt Shingle Roofing
Manufacturer: CertainTeed
Product number: XT30
Color name: Bronzed Brown
Note: My match

163

Stucco and Cedar Shingle Paint Color
Manufacturer: Benjamin Moore
Color number: 2098-10
Color name: Barrel Brown

Window, Frames, Columns, and Half-Timber Paint Color
Manufacturer: Benjamin Moore
Color number: OC-95
Color name: Navajo White

Brick
Source: Gavin Historical Brick
Product name: South Bend Paver
Note: All my matches

164

Stucco Paint Color
Manufacturer: Kelly-Moore
Color number: AC-18N
Color name: Russet Red

Door and Window Paint Color
Manufacturer: Kelly-Moore
Color number: KM503-M
Color name: Joshua Tree

Half-Timber and Window Frame Paint Color
Manufacturer: Kelly-Moore
Color number: AC-90N
Color name: Vermeer's Fields

Composition Asphalt Shingle Roofing
Manufacturer: CertainTeed
Product: Landmark Premium
Color name: Hearthstone
Note: This selection is different than photo.

165

Stucco Paint Color
Manufacturer: Kelly-Moore
Color number: KM693-L
Color name: Pewter Pot

Window and Window Frame Paint Color
Manufacturer: Kelly-Moore
Color number: 25
Color name: Blanco

Door Shutters and Half-Timber Paint Color
Manufacturer: Kelly-Moore
Color number: 174
Color name: Charcoal Gray

Composition Asphalt Shingle Roofing
Manufacturer: CertainTeed
Product name: Landmark Series
Color name: Colonial Slate
Note: My match

Pavers
Materials: Red brick; square and rectangular concrete pavers
Note: All my matches

166

Stone Facing
Material: Wissahickon schist
Note: Available at: Chestnut Hill Stone, Ltd. Glenside, Pennsylvania
Note: Home also features old red brick on the facade.

Stucco Paint Color
Manufacturer: Benjamin Moore
Color number: 194
Color name: Hathaway Gold
Note: My match

Window and Mud Room Paint Color
Manufacturer: Benjamin Moore
Color number: OC-95
Color name: Navajo White
Note: Large picture window is Benjamin Moore, Tudor Brown.
Note: My match

Window Frame, Half-Timber and Clapboard Siding Paint Color
Manufacturer: Benjamin Moore
Color number: EXT. RM.
Color name: Tudor Brown
Note: My match

Door
Material: Old oak

Varnish
Manufacturer: McCloskey
Product: Man O'War Spar Marine Varnish
Note: The finish has naturally yellowed over time. My match.

Ceramic Tile in Mud Room
Manufacturer: The Moravian Pottery and Tile Works
Product: 2"x2" quarry pavers
Finish: Smoked
Note: These are reproductions of the work of Henry Mercer of Doylestown, Pennsylvania.

Roof Tile
Product: Slate.
Note: Original to old house

167

Stucco Paint Color
Manufacturer: Fuller O'Brien
Color number: 2W17-4
Color name: Chatham Tan

Window and Door (Not Shown) Paint Color
Manufacturer: Fuller O'Brien
Color number: 2C19-5
Color name: Iron Sides

Window Frame and Trim Paint Color
Manufacturer: Fuller O'Brien
Color number: 5WA22-6
Color name: Ebony Brown

Roof Tile
Source: Eurocal Slate Centers
Product: Slate tile
Product number: RBC101
Color name: China Multicolor

Paving
Manufacturer: Matcrete Decorative Concrete Products
Product: Stamped concrete
Pattern: UK Cobblestone
Color name: Gray Stone

Sealer
Name: Conseal
Note: Product available from Matcrete. Dries to a clear transparent finish. Cures, seals and waterproofs.
Instructions: The concrete is placed in forms in a conventional manner and then screed and floated to a level surface. Dry-shake color hardener is applied. When the concrete has set to the right consistency, a colored mold is applied, which starts the stamping process. The concrete is cured for two to three days, and then is swept and washed off to expose the finished product. See manufacturer's Web site for more detailed information on this process. Color is my match.

168

Stucco Paint Color
Manufacturer: Kelly-Moore
Color name: Custom
Product: Terpolymer Elastomeric Paint
Tinting base: Deep base, 05-1097
Five gallon formula:
B 5
F 30
C 3Y16
LY 19
KX 30

Door, Window, Window Frame, Half-Timber, and Chevron Pattern (on Panel) Paint Color
Manufacturer: Kelly-Moore
Color name: Custom
Medium base: 1250-222
One gallon formula:
B 4
I 16
C 3Y
L 2Y28
Note: Most windows are leaded glass.

Pavers
Material: Antique reclaimed brick
Source: Gavin Historical Brick
Note: My match. Check for local sources.

Roof Tile
Manufacturer: DaVinci Roofscapes
Product: Slate Shingles
Color name: European Blend

169

Stucco Paint Color
Manufacturer: Kelly Moore
Color name: Custom
Product: Elastomeric Paint
Tinting base: 1118-331
One gallon formula:
C 29
L 24
I 4 1/2

Window, Window Frame, and Trim Paint Color
Manufacturer: Benjamin Moore
Color number: EXT. RM.
Color name: Black Forest Green

Window Sill Paint Color
Manufacturer: Benjamin Moore
Color number: EXT. RM.
Color name: Chrome Green
Note: My match

Cast Stone Portal Surround and Shutter Paint Color
Manufacturer: Benjamin Moore
Color number: EXT. RM.
Color name: Country Redwood

Half-Timber and Shutter Frame Stain Color
Manufacturer: Cabot
Color name: Custom
Tinting base: 6306
One gallon formula:
B 25
C Y32
F Y3
KX 12

Door Wreath
Product: Handmade by homeowner
Material: Grape vine wreath and decorative materials from a craft store

Roof Tile
Material: Natural cedar shingle

Pavers
Material: Red brick

Paving
Manufacturer: Davis Colors
Product: Colored concrete
Level: Premium
Color number: 1117
Color name: Tile red
Note: Original to the house
Note: My match

Color Consultant
Bob Crowe
Color Therapy for Your Walls
Oakland, California

170

Stucco Paint Colors
Upper
Manufacturer: Benjamin Moore
Color name: Custom
Tinting base: N103-3B
One gallon formula:
OY 2X
RX 27
BB 26
TG 6

MA 6
WH 3X
Lower
Manufacturer: Benjamin Moore
Color: Custom
Tinting base: N103-3B
One gallon formula:
OY 1 x 15
RX 7.75
BK 1 x 1
GY 1 x 1
WH 1 x 8
Window Paint Color
Manufacturer: Benjamin Moore
Color name: Custom
Tinting base: N096-1B
One gallon formula:
0Y 1 x 15
RX 2
BK 5
GY 2
Window Frame (Interior), Projecting Eave, Door, and Garage Door Paint Color
Manufacturer: Benjamin Moore
Color name: Custom "red"
Tinting base: N103-4B
One gallon formula:
0Y 2 x 16
MA 5 x 8
BK 2 x 8
OG 1x
WH 16
RX 1 x 8
Door and Garage Door Frame, Half-Timber, and Trim Paint Color
Manufacturer: Benjamin Moore
Color number: EXT. RM.
Color name: Black Forest Green
Pavers
Material: Red brick
Color Consultant
Bob Buckter
San Francisco, California

171

Faux Finish (on Stucco) Paint Color
Base Coat
Manufacturer: Sherwin Williams
Product: Elastomeric Paint
Color number: SW6381
Color name: Anjou Pear
Color Wash/Tinted Sealer
Instructions: There is no exact formula because it was mixed at the job site by professional faux painters, but the color wash is a bright orange made from a combination of the following colorants:
Manufacturers: Benjamin Moore and/or Kelly Moore paints
Product: Universal Colorants
Colors: Orange, light-fast yellow, raw umber (universal colorants)
Colorants are mixed into:
Manufacturer: UGL
Product: DryLok Masonry Treatment (a clear acrylic sealer)
Note: The more layers of sealer that are used, the more intense the color will become. This is a labor-intensive process, but once completed, it requires little care.

The color can be maintained by periodically using clear caulk in new cracks in the stucco and applying untinted DryLok Sealer every two to three years over all of the painted surfaces.

Window Paint Color
Manufacturer: Sherwin Williams
Color number: SW2816
Color name: Rookwood Dark Green
Note: The exception is the large picture window, which is stained with TWP Black Walnut. My match.

Window Frame, Half-Timber, and Exposed Rafters Paint Color
Manufacturer: TWP (Total Wood Preservative)
Product: 100 Series
Number: 104
Color name: Black Walnut

Two Entry Doors
Material: Mahogany
Finish
Note: One coat of sprayed-on varnish
Manufacturer: Pratt & Lambert
Product: Vitralite Spar Varnish
Color name: Clear
Note: Both doors are the same finish but the leaded-glass door has been bleached from direct sun exposure.

Roof Tile
Note: The multicolored slate roof tiles are vintage and are original to the house (built in 1929). They have a fishscale pattern. Similar product is available from American Slate Company.

Pavers and Steps
Material: Old uncut, no-course stone

Stone Walls
Material: Old rough-cut, irregular course and uncut, no-course rubble

Architectural Color Consultant and Specialist Painters
Sharon Stanbridge
Caton & Associates
Emeryville, California

172

Stucco Paint Color
Manufacturer: Pratt & Lambert
Color number: 2267
Color name: Clove Dust

Half-Timber and Garage Door Paint Color
Manufacturer: Pratt & Lambert
Color number: 2260
Color name: Stonehenge

Door
Material: Old oak
Protectant
Manufacturer: TWP (Total Wood Protectant)
Product: TWP 200 Series
Color name: Natural
Note: My match

Composition Asphalt Shingle Roofing
Manufacturer: CertainTeed
Product: Landmark Series

Color name: Black Walnut
Note: My match
Windows and Back Door Paint Color
Manufacturer: Pratt & Lambert
Color number: 2007
Color name: Sequoia

Pavers (Backyard)
Material: Arizona Flagstone
Note: My match

Color Consultant
Una Gallagher
Metamorphose Interiors
Felton, California

173

Field Paint Color
Manufacturer: Behr
Color name: Custom "red"
Tinting base: 5340, deep
One quart formula:
C 24 1/96
KX 20 1/96
L 16 1/96
V 1Y34

Window Frame, Door Frame, Porch Railing, and Step Risers Paint Color
Manufacturer: Behr
Color name: Custom "yellow"
Tinting base: 5450, pure white
One quart formula:
F 1/96
T 26 1/96

Door and Window Paint Color
Manufacturer: Behr
Color name: Custom "green"
Tinting base: 5340, deep
One quart formula:
AX 5
D 5 1/96
KX 11
L 2Y1
Note: These are all quart formulas. They can easily be turned into gallon formulas at the paint center.

My alternate color matches:
Field Paint Color
Manufacturer: Benjamin Moore
Color number: 2085-20
Color name: Pottery Red
Note: My match

Window Frame, Door Frame, Porch Railing, and Step Risers Paint Color
Manufacturer: Benjamin Moore
Color number: 2155-50
Color name: Suntan Yellow
Note: My match

Door and Window Paint Color
Manufacturer: Behr
Color number: 2139-20
Color name: Dakota Woods Green
Note: My match

Porch Floor Paint Color
Manufacturer: Behr
Product: Porch & Floor Collection
Color number: PPF-43
Color name: Shady Oak
Note: My match

Hanging Light Pendant
Manufacturer: Arroyo Craftsman
Product: Berkeley
Color number: BH-8WO-G

Glass: White Opalescent
Finish: Graphite metal
Note: My match

174

Field Paint Color
Manufacturer: Fuller O'Brien
Color number: 2C20-4
Color name: Rosemary Gray

Windows, Window Frames, Door Frame, Sidelights, Picket Fence, and Trellis Paint Color
Manufacturer: Fuller O'Brien
Color number: 2C20-1
Color name: Woodland Snow

Door, Screen Door, and Shutter Paint Color
Manufacturer: Fuller O'Brien
Color number: 2C20-6
Color name: Northwest Green

175

Field Paint Color
Manufacturer: Benjamin Moore
Color number: 508
Color name: Tree Moss

Window, Window Frame, and Trim Paint Color
Manufacturer: Benjamin Moore
Color number: 512
Color name: Light Breeze

Door Paint Color
Manufacturer: Benjamin Moore
Color number: EXT. RM.
Color name: Black

Door Handle Set
Manufacturer: Kwikset
Product: Ultramax Signature, Sheridan
Finish: Polished Chrome

Steps
Material: Existing terrazzo
Color name: Cream
Note: My match

176

Field Paint Color
Manufacturer: ICI
Color name: Custom "thalo blue"
Tinting base: SA 1345 Clear
One gallon formula:
BLK 1 P59
TBL 5 P27
MAG 3 P6
WHT 1 P36
Note: This custom formula was matched to:
Manufacturer: Ralph Lauren
Product number: TH64
Product name: Yacht Blue
Note: This is an interior color but can be matched to any exterior paint manufacturer. Ralph Lauren makes interior paint only.

Window Paint Color
Manufacturer: Benjamin Moore
Color number: 2114-10
Color name: Bittersweet Chocolate

Window Frame Paint Color
Manufacturer: ICI
Color number: 610

Color name: Sisal
Lightest Trim Paint Color
Manufacturer: ICI
Color number: 713
Color name: Georgian Ivory

Door and Molding Paint Color
Manufacturer: Benjamin Moore
Color number: 2093-10
Color name: Cimarron

Dentil Paint Color
Manufacturer: ICI
Color number: 609
Color name: Honeybee

Composition Asphalt Shingle Roofing
Manufacturer: CertainTeed
Product: Landmark 50 Series
Color name: Terra Cotta

Pavers
Material: Old red brick

Design and Color Consultant
Penelope De Paoli
Design Planning
San Francisco, California

177

Field Paint Color
Manufacturer: Benjamin Moore
Color number: HC-138
Color name: Covington Blue

Door, Window, and Panel Trim Paint Color
Manufacturer: Benjamin Moore
Color number: HC-156
Color name: Van Duesen Blue

Window Frame, Portico, and Trim Color
Manufacturer: Benjamin Moore
Color number: HC-27
Color name: Monterey White

Vestibule Paint Color
Base Coat
Manufacturer: Benjamin Moore
Color number: 154
Color name: Mango Punch
Glazing Formula
Material: Glazing Liquid
Manufacturer: Benjamin Moore
Product: Alkyd Glazing Liquid 409
Instructions: This glazing formula should be applied over the paint coat. Add 1 ounce each of sienna and burnt umber (universal colorants) and about 2 tablespoons of mineral spirits to the glazing liquid. Roll the mixture onto the painted surface and then stipple it in small sections with a specialist stippling brush. Moving quickly, keep the area wet while rolling or brushing out an adjacent area. Work in 2-foot-square areas to keep the color consistent and smooth.
Varnish
Manufacturer: Pratt & Lambert
Product: 38 Clear Alkyd Stain Varnish

Porch and Steps Paint Color
Manufacturer: Benjamin Moore
Product: Porch and Floor Paint
Color number: 678
Color name: Pacific Rim

Paneled Fascia Boards, Carved Panels and Trim Paint Color
Manufacturer: Benjamin Moore
Color number: HC-150
Color name: Yarmouth Blue

Gold Leaf Accents
Material: Gold Leaf
Manufacturer: The Gold Leaf Company
Note: My match

Color Consulting and Painting Specialist
Paul d'Orleans
Paul d'Orleans Painting
San Francisco, California

178

Field Paint Color
Manufacturer: Farrow and Ball
Color number: 41
Color name: Drab
Finish: Oil—Eggshell

Window Frame, Door Frame, Cornice, Gate, Railing, and Portal Paint Color
Manufacturer: Farrow and Ball
Color number: 221
Color name: Pantalon
Finish: Oil—Full Gloss

Door and Window Paint Color
Manufacturer: Fine Paints of Europe
Product name: Hollandlac
Finish: Brilliant Enamel
Collection: Historical Colors
Match color to:
Manufacturer: California Paints
Color name: Moss Glen
Note: "Fine Paints of Europe" is only sold in quarts in some states because of EPA standards. Check for restricted use of this product in your area.

Door Knob
Material: Brass
Note: This is a circa 1885 antique from manufacturer F. C. Linde in Cresskill, New Jersey, which went out of business years ago. Search antique shops or online auction sites for similar products.

Pendant Light Fixture
Material: Brass and colored glass panels
Note: This is a circa 1880 antique found at an antique store in Healdsburg, California.

Bridge Floor Boards
Material: Redwood
Finish: Linseed Oil

Mailbox
Manufacturer: Smith and Hawken
Material: Brass and Copper

House Numbers
Manufacturer: Restoration Hardware
Material: Bronze

Color Consultant
Leslie Kalish
Moraga, California

Architect
Steve Rynerson
Rynerson O'Brien Architecture
Oakland, California

Specialty Painter
Robert Dufort
Magic Brush Paint Company
San Francisco, California

179

Field Paint Color
Manufacturer: Benjamin Moore
Color number: HC-83
Color name: Grant Beige

Window, Window Frame, Portico, and Railing Paint Color
Manufacturer: Benjamin Moore
Color number: HC-27
Color name: Monterey White

Door Paint Color
Manufacturer: Benjamin Moore
Color number: EXT.RM.
Color name: Black

Wrought-Iron Balcony, Railings, and Gate Paint Color
Manufacturer: Rust-Oleum
Product: Satin Enamel Finish
Number: 7777
Color name: Satin Black
Note: My match

Garage Door
Manufacturer: Carriage House Doors
Product: Classic Line
Style: Recessed Panel
Note: My match

Paint Color
Manufacturer: Benjamin Moore
Color name: Custom
Tinting base: N096-2B
One gallon formula:
  BK 1 x 13
  BR 0.5
  MA 0.5
  OY 2 x 30
  RX 7

Cornice Horizontal Trim Paint Color
Manufacturer: Benjamin Moore
75% of formula:
Color number: HC-86
Color name: Kingsport Gray
Note: My match

Steps
Material: White marble

Hanging Light Fixture
Manufacturer: Sea Gull Lighting
Product name: Lancaster
Product number: 6039-12
Color: Black
Material: Solid brass
Glass: Clear curved, beveled
Note: My match

180

Field
Material: Old red brick

Window
Manufacturer: Sugarcreek Industries
Type: Triple track storm window
Product: Town & Country
Product number: 520
Color: Sandpiper beige
Note: My match

Window Frame, Porch Support Columns, Projecting Eave, and Trim Paint Color
Manufacturer: Benjamin Moore

Color number: 2140-40
Color name: Storm Cloud Gray

Door Paint Color
Manufacturer: M.A.B.
Color number: 496
Color name: Town & Country Red

Shutter, Adirondack Chairs, and Porch Floor Paint Color
Manufacturer: Benjamin Moore
Color number: EXT. RM.
Color name: Black Forest Green
Note: For the porch floor paint, mix the color into an exterior floor paint product.

Porch "Support Bracket" Paint Color
Manufacturer: Benjamin Moore
Color number: 2141-50
Color name: Horizon Gray

Metal Roof
Manufacturer: Calbar, Inc.
Product: Tin-O-Lin metal paint
Color name: Tinner's Red

Roof Tile
Material: Slate
Color: Gray (original to the house)

181

Field Paint Color
Manufacturer: Fuller O'Brien
Color name: Custom
Tinting base: 668-92
One gallon formula:
  BLK-3P18
  YOX-2P36
  TBL-40

Window, Window Frame, Fascia Board, Railing, and Trim Paint Color
Manufacturer: Fuller O'Brien
Color number: 3W16-1
Color name: Siam Sand

Door Paint Color
Manufacturer: Fuller O'Brien
Color name: Custom
Tinting base 668-95
One gallon formula:
  BLK-3P18
  YOX-30
  FFR-9P
  WHT-P8

Porch and Floor Paint
Manufacturer: Fuller O'Brien
Product: Porch and Floor Paint
Color name: Custom
Tinting base: 606-93
One gallon formula:
  BLK-3P24
  YOX-2P40
  TBL-42

Composition Asphalt Shingle Roofing
Manufacturer: CertainTeed
Product: Landmark TL
Color name: Moire Black
Note: My match

182

Field Paint Color
Manufacturer: Benjamin Moore
Color number: HC-156
Color name: Van Deusen Blue

Window Paint Color

Manufacturer: Benjamin Moore
Color number: INT. RM.
Color name: Bone White
Note: Mix interior paint into exterior paint product.

Window Frames, Portico, Railings, Stair Risers, Porch Floor, and Trim Paint Color
Manufacturer: Benjamin Moore
Color name: Montgomery White
Note: For the porch, mix into a porch and floor paint product.

Door
Material: Mahogany
Stain
Manufacturer: Cabot
Product: Semi-Solid Stain
Color name: Plum Island

Composition Asphalt Shingle Roofing
Manufacturer: CertainTeed
Product number: XT25
Color name: Black Pewter
Note: All my matches

183

Field Paint Color
Manufacturer: Benjamin Moore
Color number: 171
Color name: Sweet Butter

Door, Window, and Adirondack Chair Paint Color
Manufacturer: Benjamin Moore
Color number: 1321
Color name: Holly Berry

Window Frame, Fence, Porch Columns, and All Trim Paint Color
Manufacturer: Benjamin Moore
Color name: Custom
Tinting base: N103-1B
One gallon formula:
  OY 1/8
  GY 3 1/4

Porch Floor
Material: Untreated redwood
Note: My match

Pavers
Material: Old salvaged brick (from the San Francisco 1906 earthquake and fire) and railroad ties

184

Field Paint Colors
Upper
Manufacturer: ICI
Color number: 1218
Color name: Botany Bay
Lower
Manufacturer: ICI
Color number: 1213
Color name: Duck Pond

Door, Window, Window Frame, Ceiling, Railing, and Trim Paint Color
Manufacturer: ICI
Color number: 815
Color name: Natural White
Note: My match. Leaded glass window in front door.

Steps
Material: Redwood

Stain
Manufacturer: Behr
Product: Deck Plus Semi-Transparent Stain
Number: DP534
Color name: Redwood Naturaltone
Note: My match

185

Field Paint Color
Manufacturer: Pratt & Lambert
Color number: 1712
Color name: Ivory Mist
Note: My match

Window, Window Frame, Door, Door Frame, Projecting Eave, Bracket, and Trim Paint Color
Manufacturer: Pratt & Lambert
Color number: 2314
Color name: Seed Pearl
Note: My match

French Doors
Manufacturer: Marvin Doors
Product: Ultimate Swinging French Doors (in swing)
Hardware
Manufacturer: Valli & Valli
Product number: H1003
Finish: Brass
Note: This hardware selection is a stock selection from Marvin Doors.

Specialty Glass in Front Door
Manufacturer: Vitro America/ACI Distribution
Product: Tempered Obscure Glass
Pattern: Rain

Porch Paint Color
Manufacturer: Benjamin Moore
Product: Porch and Floor Paint
Match to:
Color number: HC-134
Color name: Tarrytown Green

Paneled Fascia Board Paint Color
Manufacturer: Pratt & Lambert
Color number: 1478
Color name: Storm

186

Field Paint Colors
Siding
Manufacturer: Benjamin Moore
Color number: 268 (x 1.5)
Color name: Oatmeal
Bay Windows
Manufacturer: Benjamin Moore
Color number: 270
Color name: Straw Hat
Foundation Paint Color
Manufacturer: Benjamin Moore
Color number: 2141-10
Color name: Artichoke

Window, Window Frame, Cornice, Portico, and Trim Paint Color
Manufacturer: Benjamin Moore
Color number: 267 (x 1.5)
Color name: Canvas

Door and Garage Door Paint Color
Manufacturer: Benjamin Moore
Color number: 2140-10
Color name: Fatigue Green

Color Consultant
David vanDommelen
vanDommelen Colorworks
San Francisco, California

187

Field Paint Color
Manufacturer: Benjamin Moore
Color number: HC-107
Color name: Gettysburg Gray

Window, Window Frame, Door Frame, Portico, and Trim Paint Color
Manufacturer: Benjamin Moore
Color Number: INT. RM.
Color name: Super White
Note: Mix interior color into exterior paint product.

Door Paint Color
Manufacturer: Benjamin Moore
Color number: 2132-10
Color name: Black

Door Knocker
Material: Bronze
Note: Antique

Cobblestone
Source: Gavin Historical Brick
Product: Antique granite cobblestone
Color name: Gray
Note: My match

Planter Boxes (at Entry)
Source: A. Silvestri
Product: Lion Square Rolled Rim Planter
Material: Cast Stone
Finish: Terra-cotta
Note: My match

188

Field
Material: Old red brick

Window Paint Color
Manufacturer: Sherwin Williams
Color number: SW2802
Color name: Rookwood Red

Window Frame, Cornice, Columns, Fascia Boards, and Architectural Detailing Paint Color
Manufacturer: Sherwin Williams
Color number: SW2815
Color name: Renwick Olive

Door and Shutters Paint Color
Manufacturer: Benjamin Moore
Color number: EXT. RM.
Color name: Essex Green

Bracket and Accent Paint Color
Manufacturer: Sherwin Williams
Color number: SW2817
Color name: Rookwood Amber

Porch Ceiling
Material: Natural pine
Protectant
Manufacturer: Cabot
Product: Harbormaster Polyurethane
Finish: Satin
Note: My match

Roof Tile
Material: Old original slate roof. Similar products can be found at American Slate Company.
Note: My match

Color Consultant
Ron Walker
Lambertville, New Jersey

189

Field Paint Color
Manufacturer: ICI
Color number: 521
Color name: Deacon's Bench

Door and Window Paint Color
Manufacturer: ICI
Color number: 1673
Color name: Dark Secret

Window Frame, Railing (Steps), and Accent Paint Color
Manufacturer: ICI
Color name: Custom
Tinting base: 2406-0110
One gallon formula:
  YOX 0 P44+
  OXR 0 P6
  BLK 0 P21

Steps and Inset Panels (under Cornice) Paint Color
Manufacturer: Sherwin Williams
Color number: SW2716
Color name: Deep Ruby

Wrought Iron Fence Paint Color
Manufacturer: ICI
Color number: 1673
Color name: Dark Secret
Finish: Semi-Gloss
Note: Use an exterior rust preventing primer undercoat.

Gold Leaf on Colonnettes and Fence Post
Manufacturer: Gold Leaf Company
Note: My match

Roof Tile
Material: Natural cedar shingles (diamond pattern)
Stain
Manufacturer: Cabot
Product: Semi-solid wood stain
Color number: 0138
Color name: Bark

190

Upper Field and Planter Box Panel Paint Color
Manufacturer: Benjamin Moore
Color number: 1483
Color name: Cos Cob Stonewall

Lower Field, Garage Door, Wall (at Steps), and Planter Box Paint Color
Manufacturer: Benjamin Moore
Color number: 1484
Color name: Ashwood Moss

Door Paint Color
Manufacturer: Benjamin Moore
Color number: 2012-10
Color name: Tawny Day Lily
Note: Door window has an ornate leaded glass window pattern.

Window, Window Frame, Portico, Railing (over Garage), and Trim Paint Color
Manufacturer: Benjamin Moore
Color number: OC-45
Color name: Swiss Coffee
Note: All my matches

Entry steps
Source: Gavin Historical Bricks
Material: Antique mixed red pavers
Note: My match

191

Field Paint Color
Manufacturer: Finnaren & Haley
Color name: Custom
Tinting base: Medium
One gallon formula:
  H 24
  I 26
  V 1

Window, Window Frame, Door Frame, Porch Column Supports, Cornice, and Trim Paint Color
Manufacturer: Finnaren & Haley
Product: House & Trim
Color name: High Hide White

Door, Screen Door, Shutters, Brackets, Fascia Boards, and Trim Paint Color
Manufacturer: Finnaren & Haley
Color name: Custom
Tinting base: Deep
One gallon formula:
  F 36
  I 44
  L 3Y32
  V 3Y6

Porch Paint Color
Manufacturer: Finnaren & Haley
Product: Porch & Floor Paint
Color name: Gunmetal Gray

Composition Asphalt Shingle Roofing
Manufacturer: CertainTeed
Product number: XT25
Color name: Moire Black
Note: My match

192

Field Paint Color
Manufacturer: Benjamin Moore
Color number: 1510
Color name: Dried Basil

Brick Facade (Lower)
Type: Clinker brick
Note: Red brick was salvaged from the San Francisco earthquake and fire of 1906.

Door, Window, Columns, Garage Door, Projecting Eave, and "Medium Green" Trim Paint Color
Manufacturer: Benjamin Moore
Color number: 462
Color name: Vintage Vogue

Window Frame, Cornice, and "Creamy White" Trim Paint Color
Manufacturer: Benjamin Moore
Color number: 924
Color name: San Mateo Beaches

Steps and Landing
Material: Old white marble

Hanging Light Fixture
Product: Antique
Finish: Old brass

Glass: Amber

Gold Leaf Details
Manufacturer: Gold Leaf Company
Staten Island, New York
Note: My match

193

Field, Porch Ceiling, and Floor Paint Color
Manufacturer: M.A.B.
Color name: Custom
Tinting base: 060-1971 medium
One gallon formula:
  B 14
  C 18
  E 4
  L 9
Note: Mix porch floor paint into exterior wood floor paint product.

Window, Window Frame, Porch, Railing, and all "White" Trim Paint Color
Manufacturer: M.A.B.
Color number: 90155PG
Color name: Pale Sisal
Note: My match

Door, Shutter, and Paneled Fascia Board Paint Color
Manufacturer: M.A.B.
Color name: Custom
Tinting base: deep base 024-1941
One gallon formula:
  AXN 8
  B 2Y34
  E 46

194

Field and Fence Paint Color
Manufacturer: Benjamin Moore
Color number: 1302
Color name: Sweet Rosy Brown

Door, Window, and Fascia Board Paint Color
Manufacturer: Pratt & Lambert
Color number: 2041
Color name: Fedora

All "Creamy White" Trim Paint Color
Manufacturer: Benjamin Moore
Color number: OC-36
Color name: Niveous

Roof Paint Color
Manufacturer: Benjamin Moore
Color number: 1302
Color name: Sweet Rosy Brown
Note: Painted cedar shingles

Tree (at Right)
Species: Plum
Note: All my matches

Resources

Note: Use the manufacturer's Web site to find local dealers and/or distributors for products available in your area.

Antiques

Foster & Gwin Antiques
38 Hotaling Pl.
San Francisco, CA 94111
Phone: 415-397-4986
Web site: www.fostergwin.com

Habite
963 Harrison St.
San Francisco, CA 94107
Phone: 415-543-3515
Fax: 415-543-4611
E-mail: info@habite.com
Web site: www.habite.com

Architects/Architectural Designers

Allen Koster
Architect
588–10th Ave.
San Francisco, CA 94118
Phone: 415-221-5064
E-mail: toddkoster@hotmail.com

Art4 Architecture
Constance Scott
1625 Sixth St.
Berkeley, CA 94710
Phone: 510-528-0722

Baird Wheatley Design
Architecture
Baird Wheatley
843 Neptune Ave.
Leucadia, CA 92024
Phone/Fax: 760-632-5317
E-mail: bairdwheatley@mindspring.com

Bennett Christopherson
Architect
6101 Colby St.
Oakland, CA 94618
Phone: 510-658-2800 ext. 111
E-mail: benchr@pacbell.net

Christiani Johnson Architects
Richard Christiani
665 Third St., Ste. 350
San Francisco, CA 94107
Phone: 415-243-9484
Fax: 415-243-9485
E-mail: rchristiani@cjarchs.com
Web site: www.cjarchs.com

Doane and Doane Architects
Babac Doane
1842 Reliez Valley Rd.
Lafayette, CA 94549
Phone: 925-934-1698
Fax: 925-943-7608
E-mail: b.doane@doane-arch.com

Feldman Architecture, LLP
Jonathan Feldman
Lisa Lougee, Designer
1126 Folsom St. Ste. 4
San Francisco, CA 94103
Phone: 415-252-1441
Fax: 415-252-1442
E-mail: jon@FeldmanArchitecture.com
Web site: www.FeldmanArchitecture.com

Gustave Carlson Design
Architecture
1051 Cragmont Ave.
Berkeley, CA 94708
Phone: 510-524-5181
E-mail: gac@studionumbersix.com
or gustavecarlson@sbcglobal.net

Halperin and Christ
Architecture
224 Greenfield Ave., Ste. B
San Anselmo, CA 94960
Phone: 415-457-9185
Fax: 415-485-6062
Web site: www.halperinandchrist.com

Hanns Kainz & Associates
Architecture
1099 Folsom St.
San Francisco, CA 94103
Phone: 415-552-2600
E-mail: ArchKainz@aol.com

Jensen/Ptaszynski
Architecture
Andre Ptaszynski
3449 Mt. Diablo Blvd. #A
Lafayette, CA 94549
Phone: 925-284-4398
E-mail: andre@JandPArchitects.com
Web site: www.JandParchitects.com

Kava Massih Architects
Gerry Tierney
2830 9th St.
Berkeley, CA 94701
Phone: 510-644-1920
Fax: 510-644-1929
E-mail: gerryt@kavamassiharchitects.com
Web site: www.kavamassiharchitects.com

Kotas-Pantaleoni Architects
Tony Pantaleoni
70 Zoe, Ste. 200
San Francisco, CA 94107
Phone: 415-495-4051

Lanier-Sherrill-Morrison Architects
Mac Morrison
381 Valencia St.
San Francisco, CA 94103
Phone: 415-626-0694
E-mail: LSMArchs@msn.com

Mark Becker, Inc.
Architectural Design Services
Mark Becker
420–40th St., Ste. 1
Oakland, CA 94609
Phone: 510-658-6889
Web site: www.markbecker.com

Matthew R. Mills
Architect, AIA
15 Birkdale Way
Pinehurst, NC 28374
Phone: 910-246-2787
Fax: 910-246-2789
E-mail: mmills59@earthlink.net

Origins Design Network
Architecture
Alexandra Martynetz and Arnold Mammarella
110 Linden St.
Oakland, CA 94605
Phone: 510-763-4332

Phillip O. Perkins Architectural Design
Phillip Perkins
5272 Golden Gate Ave.
Oakland, CA 94618
Phone: 510-658-8888

Regan Bice Architects
Regan Bice
950 Grayson St.
Berkeley, CA 94710
Phone: 510-549-1499
Fax: 510-845-1901
E-mail: regan@reganbice.com

Robert Nebolon
Architect
801 Camelia St., Ste. E
Berkeley, CA 94710
Phone: 510-525-2725
Fax: 510-527-5999
E-mail: rnebarch@aol.com
Web site: www.RNarchitect.com

Rupel, Geiszler & McLeod Architects
Duncan McLeod
81 Langton St., #7
San Francisco, CA 94103
Phone: 415-575-0888
Fax: 415-575-0880

Rynerson O'Brien Architecture
Steve Rynerson
1512 Franklin St., Ste. 200
Oakland, CA 94612
Phone: 510-452-9152
Fax: 510-452-9155
E-mail: info@rynersonobrien.com
Web site: www.rynersonobrien.com

Stephen Swearengen
Architect
717 Caldwell Rd.
Oakland, CA 94611
Phone: 510-559-1700
Fax: 510-559-1701
E-mail: steves@morethanacarpenter.com
Web site: www.morethanacarpenter.com

Taylor Lombardo Architects
529 Commercial St., Ste. 400
San Francisco, CA 94111

Phone: 415-433-7777
Fax: 415-433-7717
E-mail: info@taylorlombardo.com
Web site: www.taylorlombardo.com
Offices also in Oakville, CA

Twelve 13 Architecture
Russ Beaudin and Emma Kim
1924 Union St., #14
Oakland, CA 94706
Phone: 510-208-3791
Fax: 510-208-3793
E-mail: russ@twelve13.com,
emma@twelve13.com
Web site: www.twelve13.com

Veverka Architects
Jerry Veverka
645 Harrison St., Ste. 101
San Francisco, CA 94107
Phone: 415-777-3150
Fax: 415-648-4228
E-mail: info@veverka.com
Web site: www.veverka.com

Volkamer Architecture
Chris Volkamer
7007 Broadway Terrace
Oakland, CA 94611
Phone: 510-654-3019
Fax: 510-654-3080
E-mail: Volkarch@aol.com

Zack/deVito Architecture
Jim Zack
156 South Park
San Francisco, CA 94107
Phone: 415-495-7889 ext. 201
Fax: 415-495-7869
E-mail: jim@zackdevito.com
Web site: www.zackdevito.com

Architectural Metals

King Architectural Metals
PO Box 271169
Dallas, TX 75227
Phone: 800-542-2379
Fax: 214-388-1048
Web site: www.kingmetals.com

Awnings

Sunbrella
Glen-Raven Custom Fabrics, LLC
1831 North Park Ave.
Glen Raven, NC 27217
Phone: 336-221-2211
Web site: www.sunbrella.com

Brickyards

McNear Brick and Block
1 McNear Brickyard Rd.
San Rafael, CA 94901
Phone: 415-454-6811
Web site: www.mcnear.com

Gavin Historical Bricks
Antique Granite Cobblestone
2050 Glendale Rd.
Iowa City, IA 52245

Phone: 319-354-5251
E-mail: info@historicalbricks.com
Web site: www.historicalbricks.com

Building Systems

NCI Building Systems
Metal Building Components
10943 N. Sam Houston Pkwy. W.
Houston, TX 77064
Phone: 888-624-8678
Fax: 281-477-9674
Web site: www.ncilp.com

Carpenters/Cabinetmakers

Fiorella Woodworking
20 E. Herman St.
Philadelphia, PA 19144
Phone: 215-843-5870

Olson Brothers
Gordon Olson
706 Rincon Rd.
El Sobrante, CA
Phone: 510-669-9211

JC Cabinets, Inc.
John Chow
619–85th Ave.
Oakland, CA 94621
Phone: 510-569-8937

Jeff Ward
1001 Pardee St.
Berkeley, CA 94710
Phone: 510-666-1386

Cast Stone

Architectural Facades Unlimited
Precast Concrete Columns and Products
600 East Luchessa Ave.
Gilroy, CA 95020
Phone: 408-846-5350
Web site: www.architecturalfacades.com

Napa Valley Cast Stone
111 Green Island Rd.
American Canyon, CA 9588
Phone: 707-258-3340
Fax: 707-258-3350
Web site: www.napavalleycaststone.com

William Bowman
Architectural Specialist in Cast Stone
PO Box 1713
Suisun City, CA 94585
Phone: 707-429-3177
Fax: 707-429-2331
E-mail: info@williambowman.net
Web site: www.williambowman.net

Color Consultants/Designers

Note: All of the designers listed also offer color consulting services.

Bauer Interior Design
Lou Ann Bauer
3886–17th St.
San Francisco, CA 94114
Phone: 415-621-7262
Fax: 415-621-3661

Bob Buckter
Color Consulting
3877–20th St.
San Francisco, CA 94114
Phone: 415-922-7444
E-mail: drcolor@drcolor.com
Web site: www.drcolor.com

Caton & Associates
Architectural Color Consulting and Specialty Painting
Sharon Stanbridge
4065 Horton St.
Emeryville, CA 94608
Phone: 510-547-1419
Fax: 510-547-0159
E-mail: sharon@catonandassociates.com

Color Consulting for Your Walls
Bob Crowe
1560 Alice St.
Oakland, CA 94612
Phone: 510-867-9975
E-mail: bob@croweondesign.com
Web site: www.CroweOnDesign.com

Debra Cibilich Design
Interior Design
Debra Cibilich
2728 Gough St., #3
San Francisco, CA 94123
Phone: 415-922-4450
Fax: 415-922-4490

DeMartini Arnott Painting Company
Color Consulting
San Francisco, CA
Phone: 415-362-0849

Design Planning
Penelope Di Paoli
701 Castro St.
San Francisco, CA 94114
Phone: 415-826-7895
Fax: 415-826-7893
E-mail: designplanning@earthlink.net

Devine Paint Center
Color Consulting
917 Lincoln Ave.
Napa, CA 94559
Phone: 707-226-5211

Eileen Connery Design
Color Consulting
7 Corona Court
Novato, CA 94945
Phone: 415-269-6229
E-mail: econnerydesign@comcast.net

Garner Chinn 8
Interior Design and Color Consulting
Susan Garner Bottorf & Arthur Chinn
1133 Sunnyhills Rd.
Oakland, CA 94610
Phone/Fax: 510-763-7229
E-mail: gc8@sbcglobal.net

Garry Bratman
Color Consulting
9221 Oneal Rd.
Raleigh, NC 27613
Cell: 415-513-2733
E-mail: ta2trksf@aol.com

Jody Suden Color Design
Jody Suden
Color Consulting
28 Whitehall Park Rd.
London W4 3NE
England
Phone: 44 20 8400 5849
E-mail: jsuden@blueyonder.co.uk

John Wheatman & Associates, Inc.
Interior Design
John Wheatman
1933 Union St.
San Francisco, CA 94123
Phone: 415-346-8300

Kittredge Opal
Color Consulting
PO Box 756
Kentfield, CA 94914
Phone: 415-925-9596

Leslie Kalish
Color Consulting
3961 Paseo Grande
Moraga, CA 94556
Phone: 925-284-8271

Lois Wachner-Solomon
Color Consulting
Piedmont, CA
Phone: 510-207-6335
E-mail: lois3449@aol.com

M. B. Jessee Painting and Decorating
Color Consulting and Specialty Finishes
1552 Beach St., Ste. G
Oakland, CA 94608
Phone: 510-655-7000
Fax: 510-655-7317
E-mail: info@mbjessee.com
Web site: www.mbjessee.com

Metamorphose Interiors
Interior Design and Color Consulting
Una Gallagher
681 Felton-Empire Rd.
Felton, CA 95018
Phone: 831-335-2879
Fax: 831-335-8144
E-mail: darkmoon@cruzio.com

Paul d'Orleans Painting
Color Consulting
Paul d'Orleans
1682–39th Ave.
San Francisco, CA 94122
Phone: 415-378-8787
E-mail: pdopaint@aol.com

R. Boyle Painting
Painting and Color Consulting
Rory Boyle
842 Reina del Mar
Pacifica, CA 94044
Phone: 650-359-1834

Re:Design, LLC
Color Consulting and Staging
Claudia Ellinghaus
6114 LaSalle Ave., No. 615
Oakland, CA 94611
Phone: 510-452-2737
Fax: 510-452-2535
Email: redesignLLC@comcast.net

Ron Walker
Color Consulting
42 Coryell St.
Lambertville, NJ 08530
Phone: 609-397-1946
E-mail: fenwickpew@comcast.net

Stephen Moore Interior Design
Stephen Moore
4695–18th St.
San Francisco, CA 94114
Phone: 415-621-4695
Fax: 415-863-1604
E-mail: stephen@stephenmoorehomes.com

STUDIO+ONE:DESIGN
Interior Architecture/Design, Decorating, and Color Consulting
Susan Hershman
1395 Trestle Glen Rd.
Oakland, CA 94610
Phone: 877-832-9990
Phone/Fax: 510-986-0200
E-mail: susan@studio-one-design.com,
shershman@pacbell.net
Web site: www.studio-one-design.com

The Colour Studio
Corporate Color Consulting
Jill Pilaroscia
446 Geary St., Ste. 501
San Francisco, CA 94102
Phone: 415-292-6376
Fax: 415-292-5638
E-mail: info@colourstudio.com
Web site: www.colourstudio.com

Thomas Woodend
Color Consulting and Painting
PO Box 1001
Medford, NJ 08055
Phone: 609-654-6065

Troon Pacific, Inc.
Development and Design
Charlot D. Malin, Interior Designer
4924–17th St.
San Francisco, CA 94117
Phone: 415-294-4093
Fax: 415-504-8110
E-mail: cdm@troonpacific.com

Valerie Bianquis
Interior Architecture and Color Consulting
1721–20th St.
San Francisco, CA 94107
Phone: 415-285-4503
Fax: 415-826-9378
E-mail: vbianquis@aol.com

vanDommelen Colorworks
Color Consulting
David vanDommelen
1031 Florida St.
San Francisco, CA 94110
Phone: 415-641-4783
Fax: 415-642-3755
E-mail: david@vandommelencolorworks.com

Village Design Group
Interior Design
Cynthia Kent-Mills
1495 Highway 15/501
Southern Pines, NC 28387

Phone: 910-692-1999
E-mail: ckmills@villagedesigngroup.com

Color Systems

Pantone, Inc.
System for Accurate Color Communication
590 Commerce Blvd.
Carlstadt, NJ 07072
Phone: 201-935-5500
Fax: 201-935-3338
Web site: www.pantone.com

Concrete Products and Consultants

Architectural Facades Unlimited
See listing under Cast Stone

Baselite Concrete Products
605 Industrial Way
Dixon, CA 95620
Phone: 800-776-6690
Fax: 707-678-6268
Web site: www.baselite.com

Calstone
Concrete Pavers
1155 Aster Ave.
Sunnyvale, CA 94086
Phone: 408-984-8800
Fax: 408-984-2648
Web site: www.calstone.com

Flagstone Pavers, Inc.
9070 Old Cobb Rd.
Brooksville, FL 34601
Phone: 352-799-7933
Fax: 352-799-6844
E-mail: flagsales@tampabay.com
Web site: www.flagstonepavers.com

Matcrete Decorative Concrete Products
1495 Hudson Ave.
Ontario, CA 91761
Phone: 800-777-7063
Web site: www.matcrete.com

McNear Brick and Block
Concrete Paving
See listing under Brickyards

Steven's Concrete, Inc.
Colored Concrete Consultant
Hurshal Woodruff
1078 Fulton Ln.
St. Helena, CA 94574
Phone: 707-963-3412
E-mail: hurshal@stevensconcrete.com

Sunny Brook Pressed Concrete Company
3586 Sunny Brook Rd.
Kent, OH 44240
Phone: 888-677-3100
Fax: 330-677-3103
E-mail: sbconcrete@aol.com
Web site: www.sunnybrookpressedconcrete.com

Concrete Stains

Davis Colors
Color for Concrete
3700 East Olympic Blvd.
Los Angeles, CA 90023
Phone: 800-356-4848
Fax: 323-269-1053
Web site: www.daviscolors.com

L. M. Scofield Company
Color for Concrete
6533 Bandini Blvd.
Los Angeles, CA 90040
Phone: 800-800-9990
Fax: 323-720-6060
Web site: www.scofield.com

Superdeck Brand Products
Mason's Select Transparent Concrete Stain
Phone: 800-825-5382
E-mail: customerservice@superdeck.com
Web site: www.superdeck.com

Dampers, Diffusers, Louvers, and Registers

Seiho
120 W. Colorado Blvd.
Pasadena, CA 91105
Phone: 800-248-0030
Fax: 626-395-7290
E-mail: info@seiho.com
Web site: www.seiho.com

Decorative Painters

see Specialty Painters

Door Hardware

Baldwin Hardware Corporation
841 E. Wyomissing Blvd.
PO Box 15048
Reading, PA 19612
Phone: 800-566-1986
Fax: 610-916-3230
Web site: www.baldwinhardware.com

Bianchi Lamberto
Bronze Reproductions and Restoration Artists
Via dei Serragli, 10r
50124 Florence, Italy
Phone: 29.46.94

Bouvet
540 De Haro St.
San Francisco, CA 94107
Phone: 415-864-0273
Fax: 415-864-2068
E-mail: request@bouvet.com
Web site: www.bouvet.com

Clausen Sculptural Iron
Master Blacksmith
Eric Clausen
5401 Claremont Ave.
Oakland, CA 94618
Phone/Fax: 510-655-8428
E-mail: eric@clauseniron.com
Web site: www.clauseniron.com

Colonialworks
Period Hardware
23679 Calabasas Rd., #801
Calabasas, CA 91302
Phone: 888-784-7399

Fax: 888-778-7889
E-mail: worldlinkdistribution@yahoo.com
Web site: www.period1.com

Craftsmen Hardware Company
PO Box 161
Marceline, MO 64658
Phone: 660-376-2481
Fax: 660-376-4076
E-mail: craftsm@shighway.com
Web site: www.craftsmenhardware.com

Double Hill
2750 E. Regal Park Dr.
Anaheim, CA 92806
Phone: 714-630-5588
Fax: 714-630-5578
E-mail: sdh@doublehillusa.com
Web site: www.doublehillusa.com

Emtek Products, Inc.
Phone: 800-356-2741
Fax: 800-577-5771
Web site: www.emtekproducts.com

Forms and Surfaces
30 Pine St.
Pittsburgh, PA 15223
Phone: 800-451-0410
Fax: 412-781-7840
E-mail: marketing@forms-surfaces.com
Web site: www.forms-surfaces.com

Hoppe North America, Inc.
205 East Blackhawk Dr.
Fort Atkinson, WI 53538
Phone: 888-485-4885
Fax: 920-563-4408
Web site: www.hoppe.com

Kwikset
19701 DaVinci
Lake Forest, CA 92610
Phone: 800-327-5625
Web site: www.kwikset.com

Omnia Industries, Inc.
5 Cliffside Dr.
Cedar Grove, NJ 07009
Phone: 973-239-7272
Fax: 973-239-5960
E-mail: info@omniaindustries.com
Web site: www.omniaindustries.com

Period Brass
955 Godfrey Ave. S.W.
Grand Rapids, MI 49503
Phone: 800-332-6677
Fax: 800-215-8837
E-mail: customerservice@belwith.com
Web site: www.periodbrassusa.com

Rejuvenation Hardware and Lighting
Period Hardware
2550 NW Nicolai St.
Portland, OR 97210
Phone: 888-401-1900
Fax: 800-526-7329
E-mail: info@rejuvenation.com
Web site: www.rejuvenationhardware.com

Rocky Mountain Hardware
PO Box 4108
1030 Airport Way
Hailey, ID 8333

Phone: 888-788-2013
Fax: 208-788-2577
E-mail: info@rockymountainhardware.com
Web site: www.rockymountainhardware.com

Schlage Lock Company
2119 E. Kansas City Rd.
Olathe, KS 66051
Phone: 800-847-1864
Web site: www.schlage.com

spOre incorporated
Doorbells and House Numbers
PO Box 4758
Seattle, WA
Phone: 206-624-9573
Fax: 206-625-4223
E-mail: info@sporeinc.com
Web site: www.sporeinc.com

Stone River Bronze
PO Box 3513
Logan, UT 84323
Phone: 435-755-8100
Fax: 866-713-0117
E-mail: info@stoneriverbronze.com
Web site: www.stoneriverbronze.com

Sun Valley Bronze
PO Box 3475
Hailey, ID 83333
Phone: 866-788-3631
E-mail: svbronze@sunvalley.net
Web site: www.svbronze.com

Valli & Valli
150 E. 5th St., 4th Floor
New York, NY 10022
Phone: 212-326-8811
Fax: 212-326-8816
Web site: www.vallievalli.com

Wild West Hardware
2008 W. Lincoln Hwy., #569
Merriville, IN 46410
E-mail: sales@wildwesthardware.com
Web site: www.wildwesthardware.com

Doors and Windows

All Weather Architectural Aluminum
777 Aldridge Rd.
Vacaville, CA 95688
Phone: 707-452-1600
Fax: 707-452-1616
E-mail: info@allweathersweb.com
Web site: www.allweathersweb.com

4th Street Woodworking Company
1266–45th St.
Emeryville, CA 94608
Phone: 510-655-6700

Blomberg Window Systems
1453 Blair Ave.
PO Box 2248
Sacramento, CA 95822
Phone: 800-884-2566
Fax: 916-422-1967
E-mail: bwsmfg@sbcglobal.net
Web site: www.cabec.org/blomberg.php

Bonelli Doors and Windows
330 Corey Way

South San Francisco, CA 94080
Phone: 650-873-3222
E-mail: mail@bonelli.com
Web site: www.bonelli.com

Builders Door & Window Supply
4275 Phillips Ave.
Burnaby, BC V5A 2X4
Canada
Phone: 877-441-6693
Fax: 604-444-6694
E-mail: denis@woodwindows.com
Web site: www.woodwindows.ca

Craftsmen in Wood Mfg.
5441 W. Hadley St.
Phoenix, AZ 85043
Phone: 602-296-1050
Fax: 602-296-1052
Web site: www.craftsmeninwood.com

Fevreco Door Products
International Wood Products (IWP)
7312 Convoy Court
San Diego, CA 92111
Phone: 322-384-9205
Fax: 322-706-2340
E-mail: info@fevreco.com
Web site: www.fevreco.com

Fleetwood Windows and Doors
2845 Railroad St.
Corona, CA 92880
Phone: 800-736-7363
Web site: www.fleetwoodusa.com

Golden Gate Door & Window
1460 Wallace Ave.
San Francisco, CA 94124
Phone: 415-822-9663
Fax: 415-822-1753

Greenbridge Doors
520 W. Erie St., Ste. LL100
Chicago, IL 60610
Phone: 888-366-7798
Fax: 312-893-2255
E-mail: service@greenbridgedoors.com
Web site: www.greenbridgedoors.com

JC Cabinets & Doors
See listing under Carpenters/Cabinetmakers

JELD-WEN Windows & Doors
PO Box 1329
Klamath Falls, OR 97601
Phone: 800-535-3936
Web site: www.jeld-wen.ca

Liberty Valley Doors
6005 Gravenstein Hwy.
Cotati, CA 94931
Phone: 707-795-8040
Fax: 707-795-9258
E-mail: info@libertyvalleydoors.com
Web site: www.libertyvalleydoors.com

Loewen Doors
77 Highway 52 W.
Box 2260
Steinbach, Manitoba R5G 1B2
Canada
Phone: 800-563-9367
Web site: www.loewen.com

Marvin Windows and Doors
PO Box 100
Warroad, MN 56763
Phone: 888-537-7828
Web site: www.marvin.com

Milgard Windows
1010–54th Ave. E.
Tacoma, WA 98424
Phone: 800-MILGARD
Web site: www.milgard.com

Ocean Sash and Door Company
3154–17th St.
San Francisco, CA 94110
Phone: 415-863-1256
Fax: 415-863-6218
E-mail: mikeyork@oceansashanddoor.com
Web site: www.oceansashanddoor.com

Rustica Arts
336 S. Fairview Ave.
Goleta, CA 93117
Phone: 805-692-8865
Fax: 805-692-8895
E-mail: moredoor@aol.com
Web site: www.rusticaarts.com

Schweiss Bi-Fold Doors
Airplane Hangar Doors
Box 220
Fairfax, MN 55332
Phone: 800-746-8273
Fax: 507-426-7408
E-mail: schweiss@bifold.com
Web site: www.bifold.com

Sierra Pacific Windows
11605 Reading Rd.
Red Bluff, CA 96080
Phone: 800-824-7744
Fax: 530-527-4438
E-mail: windows@spi-ind.com
Web site: www.sierrapacificwindows.com

Simpson Door Company
400 Simpson Ave.
McCleary, WA 98557
Phone: 800-952-4057
E-mail: simpsondoor@brander.com
Web site: www.simpsondoor.com

Sugarcreek Industries
Storm Windows
425 S. Broadway St.
Sugarcreek, OH 44681
Phone: 800-837-2417
Fax: 330-852-2490
E-mail: sicustser@sugarcreekindustries.com
Web site: www.precisionentry.com

Summit Woodworking
13663 Holcomb Blvd.
Oregon City, OR 97045
Phone: 800-727-7978
E-mail: summitww@aol.com
Web site: www.summitwoodworking.com

T. M. Cobb Company
500 Palmyrita Ave.
Riverside, CA 92507
Web site: www.tmcobbco.com

Tom Ehine
Custom Doors and Millworking
674 Arkansas St.
San Francisco, CA 94107
Phone: 415-826-1036
E-mail: teline@hotmail.com

Well Hung Doors, Inc.
7820 Enterprise Dr.
Newark, CA 94560
Phone: 510-795-1118

Etching

Etchings
Bonnie Brown
45 Mitchell Blvd., Ste. F
San Rafael, CA 94903
Phone: 415-492-8986

Paige Glass Company
1531 Mission St.
San Francisco, CA 94103
Phone: 415-621-3858

Garage Doors

Amarr Garage Doors
165 Carriage Court
Winston-Salem, NC 27105
Phone: 800-503-DOOR
Fax: 336-767-3805
E-mail: marketing@amarr.com
Web site: www.amarr.com

BP Glass Garage Doors
9412 Gidley St.
Temple City, CA 91780
Phone: 626-442-1716
Fax: 626-579-5320
E-mail: service@bpcompany.net
Web site: www.glassgaragedoors.com

Carriage House Doors
1421 Richards Blvd.
Sacramento, CA 95814
E-mail: sales@carriagehousedoors.com
Web site: www.carriagedoor.com

Clopay
8585 Duke Blvd.
Mason, OH 45040
Phone: 800-225-6729
Web site: www.clopaydoor.com

Norman Overhead Doors
8 Laurel Grove Ave.
Kentfield, CA 94904
Phone: 415-642-7980

Ranch House Doors
Custom Overhead Garage Doors
1527 Pomona Rd.
Corona, CA 92880
Phone: 951-278-2884
Fax: 951-278-2686
Web site: www.ranchhousedoors.com

Glass

(Architectural Glass and Etching Services)

Bendheim Glass
Specialty Glass

122 Hudson St.
New York, NY 10013
Phone: 800-606-7621
Fax: 212-431-3589
Web site: www.bendheim.com

Stained Glass Garden
Stained Glass Materials for Construction
1800 Fourth St.
Berkeley, CA 94710
Phone: 510-841-2200
Fax: 510-644-0945
E-mail: feedback@stainedglassgarden.com
Web site: www.stainedglassgarden.com

Vitro America
ACI Distribution
Laminated and Insulated Glass Products
965 Ridge Lake Blvd.
PO Box 171173
Memphis, TN 38187
Phone: 800-238-6057
E-mail: info@vitroamerica.com
Web site: www.vvpamerica.com

Granite, Marble, Slate, and Stone

Alpha Granite and Marble
2303 Merced St.
San Leandro, CA 94577
Phone: 800-510-ALPHA
Fax: 510-357-6365
E-mail: sales@alphagranite.com
Web site: www.alphagranite.com

American Slate Company
Tile and Slate Roofs
1900 Olympic Blvd.
Walnut Creek, CA 94590
Phone: 800-553-5611
Fax: 925-977-4885
E-mail: slatexpert@americanslate.com
Web site: www.americanslate.com

American Soil Products
2121 San Joaquin St.
Richmond, CA 94804
Phone: 510-292-3000
E-mail: richmond@americansoil.com,
sanrafael@americansoil.com
Web site: www.americansoil.com

Bouquet Canyon Stone Company
Phone: 661-250-7171
E-mail: joseph-bouquet@earthlink.net
Web site: www.bouquetcanyonstone.com
See Web site for dealer locations

Calstone
See listing under Concrete Products and Consultants

Chestnut Hill Stone, Ltd.
1A Waverly St.
Glenside, PA 19038
Phone: 215-572-7000
Fax: 215-572-7100

Daltile
7834 C. F. Hawn Fwy.
Dallas, TX 75217
Phone: 214-398-1411

Web site: www.daltileproducts.com

Delaware Quarries, Inc.
6603 Rte. 202
PO Box 778
New Hope, PA 18938
Phone: 800-533-4954
Fax: 215-862-1680
Web site: www.delawarequarries.com

Echeguren Slate
1495 Illinois St.
San Francisco, CA 94107
Phone: 415-206-9343
Fax: 415-206-9353
E-mail: slate@echeguren.com
Web site: www.echeguren.com

Eldorado Stone
Architectural Stone Veneer
1370 Grand Ave., Building B
San Marcos, CA 92078
Phone: 800-925-1491
E-mail: customerservice@eldoradostone.com
Web site: www.eldoradostone.com

Eurocal Slate Centers
3478 Buskirk Ave., Ste. 260
Pleasant Hill, CA 94523
Phone: 510-943-6992
Fax: 925-930-0752

Floor + Stone Depot
1201 Minnesota St.
San Francisco, CA 94107
Phone: 415-282-8600

GMS Global, Inc.
2480 Verna Ct.
San Leandro, CA 94577
Phone: 510-352-8112
Fax: 510-352-8113
E-mail: gms@gmsglobal.com
Web site: www.gmsglobal.com

Graniterock
350 Technology Dr.
Watsonville, CA 95076
Phone: 888-ROCK-100
Fax: 831-768-2201
E-mail: mainoffice@graniterock.com
Web site: www.graniterock.com

Montana Rockworks Inc.
1107 Rose Crossing
Kalispell, MT 59901
Phone: 406-752-7625
Fax: 406-752-7645
E-mail: info@montanarock
works.com
Web site: www.montanarock
works.com

Mt. Moriah Stone
HCR 310 Gandy Rd.
Garrison, UT 84728
Phone/Fax: 435-855-2232
Web site: www.mtmoriahstone.net

Pave Tile and Stone, Inc.
10 West St.
West Hatfield, MA 01088
Phone: 800-239-6437
Fax: 800-560-5787
E-mail: info@pavetile.com

Web site: www.pavetile.com

Shamrock Materials, Inc.
181 Lynch Creek Way
Petaluma, CA 94954
PO Box 808044
Petaluma, CA 94975
Phone: 707-781-9000
Fax: 707-781-9055
E-mail: admin@shamrockmaterials.com
Web site: www.shamrockmat.com

Vermont Structural Slate Company, Inc.
3 Prospect St.
PO Box 98
Fairhaven, VT 05743
Phone: 800-343-1900
Fax: 802-265-3865
E-mail: info@vermontstructuralslate.com
Web site: www.vermontstructuralslate.com

House Numbers and Plaques

Armador Memorial
Custom Granite and Marble House
Number Plaques
4435 Piedmont Ave.
Oakland, CA 94611
Phone: 510-652-5147
E-mail: amadormemorial@earthlink.net

Canterbury Designs
8014 Horse Chestnut Ln.
Charlotte, NC 28277
Phone: 704-540-7009
Fax: 704-540-8870
E-mail: canterburyd2001@aol.com
Web site: www.canterburydesignsltd.com

Customhousenumbers.com
Phone: 888-868-3567
Fax: 707-581-7321
E-mail: info@customhousenumbers.com
Web site: www.customhousenumbers.com

Gemini Incorporated
103 Mensing Way
Cannon Falls, MN 55009
Phone: 1-800-LETTERS
Web site: www.signletters.com

Hewi USA
Distributed by Hafele America Co.
3901 Cheyenne Dr.
PO Box 4000
Archdale, NC 27263
Phone: 800-423-3531
Fax: 336-431-3831
Web site: www.hafeleonline.com

Matthews International Corporation
Bronze Division
1315 West Liberty Ave.
Pittsburgh, PA 15226
Phone: 800-950-1317
Fax: 412-571-5561
Web site: www.matthewsbronze.net

spOre incorporated
See listing under Door Hardware

Steel Art Co., Inc
75 Brainerd Rd.
Boston, MA 02134

Phone: 800-322-2828
Fax: 888-783-5335
E-mail: sales@steelartco.com
Web site: www.steelartco.com

Vietri
343 Elizabeth Brady Rd.
Hillsborough, NC 27278
Phone: 866-327-1279
Email: customerservice@vietri.com
Web site: www.vietri.com

WestOn
7259 N. Atoll Ave.
West Hollywood, CA 91605
Phone: 818-503-9472
Fax: 818-503-9475
Web site: www.westonletters.com

Landscape Architects/Designers

Bradley Burke
Landscape Architecture
609 Connecticut St.
San Francisco, CA 94107
Phone: 415-824-9119
E-mail: brad@bradleyburke.com
Web site: www.bradleyburke.co

David Bigham
Landscape Architecture
1542 La Loma Ave.
Berkeley, CA 94708
Phone: 510-843-4247

Enchanting Planting
Richard Sullivan
26 Camino Del Diablo
Orinda, CA 94563
Phone: 925-258-5500

Goodman Landscape Design
Linda Goodman
140 Montrose Rd.
Berkeley, CA 94707
Phone: 510-528-8950
E-mail: goodland@earthlink.net
Web site: www.goodmanlandscape.com

Hansen McArdle
Landscape Architecture
Karen and Paul McArdle
3400 Mt. Diablo Blvd., Ste. 209
Lafayette, CA 94549
Phone: 925-283-5520
Fax: 925-283-9476
E-mail: info@hansenmcardle.com

Indigo Design Group
Landscape Architecture/Architecture
Kristin Personett
801 Camilla St., Ste. E
Berkeley, CA 94710
Phone: 510-697-4289
Fax: 510-655-3705
E-mail: indigodesigngroup@gm.com
Web site: indigo-design-group.com

Jack Chandler and Associates
Landscape Architecture
Jack Chandler
PO Box 2654

Yountville, CA 94599
Phone: 707-253-8266
Fax: 707-253-0166
E-mail: office@chandler2.com
Web site: www.jackchandler.com

Jay Thayer
Landscape Design
10 Arkansas St., #C
San Francisco, CA 94107
Phone: 415-626-2636

Julian Design
Landscape Architecture
Doug Julian
570 Pebble Hill Rd.
Doylestown, PA 18901
Phone: 215-345-1989

Magrane Associates
Landscape Design
Penney Magrane
225 Hoffman Ave.
San Francisco, CA 94114
Phone: 415-821-0233
Fax: 415-821-7438
E-mail: tech@magrane.com
Web site: www.magrane.com

Miller Company Landscape Architects
Jeff Miller
1585 Folsom St.
San Francisco, CA 94103
Phone: 415-252-7288
Fax: 415-252-7289
E-mail: jmiller@millercomp.com
Web site: www.millercomp.com

Paul McArdle
Landscape Architecture
836 Creed Rd.
Oakland, CA 94610
Phone: 925-284-4916
Fax: 925-283-9476
E-mail: pmlarch@cs.com
Web site: www.paulmcardle.com

Rayner Landscaping
Theresa Zaro
366 Bel Marin Key Blvd.
Novato, CA 94949
Phone: 415-382-9014
Fax: 415-382-9015
E-mail: theresazaro@hotmail.com
Web site: www.raynerlandscaping.com

Vince Mackel, Inc.
Landscape Architecture
Vince Mackel
186 Donahey Rd.
Coupeville, WA 98239
Phone: 800-845-7912
E-mail: vmidp@pacbell.net
Web site: www.vmilandarch.com

Wake and Bake Landscape
Landscape Architecture
Julie Calandra
5030 Mountain Blvd.
Oakland, CA 94519
Phone: 510-482-6426

Wilson Landscaping
Landscaping Design and Care

Richard & Robert Wilson
442 Red Lion Rd.
Huntingdon Valley, PA 19006
Phone: 215-601-9123

Lighting

20th Century Lighting, Inc.
1668 Euclid Ave.
Santa Monica, CA 90404
Phone: 310-581-1923
Web site: www.20thcenturylighting.com

Arroyo Craftsman
4509 Little John St.
Baldwin Park, CA 91706
Phone: 800-400-2776
Fax: 888-960-9521
Web site: www.arroyo-craftsman.com

Artistic Lighting & Design
PO Box 379
Norcross, GA 30091
Phone: 770-209-9449
Fax: 770-209-9466
E-mail: artisticlt@aol.com
Web site: www.artisticlighting.com

Baselite Corporation
12260 East End Ave.
Chino, CA 91710
Phone: 877-999-1990
Fax: 909-548-4774
E-mail: sales@baselite.com
Web site: www.baselite.com

Brass Light Gallery
PO Box 674
Milwaukee, WI 53201
Phone: 800-243-9595
Fax: 800-505-9404
E-mail: customerservice@brasslight.com
Web site: www.brasslight.com

Coe Studios
Architectural Lighting
1214 Fourth St.
Berkeley, CA 94710
Phone: 510-527-2950
Fax: 510-527-0103
E-mail: info@coestudios.com
Web site: www.coestudios.com

CX Design
550 Broadway FL4
New York, NY 10012
Phone: 888-431-4242
Fax: 212-431-4286
E-mail: info@cxny.com
Web site: www.cxny.com

English Garden Furniture
128 Mitchell Blvd.
San Rafael, CA 94903
Phone: 415-492-1051
Fax: 415-492-9705
Web site: www.englishgardenfurniture.com

H. A. Framburg & Company
941 Cernan Dr.
Bellwood, IL 60104
Phone: 800-796-5514
Fax: 800-423-0098
E-mail: Framburg@framburg.com

Web site: www.framburg.com

Hilite Manufacturing
13450 Monte Vista Ave.
Chino, CA 91710
Phone: 800-465-2011
Fax: 909-465-0907
E-mail: sales@hilitemfg.com
Web site: www.hilitemfg.com

Hinkley Lighting
12600 Berea Rd.
Cleveland, OH 44111
Phone: 216-671-3300
Fax: 216-671-4537
E-mail: info@hinkleylighting.com
Web site: www.hinkleylighting.com

Hubbardton Forge
154 Route 30 S.
PO Box 827
Castleton, VT 05735
Phone: 800-468-3090
Fax: 802-468-3284
E-mail: info@vtforge.com
Web site: www.vtforge.com

Kichler Lighting
7711 E. Pleasant Valley Rd.
PO Box 318010
Cleveland, OH 44131
Phone: 800-875-4216
Fax: 216-573-1003
E-mail: dancer@kichler.com
Web site: www.kichler.com

LBL Lighting
320 W. 20th St.
Chicago Heights, IL 60411
Phone: 708-755-2100
Web site: www.lbllighting.com

Louis Poulsen Lighting, Inc.
3260 Meridian Pkwy.
Ft. Lauderdale, FL 33331
Phone: 954-349-2525
Fax: 954-349-2550
E-mail: info@louispoulsen.com
Web site: www.louis-poulsen.com

LSI Industries
10000 Alliance Rd.
Cincinnati, OH 45242
Phone: 800-436-7800
Fax: 513-984-1335
Web site: www.lsi-industries.com

Minka Group
1151 West Bradford Court
Corona, CA 92882
Phone: 800-221-7977
Fax: 951-735-9758
E-mail: sales@minkagroup.net
Web site: www.minkagroup.net

Moravian Book Shop
428 Main St.
Bethlehem, PA 18018
Phone: 888-661-2888
Fax: 610-868-8330
E-mail: info@moravianbookshop.com
Web site: www.moravianbookshop.com
Note: Source for hanging Moravian star exterior light fixture.

Murray Feiss
125 Rose Feiss Blvd.
Bronx, NY 10454
E-mail: customerservice@feiss.com
Web site: www.feiss.com

Murray's Iron Works
1801 E. 50th St.
Los Angeles, CA 90058
Phone: 323-521-1100

Old California Lantern Company
975 N. Enterprise St.
Orange, CA 92867
Phone: 800-577-6679
Fax: 714-771-5714
E-mail: ocsales@oldcalifornia.com
Web site: www.oldcalifornia.com

Progress Lighting
PO Box 5704
Spartanburg, SC 29304
Phone: 864-599-6000
Fax: 864-599-6151
Web site: www.progresslighting.com

RAB Lighting, Inc.
170 Ludlow Ave.
Northvale, NJ 07647
Phone: 888-RAB-1000
Fax: 888-RAB-1232
E-mail: custserv@rabweb.com
Web site: www.rabweb.com

Rejuvenation Hardware and Lighting
See listing under Door Hardware

Restoration Hardware
Phone: 800-910-9836
Web site: www.restorationhardware.com

Santa Maria Lighting
2943 Hope Ave.
Carlsbad, CA 92008
Phone: 760-473-9244
Fax: 760-281-8430
E-mail: lulu@santamariadesign.net
Web site: www.santamariadesign.net

Sea Gull Lighting Products
301 W. Washington St.
Riverside, NJ 08075
Phone: 800-347-5483
Fax: 800-877-4855
E-mail: info@seagulllighting.com
Web site: www.seagulllighting.com

Shaper Lighting (Division of Cooper Industries)
1121 Highway 74, S.
Peachtree City, GA 30269
Web site: www.shaperlighting.com

Steven Handelman Studios
716 W. Milpitas St.
Santa Barbara, CA 93103
Phone: 805-962-5119
Fax: 805-966-9529
E-mail: shssales@verizon.net
Web site: www.stevenhandelmanstudios.com

Teka Illumination
40429 Brickyard Dr.
Madera, CA 93636
Phone: 805-434-3511

Fax: 805-434-3512
E-mail: info@teka-illumination.com
Web site: www.tekaillumination.com

Troy Lighting
RLM
14625 E. Clark Ave.
City of Industry, CA 91745
Phone: 626-336-4511
Fax: 626-330-4266
Web site: www.troy-lighting.com

Mailboxes

see also Patio and Garden

Frontgate Catalogue
5566 West Chester Rd.
West Chester, OH 45069
Phone: 888-263-9850
Fax: 800-436-2105
E-mail: ps@frontgate.com
Web site: www.frontgate.com

Mahvelous Mailboxes & More
N89 W16750 Appleton Ave.
Menomonee Falls, WI 53051
Phone: 888-675-MAIL
Web site: www.mahvelousmailboxes.com

Mailbox Shoppe
910 West Jericho Turnpike
Smithtown, NJ 11787
Phone: 800-330-3309
Fax: 631-493-0605
Web site: www.mailboxnet.com

The Mailbox Works
1743 Quincy Ave., Ste. 151
Naperville, FL 60540
Phone: 800-824-9985
Fax: 630-355-9619
E-mail: info@mailboxworks.com
Web site: www.mailboxworks.com

Salisbury Industries
1010 E. 62nd St.
Los Angeles, CA 90001
Phone: 800-624-5269
Fax: 800-624-5299
E-mail: salisbury@mailboxes.com
Web site: www.mailboxes.com

Smith & Hawken
PO Box 8690
Pueblo, CO 81008
Phone: 800-940-1170
E-mail: smithandhawkencustomerservice@innotrac.com
Web site: www.smithandhawken.com

Marble

see Granite, Marble, Slate, and Stone

Metal/Iron Fabricators

Ace Iron, Inc.
31626 Hayman St.
Hayward, CA 94544
Phone: 510-324-3300
Fax: 510-324-3322
Web site: www.aceironinc.com

Bayshore Metals
Hot Rolled Carbon Products
244 Napoleon St.
San Francisco, CA 94124
Phone: 800-533-2493
Fax: 415-285-5759
E-mail: baymetals@sbcglobal.net
Web site: www.bayshoremetals.com

Bianchi Lamberto
See listing under Door Hardware

Blank and Cable
950 63rd St.
Emeryville, CA 94608
Phone: 510-648-3842

Clausen Sculptural Iron
See listing under Door Hardware

Copper Iron Designs, Inc.
Custom Metalwork, Ornamental Gates, Rails,
and Furniture
1900 Camino Oruga, Studio J
Napa, CA 94558
Phone: 707-252-1949
Fax: 707-252-6377
E-mail: andycufe@aol.com
Web site: www.copperirondesigns.com

Dan Nelson
1699 Hawes St.
San Francisco, CA 94124
Phone: 415-822-1300
Fax: 415-822-1301

Dennis Luedeman
4320 Helen St.
Oakland, CA 94608
Phone: 510-658-9435

Eandi Metal Works, Inc.
976–23rd Ave.
Oakland, CA 94606
Phone: 510-532-8311

Harrison & Bonini
Specialty Fastening Hardware
1122 Harrison St.
San Francisco, CA 94103
Phone: 866-442-2658
Fax: 415-552-0796
E-mail: info@hbbolt.com
Web site: www.hbbolt.com

Jack Chandler and Associates
Custom Metalwork/Gates
See listing under Landscape
Architects/Designers

James Patock
Metalwork
San Francisco, CA
Phone: 415-595-8553
E-mail: madfab@sbcglobal.net

John White Service
113 E. Main St.
Fowler, CA 93625
Phone: 559-834-3306

Kyle Reicher
Designer and Builder of Metal Sculpture
2216 Bonar St.
Berkeley, CA 94702
Phone: 510-812-9141

Fax: 510-215-9908
E-mail: kyle_reicher@yahoo.com

Mexico City Ironworks
1385 Fitzgerald
San Francisco, CA 94124
Phone: 415-861-2985

Michael Wentworth
Architectural Metalwork and Design
7015 Buckingham Blvd.
Berkeley, CA 94705
Phone: 510-843-9245
E-mail: mbwentworth@comcast.net
Web site: www.michaelwentworth.com

Murray's Iron Works
See listing under Lighting

Nueva Castilla Company
895 Innes Ave., #100
San Francisco, CA 94124
Phone: 415-282-6767
Fax: 415-282-3442
E-mail: info@nuevacastilla.com
Web site: www.nuevacastilla.com

Olszewski Iron Design
Janusz Olszewski
Custom Metalwork for Gates, Grilles, and
Railings
1949 Arnold Industrial Way
Concord, CA 94520
Phone: 925-687-8840

One Off Design
Metal Design
Mary Revelli
285 Joost
San Francisco, CA 94131
Phone: 415-452-0456

Rotolo Design
Christine Rotolo
Artistic Custom Metalwork
911 Regal Rd.
Berkeley, CA 94708
Phone: 510-612-6364
E-mail: rotolodesign@mac.com

TGW Metals, Inc.
150 W. Trident Ave.
Alameda, CA 94501
Phone: 510-523-4417

Villa Iron Works, Inc.
7610 Brighton Ave.
Sacramento, CA 95826
Phone: 916-457-2605

Millworkers

4th Street Woodworking Company
See listing under Doors and Windows

Outdoor Fabric

Sunbrella
See listing under Awnings

Outdoor Furniture

see also Patio and Garden

Charleston Gardens
650 King St.

Charleston, NC 29403
Phone: 800-469-0118
Fax: 800-532-5140
E-mail: staff@charlestongardens.com
Web site: www.charlestongardens.com

The Conran Shop
Outdoor Furniture/Outdoor Living
407 East 59th St.
New York, NY 10022
Web site: www.conran.com

English Garden Furniture
See listing under Lighting

JANUS et Cie
8687 Melrose Ave., #B-193
West Hollywood, CA 90069
Phone: 310-652-7090
Fax: 310-652-7928
Web site: www.janusetcie.com

Treillage, Ltd.
418 E. 75th St.
New York, NY 10021
Phone: 212-535-2288
Fax: 212-517-6589
E-mail: info@treillageonline.com
Web site: www.treillageonline.com

Paint Companies

Behr
3400 W. Segerstrom Ave.
Santa Ana, CA 92704
Phone: 800-854-0133
Web site: www.behrpaint.com
Note: Found at Home Depot

Benjamin Moore Paints
51 Chestnut Ridge Rd.
Montvale, NJ 07645
Phone: 800-826-2623 (cust. service),
888-236-6667 (technical services)
Web site: www.benjaminmoore.com

California Paints
150 Dascomb Rd.
Andover, MA 01810
Phone: 800-225-1141
Fax: 800-533-6788
E-mail: info@californiapaints.com
Web site: www.californiapaints.com

Dunn Edwards
4885 E. 52nd Pl.
Los Angeles, CA 90040
Phone: 888-DE-PAINT
Web site: www.dunnedwards.com

**Duron (a Division of Sherwin Williams
Paint)**
10406 Tucker St.
Beltsville, MD 20705
Phone: 800-723-8766
Fax: 301-595-3919
E-mail: information@duron.com
Web site: www.duron.com

Farrow & Ball
1054 Yonge St.
Toronto, Ontario
Canada
Phone: 888-511-1121

Fax: 416-920-1223
E-mail: farrowball@bellnet.ca
E-mail: usasales@farrow-ball.com
Web site: www.farrow-ball.com

Fine Paints of Europe
Hollandlac Paint
PO Box 419
Woodstock, VT 05091
Phone: 800-332-1556
E-mail: info@finepaints.com
Web site: www.finepaintsofeurope.com

Finnaren & Haley
901 Washington St.
Conshohocken, PA 19428
Phone: 610-825-1900
Fax: 610-825-1184
E-mail: architectural@fhpaint.com
Web site: www.fhpaint.com

Fuller O'Brien
925 Euclid Ave.
Cleveland, OH 44115
Phone: 866-391-1955
Web site: www.fullerpaint.com

The Glidden Company
925 Euclid Ave.
Cleveland, OH 44115
Phone: 800-GLIDDEN
Web site: www.gliddenpaint.com

Kelly-Moore Paints
987 Commercial St.
San Carlos, CA 94070
Phone: 888-KM COLOR
Web site: www.kellymoore.com

Lowe's
American Traditions Paint
PO Box 1111
North Wilkesboro, NC 28656
Phone: 800-445-6937
Web site: www.lowes.com

ICI Dulux Paint
925 Euclid Ave.
Cleveland, OH 44115
Phone: 800-984-5444
Web site: www.iciduluxpaints.com

M.A.B. Paints
600 Reed Rd.
Broomall, PA 19008
Phone: 800-MAB-1899
Fax: 610-353-8189
Web site: www.mabpaints.com

Martin Senour Paints
191 Prospect Ave. NW
1500 Midland Building
Cleveland, OH 44115
Phone: 800-677-5270
Web site: www.martinsenour.com

Morwear
620 Lamar St.
Los Angeles, CA 90031
Phone: 800-605-2627
Web site: www.morwear.com

Pittsburgh Paints
One PPG Pl.
Pittsburgh, PA 15272
Phone: 800-441-9695

Web site: www.pittsburghpaint.com

Pratt & Lambert
PO Box 1505
Buffalo, NY 14240
Phone: 800-289-7728
Web site: www.prattandlambert.com

Sherwin Williams Company
101 Prospect Ave.
Cleveland, OH 44115
Phone: 800-331-7979,
800-336-1110
Web site: www.sherwin.com

V.I.P. Elastomeric Paint
260 Hudson River Rd.
Waterford, NY 12188
Phone: 800-334-4674
E-mail: info@siliconeorders.com
Web site: www.gesilicones.com

Patio and Garden

Authentic Provence
222 Clematis St.
West Palm Beach, FL 33401
Phone: 561-805-9995
Fax: 561-805-5730
E-mail: info@authenticprovence.com
Web site: www.authenticprovence.com

Chilewich
Outdoor Mats
44 E. 32 St.
New York, NY 10016
Phone: 212-679-9204
Fax: 212-679-9205
Web site: www.chilewich.com

Coolaroo
Triangle Shade Sails
PO Box 951509
Lake Mary, FL 32795
Phone: 800-560-4667
Fax: 407-333-7716
Web site: www.coolaroo.com

Design within Reach
225 Bush St., 20th Fl.
San Francisco, CA 94104
Phone: 800-944-2233
Fax: 800-846-0411
Web site: www.dwr.com

Eye of the Day Garden Design Center
4620 Carpenteria Ave.
Carpenteria, CA 93013
Phone: 805-566-0778
Fax: 805-566-0478
Web site: www.eyeofthedaygdc.com

Fly Creek Studio
Garden Plaques
PO Box 211
20 Prospect Lake Rd.
North Edgermont, MA 01252
Email: david@flycreekstudio.com
Web site: www.flycreekstudio.com

Frontgate Catalogue
See listing under Mailboxes

Haddonstone
201 Heller Pl.

Bellmawr, NJ 08031
Phone: 856-931-7011
Fax: 856-931-0040
E-mail: info@haddonstone.com
Web site: www.haddonstone.com

House and Garden Accents
Flora & Fauna
12508 Lake City Way NE, Ste. 210
Seattle, WA 98125
Phone: 866-634-9022
Fax: 206-634-2662
E-Mail: info@houseandgardenaccents.com
Web site: www.houseandgardenaccents.com

Jackson and Perkins
1 Rose Ln.
Medford, OR 97501
Phone: 877-322-2300
Fax: 800-242-0329
Web site: www.jacksonandperkins.com

Kenneth Lynch & Sons
84 Danbury Rd.
PO Box 488
Wilton, CT 06897
Phone: 203-762-8363
Fax: 203-762-2999
E-mail: info@klynchandsons.com
Web site: www.klynchandsons.com

The Magazine
1823 Eastshore Hwy.
Berkeley, CA 94710
Phone: 510-549-2282
Fax: 510-549-2282
E-mail: themag@pacbell.net
Web site: www.themagazine.info

Ohmega Salvage
Architectural Salvage
2407 and 2400 San Pablo Ave.
Berkeley, CA 94702
Phone: 510-204-0767
Fax: 510-843-7123
E-mail: ohmegasalvage@earthlink.net
Web site: www.ohmegasalvage.com
Note: Source for "pillow" stepping-stones

Pottery Barn (A Division of Williams-Sonoma)
3250 Van Ness Ave.
San Francisco, CA 94109
Phone: 888-779-5176
Web site: www.potterybarn.com

Restoration Hardware Outdoor
Phone: 800-910-9836 (corporate headquarters)
Phone: 800-762-1005 (phone orders)
Web site: www.restorationhardware
outdoor.com

Room and Board
4600 Olson Memorial Highway
Minneapolis, MN 55422
Phone: 800-301-9720
E-mail: shop@roomandboard.com
Web site: www.roomandboard.com

Smith & Hawken
See listing under Mailboxes

Treillage Ltd.

See listing under Outdoor Furniture

Urban Gardener
2211 N. Elson Ave.
Chicago, IL 60615
Phone: 800-998-7330
Web site: www.urbangardenerchicago.com

West Elm (a Division of Williams-Sonoma)
45 Main St., Studio 900
Brooklyn, NY 11201
Phone: 888-922-4119
E-mail: customerservice@westelm.com
Web site: www.westelm.com

Williams-Sonoma
3250 Van Ness Ave.
San Francisco, CA 94109
Phone: 877-812-6235
Fax: 702-363-2541
Web site: www.williams-sonoma.com

Pavers

see Granite, Marble, Slate, and Stone

Polyurethane, Protective Coating, Oil, Stain, and Varnish Companies

Amteco
Maintenance and Technical Coatings
110 Jefferson Dr.
PO Box 9
Pacific, MO 63069
Phone: 800-969-4811
Fax: 636-271-2211
E-mail: amteco@aol.com
Web site: www.twp-amteco.com

Cabot
Wood Care Products
100 Hale St.
Newburyport, MA 01950
Phone: 800-US-STAIN
Web site: www.cabotstain.com

Flood
PO Box 2535
Hudson, OH 44236
Phone: 800-321-3444
E-mail: askus@flood.com
Web site: www.flood.com

FSC Coatings
5360 Eastgate Mall Rd., Ste. F
San Diego, CA 92121
Phone: 800-579-8459
Fax: 858-558-2159
E-mail: fscoatings@aol.com
Web site: www.fsccoatings.com

Minwax
10 Mountainview Rd.
Upper Saddle River, NJ 07458
Phone: 800-523-9299
E-mail: askminwax@sherwin.com
Web site: www.minwax.com

Mohawk Finishing Products
Division of RPM Wood Finishes Group, Inc.
PO Box 22000
Hickory, NC 28603

Phone: 800-545-0047
Fax: 800-721-1545
Web site: www.mohawk-finishing.com

McCloskey
Man O'War Spar Marine Varnish
See Valspar Corporation

Penofin
PO Box 1569
360 Lake Mendocino Dr.
Ukiah, CA 95482
Phone: 800-PENOFIN
Fax: 707-462-6139
E-mail: info@penofin.com
Web site: www.penofin.com

Rockler Woodworking and Hardware
Rotten Stone
4365 Willow Dr.
Medina, MN 55340
Phone: 800-279-4441
Fax: 763-478-8395
E-mail: support@rockler.com
Web site: www.rockler.com

Rust-Oleum
Specialty and Rust Preventive Paints
11 Hawthorn Pkwy.
Vernon Hills, IL 60061
Phone: 800-323-3584
Fax: 847-816-2330
E-mail: consumerservices@rustoleum.com
Web site: www.rustoleum.com

Sikkens
Woodcare Products
Phone: 866-SIKKENS
Web site: www.nam.sikkens.com

Sunnyside Corporation
Phone: 800-323-8611
E-mail: info@sunnysidecorp.com
Web site: www.sunnysidecorp.com

Superdeck Brand Products
See listing under Concrete Stains

TWP Products (Amteco)
1841 Marietta Blvd. NW, Ste. F
Atlanta, GA 30318
Phone: 800-297-7325
Fax: 404-355-5161
E-mail: info@mfgsealants.com
Web site: www.mfgsealants.com

UGL (United Gilsonite Laboratories)
PO Box 70
Scranton, PA 18501
Phone: 800-272-3235
Web site: www.ugl.com

Valspar Corporation
McCloskey
1191 Wheeling Rd.
Wheeling, IL 60090
Phone: 800-845-9061
Fax: 847-541-8584
E-mail: techsupport@valspar.com
Web site: www.valspar.com

Varathane
See Rust-Oleum

Watco
See Rust-Oleum

Woodkote Products, Inc.
8000 NE 14th Place
Portland, OR 97211
Phone: 800-843-7666
Fax: 503-285-8374
E-mail: info@woodkote.com
Web site: www.woodkote.com

ZAR
Wood Finishing Products
See UGL

Pots and Planter Boxes

Architectural Pottery
15161 Van Buren
Midway City, CA 92655
Phone: 714-895-3359
Fax: 714-898-5109
E-mail: archpot@msn.com
Web site: www.archpot.com

Asia Trade Imports
Ceramic Planter Wholesalers
109 Mayfair Ave.
Vallejo, CA 94591
Phone: 707-553-2348
Fax: 707-319-8030

A. Silvestri Company
2635 Bayshore Blvd.
San Francisco, CA 94134
Phone: 415-239-5990
Fax: 415-239-0422
E-mail: info@asilvestri.com
Web site: www.asilvestri.com

AW Pottery
601–50th Ave.
Oakland, CA 94601
Phone: 510-533-3900
Fax: 510-533-8190
Web site: www.awpotteryusa.com

Authentic Provence
See listing under Patio and Garden

Eye of the Day Garden Design Center
See listing under Patio and Garden

International Art Properties
101 Henry Adams St., #380
San Francisco, CA 94103
Phone: 800-426-6471
Fax: 415-863-3406
E-mail: iapsf@yahoo.com
Web site: www.iapsf.com

PlantContainers.com
1309 Leavenworth St.
Omaha, NE 68102
Phone: 866-342-3330
Fax: 402-342-4269
E-mail: customerservice@plantcontainers.com
Web site: www.plantcontainers.com

Smith & Hawken
See listing under Mailboxes

The Magazine
See listing under Patio and Garden

Urban Gardener
See listing under Patio and Garden

VESSEL LAUNCH
Mary Collins
501 Irish Ridge Rd.
Half Moon Bay, CA 94019
Phone: 650-868-4544
E-mail: maryround@aol.com
Web site: www.maryround.com

Powder Coatings

NIC Industries
Prismatic Powders Division
7050–6th St.
White City, OR 97503
Phone: 866-774-7628
Fax: 541-826-6372
E-mail: info@nicindustries.com
Web site: www.nicindustries.com

Tiger Drylac U.S.A., Inc.
Powder Coating
1261 E. Belmont St.
Ontario, CA 91761
Phone: 909-930-9100
Fax: 909-930-9111
Web site: www.tigerdrylac.com
See Web site for local dealers and e-mail
addresses

Rain Chains

Rainchains.com
8040 Remmet Ave., Unit 7
Canoga Park, CA 91304
Phone: 888-480-RAIN
Fax: 818-347-6450
E-mail: customerservice@rainchains.com
Web site: www.rainchains.com

Roofing Material

AEP Span Metal Roofing
5100 East Grand Ave.
Dallas, TX 75228
Phone: 800-527-2503
Fax: 214-828-1394
Web site: www.aep-span.com

American Slate Company
See listing under Granite, Marble, Slate, and
Stone

CertainTeed
PO Box 860
750 E. Swedesford Rd.
Valley Forge, PA 19482
Phone: 800-782-8777
E-mail: corporate@certainteed.com
Web site: www.certainteed.com

DaVinci Roofscapes
Synthetic Slate and Shake Shingles
1413 Osage Ave.
Kansas City, KS 66105
Phone: 800-328-4624
Fax: 913-599-0065
E-mail: info@davinciroofscapes.com
Web site: www.davinciroofscapes.com

Di Benedetto Light Weight Roof Tile Co.
410 N. Park
Kansas City, MO 64120

Phone: 816-221-1935
Fax: 816-221-9360
E-mail: info@elegantekc.com

Elk Roofing
14911 Quorum Dr., Ste. 600
Dallas, TX 75254
Phone: 888-355-5882
Fax: 972-851-0401
E-mail: webinfo@elkcorp.com
Web site: www.elkcorp.com

GAF
1361 Alps Rd.
Wayne, NJ 07470
Phone: 800-766-3411
E-mail: residentialsales@gaf.com
Web site: www.gaf.com

McElroy Metal
1500 Hamilton Rd.
Bossier City, LA 71111
Phone: 800-562-3576
Fax: 318-747-8097
E-mail: info@mcelroymetal.com
Web site: www.mcelroymetal.com

MonierLifetile
7575 Irvine Center Dr., Ste. 100
Irvine, CA 92618
Phone: 949-756-1605
Fax: 949-756-2401
Web site: www.monierlifetile.com

NCI Building Systems
See listing under Building Systems

Redland Clay Tile
24699-4 Humphries Rd.
Tecate, CA 91980
Phone: 800.354.5983
Fax: 619.478.2755
Web site: www.redlandclaytile.com

Tamko Roofing Products
220 W. 4th St.
PO Box 1404
Joplin, MO 64801
Phone: 800-641-4691
Fax: 800-841-1925
E-mail: sales@tamko.com
Web site: www.tamko.com

United States Tile Company (U.S. Tile)
909 Railroad St.
Corona, CA 92882
Phone: 800-252-9548
Fax: 951-734-9591
Web site: www.ustile.com

Shutters

Atlantic Shutter Systems
3217 Hwy. 301 N.
Lata, SC 29565
Phone: 877-437-0608
Web site: www.atlanticshuttersystems.com

Siding

ASC Profiles/AEP Span
Corrugated Metal Panels
2110 Enterprise Blvd.
W. Sacramento, CA 95691

Phone: 800-360-2477
Fax: 916-372-7606
E-mail: info@ascprofiles.com
Web site: www.ascprofiles.com

United States Steel
Corrugated Metal Panels
3010 Highland Pkwy, Ste. 575
Downers Grove, IL 60515
Phone: 800-447-4338
Web site: www.ussteel.com

Slate

see Granite, Marble, Slate, and Stone

Specialty Coating Manufacturers

Blue Pearl Paint
Metallic and Pearlescent Paint
PO Box 1173
Effingham, IL 62401
Phone: 217-347-3710
Web site: www.bluepearlpaint.com

Calbar, Inc.
Metal Roofing and Siding Paint
8000 Bristol Pike
Levittown, PA 19057
Phone: 215-949-0800
Fax: 215-949-9422
Web site: www.calbarinc.com

Diamon-Fusion International
Application for Etched or Sandblasted Glass
1046 Calle Recodo, Ste. F
San Clemente, CA 92673
Phone: 800-388-8000
Fax: 949-388-4299
Web site: www.diamon-fusion.com

Flood
See listing under Polyurethane, Protective
Coating, Oil, Stain, and Varnish Companies

GE Advanced Materials, Silicones
9930 Kincey Ave.
Huntersville, NC 28078
Phone: 800-255-8886 (technical assistance)
Phone: 877-943-7325 (customer service)
Web site: www.geadvancedmaterials.com

Gold Leaf Company
27 Fort Pl., 2nd Floor
Staten Island, NY 10301
Phone: 718-815-8802
Fax: 718-720-7027
E-mail: info@goldleafcompany.com
Web site: www.goldleafcompany.com

Insl-X
Specialty Paints
50 Holt Dr.
PO Box 693
Stony Point, NY 10980
Phone: 845-786-5000
Fax: 845-786-5831
E-mail: customercare@insl-x.com
Web site: www.insl-x.com

Modern Masters Inc.
Decorative Paints
9380 San Fernando Rd.

Sun Valley, CA 91352
Phone: 800-942-3166
Fax: 818-683-0202
E-mail: info@modernmastersinc.com
Web site: www.modernmastersinc.com

NIC Industries
Specialty Coatings
7050 Sixth St.
White City, OR 97503
Phone: 541-826-1922
Fax: 541-826-6372
Web site: www.nicindustries.com

Rust-Oleum
See listing under Polyurethane, Protective
Coating, Oil, Stain, and Varnish Companies

Sumter Coatings, Inc.
Metal Paint Primers
2410 Hwy. 15 S.
Sumter, NC 29154
Phone: 888-471-3400
Fax: 803-481-3776
E-mail: emonarch@sumtercoatings.com
Web site: www.sumtercoatings.com

Triangle Coatings, Inc.
Specialty Coatings
1930 Fairway Dr.
San Leandro, CA 94577
Phone: 800-895-8000
Fax: 510-895-8800
Email: info@tricoat.com
Web site: www.tricoat.com

Specialty Painters

Joshua McCullough
Faux Painting Specialist
1318 Pine St.
Martinez, CA 94553
Phone: 510-326-0506
E-mail: joshart@gmail.com

Magic Brush
Painting Restoration and Specialty Finishes
Robert Dufort
1500B Davidson Ave.
San Francisco, CA 94124
Phone: 415-641-8622
Fax: 415-641-8655
E-mail: magicb@pacbell.net
Web site: www.magicbrush.net

M. B. Jessee Painting and Decorating
Painting Specialists
See listing under Color Consultants/Designers

Paco's Painting
Whitewashing Specialist
Ukiah, CA
Phone: 707-485-7226

Patrick Bornemann
Decorative Paint/Lime Wash Process Specialist
31 Bay View Terrace
Mill Valley, CA 94941
Phone: 415-302-6387
E-mail: patbornemann@earthlink.net

Paul d'Orleans Painting
Specialty Painter and Color Consulting
See listing under Color Consultants/Designers

Stancil Studios
Handpainting, Patterning, Glazing, Faux Bois,
Stone, and Marquetry Artists
Elisa Stancil
365 Tehama St.
San Francisco, CA 94103
Phone: 415-243-9746
E-mail: info@elisastancil.com
Web site: www.elisastancil.com

Statuary

A. Silvestri Co.
See listing under Pots and Planter Boxes

Giannini Garden Ornaments, Inc.
225 Shaw Rd.
South San Francisco, CA 94080
Phone: 650-873-4493
Web site: www.gianninigarden.com

Stone

see Granite, Marble, Slate, and Stone

Stucco Surfacing

Dryvit Systems, Inc.
One Energy Way
PO Box 1014
West Warwick, RI 02893
Phone: 800-556-7752
Fax: 401-822-1980
E-mail: sales@dryvit.com
Web site: www.dryvit.com

LaHabra
4130 E. La Palma
Anaheim, CA 92807
Phone: 877-547-8822
Fax: 714-774-8599
E-mail: info@lahabrastucco.com
Web site: www.lahabrastucco.com

Parex
1870 Stone Mountain—Lithonia Rd.
Redan, GA 30074
Phone: 800-537-2739
Fax: 770-482-6878
E-mail: info@parex.com
Web site: www.parex.com

Quikrete
One Securities Center
3490 Piedmont Rd., Ste. 1300
Atlanta, GA 30305
Phone: 800-282-5828
Web site: www.quikrete.com

Senergy
Degussa Wall Systems
3550 St. Johns Bluff Rd., S.
Jacksonville, FL 32224
Phone: 800-221-9255
Fax: 904-996-6300
E-mail: senergyinfo@degussa.com
Web site: www.senergy.cc and
www.degussa.com

STO Corporation
3800 Camp Creek Pkwy.
Building 1400, Ste. 120
Atlanta, GA 30331

Phone: 800-221-2397
Fax: 404-346-3119
E-mail: marketingsupport@stocorp.com
Web site: www.stocorp.com

Tile

Ann Sacks
Phone: 800-278-8453
Web site: www.annsacks.com

Country Floors, Inc.
15 E. 16th St.
New York, NY 10003
Phone: 800-311-9995
Fax: 212-242-1604
E-mail: info@countryfloors.com
Web site: www.countryfloors.com

Daltile Corp.
See listing under Granite, Marble, Slate, and
Stone

Floor Gres
Florim Ceramiche
Via Canaletto, 24
41042 Fiarano, Italy
Phone: +39 0536.840111
Fax: +39 0536.840999
Web site: www.floorgres.it

Import Tile Co.
611 Hearst Ave.
Berkeley, CA 94710
Phone: 888-843-5959
Fax: 510-843-0121
Web site: www.importtile.com

Kibak Tile
1559 SE Railroad Blvd., Ste. B
Redmond, OR 94756
Phone: 541-923-0039
Web site: www.kibaktile.com
Note: Can be purchased through Ann Sacks,
www.annsacks.com.

Pave Tile and Stone, Inc.
See listing under Granite, Marble, Slate, and
Stone

Portobello America, Inc.
1205 N. Miller
Anaheim, CA 92806
Phone: 714-535-3311
Fax: 714-535-3322
Web site: www.portobelloamerica.com
Note: Other locations in Illinois, Florida, New
Jersey, and Texas. See Web site for contact
information.

Richards & Sterling Importers
Italics Showroom
1488 67th St.
Emeryville, CA 94608
Phone: 510-647-1030
E-mail: info@richardsandsterling.com
Web site: www.richardsandsterling.com

The Moravian Pottery and Tile Works
130 Swamp Rd.
Doylestown, PA 18901
Phone: 215-345-6722
E-mail:
moravianpotteryandtileworks@co.bucks.pa.us

Web site: www.mptw.go.to

Witex
1925 Vaughn Rd., Ste. 235
Kennesaw, GA 30144
Phone: 678-766-0800
Fax: 678-766-0803
E-mail: info@witexflooring.com
Web site: www.witex.com

Window Coverings

Castec, Inc.
7531 Coldwater Canyon Ave.
North Hollywood, CA 91605
Phone: 800-828-2500
Fax: 818-503-8300
E-mail: sales@castec.com
Web site: www.castec.com

Glossary

baluster—An upright post that supports a handrail.

batten—A thin strip of solid material that is usually made of wood.

battered wall—A strengthening wall that leans inward rather than outward.

bay window—A projecting bay with windows that forms an extension to the interior floor space.

broken pediment—A symmetrical break in the center of a pediment that omits the apex of the triangle.

cantilever—A beam or other structure projecting from a wall that is supported at one end and carries a load at the other end or along its length.

clapboard—Overlapping horizontal or vertical siding.

clinker brick—Bricks that have been damaged from a firing process and become irregular and distorted. They are used for their picturesque qualities for building material.

cobblestone—A naturally rounded rectangular stone usually taken from river beds; historically used for paving streets.

colonnade—A series of columns placed at regular intervals.

colonnette—A relatively small column that's used decoratively or to support an arcade.

cornice—A projecting horizontal molding that crowns or completes a building or wall. It is the uppermost part of an entablature.

dormer—A house-like structure containing a vertical window, or windows, that projects through a pitched roof and has a roof of its own.

fan light—A semicircular or elliptical window over a doorway or other window.

dentil—A decorative classical Greek detail consisting of a series of small, square, projecting blocks placed closely together beneath the cornice that are tooth-like in appearance.

entablature—The superstructure of moldings and bands, which lies horizontally above the columns, resting on their capitals. It is a major element of classical architecture.

escutcheon—A metal plate that is fitted around a handle or knob to protect, decorate, or cover the area of attachment.

exposed rafters—Visible heavy beams that support the roof of a building. Exposed rafters are a feature of many traditional styles of architecture where sloping beams project past the walls and are exposed on the outside of the house.

facade—The front elevation of a building.

fan deck—A paint manufacturer's collection of paint colors that are usually organized by color, tint, and shade; displays all of the custom colors available on a long

deck of cards. Used by professionals but also available for consumer purchase.

fascia board—A flat, horizontal band between moldings, especially in a classical entablature.

finial—A formal decorative element that emphasizes the top of an upright post of a railing.

frieze—The wide, central, horizontal band of an entablature that is below the cornice. It is a flat member that may be plain or sometimes will be enriched with ornamental sculpture.

gable—The vertical triangular portion of a wall at the end of a building that is between the lines of a sloping roof. Sometimes it refers to the entire end wall.

gingerbread—Any kind of decoration on a home found in the gables, porches, eaves, and around windows or doors. The decoration is generally created with a sawn scrollwork technique.

glazing liquid—A product that transforms an opaque wall paint into a translucent paint. Faux-finish techniques add layers of this translucent color to give depth, texture, and movement to the finished product.

grille work—A framework of metal bars used decoratively on windows and/or for protection from intruders.

half-timber—A type of construction in which the heavy timber frame-

work is exposed and the spaces between the studs are filled with plaster or brickwork. It is often seen in Tudor-style homes.

lintel—A horizontal beam of wood or stone over a door or window that supports the structure above.

louvered door—A door shutter fitted with slanting fixed or movable slats. They admit light and air while keeping out rain and snow.

lunette—A small circular or crescent-shaped opening in a vaulted roof or a semicircular space. It is usually located over a door or window that may contain another window, a sculpture, or a mural.

mullion—A vertical bar on a window or door that divides and supports the panes of glass.

muntin—A secondary framing member (horizontal, vertical, or diagonal) that holds the window panes in the sash.

niche—A small recessed area in a wall; often used to display ornamental objects.

patina—A film that naturally (or artificially, through the application of acid) forms on copper or bronze as a result of corrosion and is aesthetically valued for its color.

pediment—An ornamental triangular or rounded classical architectural element used over porticos, doorways, or windows.

pendant—A light fixture that hangs from the ceiling.

portal—An entranceway to a building

or a courtyard.

portico—A roofed area open to the air on one or more sides and supported by classical columns or posts, forming the entrance to a building.

projecting eave—The lower portion of the roof that overhangs or projects beyond the walls.

quoin—The corner stones of a building constructed with blocks that rise the entire height of the wall and are distinguished from the main construction by the use of contrasting materials.

rafters—The parallel structural framing members that support the roof.

rubble—Rough fragments of broken stone either naturally formed or quarried; used in masonry to construct walls.

rusticated—A rough surface with a textured, provincial appearance.

sash—The framework that holds the panes of a window in the window frame.

shade—The degree to which a color is mixed with black and is decreased into gradations of darkness.

shingle—A thin wedge-shaped piece of wood, slate, etc., laid in a series of overlapping rows for roofs and sides of houses. Often seen in Bungalow or Craftsman-style houses.

sidelight—Framed windows on either side of a door or window.

sill—The horizontal member that forms and bears the weight of a window frame.

stays—Horizontal stiffening elements that strengthen flat window shades.

stucco—A durable finish for exterior walls, usually consisting of a mixture of cement, sand, and lime. It is applied wet.

terra-cotta—A hard, semi-fired, waterproof, unglazed red clay used for roof tiles and decorative wall coverings.

tint—A gradation of color made lighter by adding white to lessen its saturation.

tone—The general effect of shading or tinting to soften or change a color.

transom—Horizontal glazed opening above a door or window.

truss—Method of construction using a triangular framework of timber.

topiary—A pruned and trained plant or floral arrangement in an ornamental shape.

universal colorants—Solid pigment, mixed into white base paint, that produces all paint colors.

varnish—A finish that is applied to wood or other materials as a clear coating for protection and enhanced appearance. Varnish is traditionally a combination of a drying oil, a resin, and a thinner or solvent.

vestibule—The small entrance hall between the exterior door and the interior door of a house or building.

viga—A projecting roof rafter used in Pueblo-style architecture.

wrought iron—A tough, malleable, relatively soft iron that is readily forged and welded.

Bibliography

Benjamin Moore Paints. *Color Inspiration: A Color Guide for Home Decorating.*

Blumenson, John J. G. *Identifying American Architecture*. New York: W. H. Norton & Company Publishers, 1981.

Carley, Rachel. *The Visual Dictionary of American Domestic Architecture*. New York: Henry Holt and Company and Owl Books, 1994.

Ching, Francis D. K. *A Visual Dictionary of Architecture*. New York: Van Nostrand Reinhold Publishings, Inc., 1994.

http://en.wikipedia.org/wiki/Category:Architectural_elements

http://www.answers.com

http://www.dunnedwards.com [estimation guide for estimating square foot coverage]

http://www.fullerobrien.com/NUS-BOB/colorfeatures/colorscheme.jsp [color scheme information]

http://www.ineed2know.org/roofshingles.htm [short lesson on roof shingles]

http://www.kellymoore.com/site/HowToArea [painting how-to information]

http://www.northwale.org.uk/jn/limewash.htm [information about lime wash process]

http://www.probertencyclopaedia.com

http://www.sherwinwilliams.com/do_it_yourself/paint_colors_education/why_color.jsp

Loeb, Marcia. *Art Deco Designs and Motif*. Mineola, New York: Dover Publications, 1981.

McAlester, Virginia and Lee. *A Field Guide to American Houses*. New York: Alfred A. Knopf Publishers, 1984.

Outdoor Home Idea Book. Newtown, CT: The Taunton Press, 2006.

Vandervort, Don. *Curb Appeal*. Menlo Park, California: Sunset Books, 2005.

Acknowledgments

I want to thank my family for putting up with me while I wrote, researched, and photographed this book. I asked a lot of them and they delivered, allowing me to work on it pretty much nonstop for almost three years.

I need to thank my husband, Rock Snyder, for creating a software program and database that made it possible for me to organize the massive amounts of information in an organized and cohesive fashion. He's a genius. He was there for me every day answering questions about the technical aspects of the project. Rock, I couldn't have begun to undertake this huge project without you. For your patience and for never making me feel rushed to finish it, I thank you from the bottom of my heart. I love you.

Thanks to my wonderful son, Cary Snyder, who lost his Mom for a long time. Thanks for your patience. I'll make it up to you. You're the best. You are the child of my dreams.

Thanks to Gibbs Smith, Publisher, for their incredible patience and support of this project. I can't thank the team enough for all the time spent to make this book special. Thanks go to Lisa Anderson, my editor, who organized every aspect of this book and was a pleasure to work with; Aimee Stoddard, who got the book off the ground with me and who I missed throughout the rest of the process; Suzanne Taylor and Gibbs Smith, who won me away from another publisher by offering an author-friendly environment to work in; and to the rest of the team: Marty Lee, Laura Ayrey, and the creative art department, who worked to make this book a dream come true. Thank you all for believing in this project!

I thank all of the homeowners for participating in the project and selflessly contributing and sharing design information about their homes. I feel like I know you all through our e-mails and ongoing correspondence. It took a long time to reel it all in, and I appreciate your patience with all of my nitpicky questions. I could not have done this book without you all—you are the reason that this book exists. Thank you for your support of this project and for your generosity of time, spirit, and willingness to participate.

To Francine Allyn, my dear old friend. Thank you so much for going through the tedious specifications of editing with me. I appreciate your patience and the time spent in reviewing all the details to ensure accuracy. Your friendship and support mean the world to me. Thanks and love to you and Bonnie.

Thanks to my lawyer, Phillip P. Lee of Beyer Waver & Thomas LLP, for donating time to the book and helping me to wade through the contract documents with the publisher. As a first-time writer, I was lost in the legalese until you helped me to understand and guided me through it. I can't thank you enough.

To Gretta Sladen, my dear friend and confidant, who kept me going by offering a sympathetic ear when I thought that I might be losing it, and her fabulous penthouse—complete with panoramic views—whenever I needed to think and write in complete and utter silence. Thank you. I love you. You're the best.

Thanks, love, and appreciation to Marianne Fowler for your support through this long process and being such a wonderful friend and cheerleader to me when I needed it most. Thanks for food, lodging, and sustenance while I worked in your area. Thanks to Andrew, Nick, Jake, and Milo too.

To Michael and Lynda Hershman, my baby brother and sister-in-law. You put me up and put up with me when I was working frantically in a ridiculously short period of time back East. Thanks for your love, support, and sustenance. Zack and Jess too. Michael, thanks for making me laugh when I needed it most. You are the funniest man alive. I love you all.

Thanks to my old friend Gary Price for showing me around areas unknown. You were a great support, as always. You know everything and everyone and you give with grace.

Thanks to Karen and Paul McArdle, landscape architects par excellence, who guided me with knowledgeable answers to my landscaping questions. Karen, you are a selfless giver.

Thanks to painter Ross Powers, who generously answered my questions about painting houses. His knowledgeable answers helped me to write the painting section. Ross is a local painter in Berkeley, California. His contact information is in the resource section.

A special thank you to Anna Scott, my coach and friend. You helped me immeasurably during the last stages of the book. I appreciate your support and encouragement more than words can express. It meant a lot to me.

Thanks to my dear old friend Paul Keplinger. I appreciate your generosity of time as you showed me around your old stomping grounds in search of houses for the book.

To Alden, who passed away while I was writing the book. You helped me to understand how paints are mixed and answered so many of my questions. All of the Benjamin Moore customers in our neighborhood will miss you.

Thanks to Bob Jones for being my Kelly-Moore expert who knew everything there was to know about paint and answered all of my questions with kindness, humor, and patience.

To James Miao at Benjamin Moore. You are my paint guru, answering all of my paint questions with great precision. You know your stuff and you made it fun.

A special thanks to the following manufacturers' reps who helped me along the way by answering my many questions: Matt Smith at Sherwin Williams, Michelle Gable from LaHabra Stucco, Kenneth Rhodes at Parex/LaHabra, Vicki at Finnaren & Haley, Mark Abboud and Carol Elam at Fuller O'Brien, and everyone else who graciously helped me along the way.

Thanks to Susan Bottorf and Alan Kawasaki of Garner Chinn 8 for showing me around your stomping grounds. I appreciate the time that you took for the project.

To Robert Nebolon, Jim Zack, Sharon Risedorph, Bill Brown, Cynthia-Kent Mills, and Massimiliano Bolzonella, thanks for the photographs. I appreciate your generous support.

Many thanks to Jaequeline Duval from Hearst Publishers who first believed in this project and got this book off of the ground. I appreciate what you did for me and I will never forget your professionalism and terrific support.

Thanks to all the architects, designers, and landscape designers whose accomplished work shines throughout the book. You all have created designs that allow the rest of us to dream.

Thanks to Cathleen Schwartz for lending me the book on Italian house colors. Maybe that will be my next book. I appreciate your kindness.

Thanks to architect Robert Nebolon, landscape designer Linda Goodman, and painter Mike Hayes for support above and beyond.

Thanks to Molly, my trusty Labrador-Chihuahua, who sat by my side during the thousands of hours it took to put this book together. You're the best dog a girl could ever have!

Thanks, Mom and Dad. I wish you were here to see that I wrote a book. Thanks for making me someone who could take it on. I miss you guys and wish that you were here for many reasons. I will love you always.

More Thanks

Finally, thanks to all of the dogs and cats who allowed me to come onto their property to photograph their homes. These are just some of the many four-footed friends who made it possible, and in their own inimitable way, contributed to this book too.

Photography Credits

Page 80 (both)

Cynthia Kent-Mills
Interior Designer
1495 Highway 15/501
Southern Pines, NC 28387

Page 107 (right)

Sharon Risedorph
Photographer
761 Clementina St.
San Francisco, CA 94103
Phone: 415-431-5851
Fax: 415-431-2537
E-mail: sharon@sharonrisedorph.com
Web site: www.sharonrisedorph.com

Pages 154, 155 (top left)

Massimiliano Bolzonella
Photographer
1735 Van Ness Ave., #104
San Francisco, CA
Phone: 415-563-1795
Fax: 415-651-9929

Pages 153, 160 (top, bottom left), 161, 180 (bottom right), 184 (top right)

Robert Nebolon
Architect
8701 Camelia St.
Berkeley, CA 94710
Phone: 510-525-2725
Fax: 510-527-5999
E-mail: rnebarch@aol.com
Web site: www.RNarchitect.com